The Second Language Acquisition of French Tense,
Aspect, Mood and Modality

AILA Applied Linguistics Series (AALS)

The AILA Applied Linguistics Series (AALS) provides a forum for established scholars in any area of Applied Linguistics. The series aims at representing the field in its diversity. It covers different topics in applied linguistics from a multidisciplinary approach and it aims at including different theoretical and methodological perspectives. As an official publication of AILA the series will include contributors from different geographical and linguistic backgrounds. The volumes in the series should be of high quality; they should break new ground and stimulate further research in Applied Linguistics.

For an overview of all books published in this series, please see
http://benjamins.com/catalog/aals

Editor

Rosa Manchón
University of Murcia

Editorial Board

Anne Burns
Aston University & University of South Wales

Hannele Dufva
University of Jyväskylä

Susan M. Gass
Michigan State University

Folkert Kuiken
University of Amsterdam

Susanne Niemeier
University of Koblenz-Landau

Volume 10

The Second Language Acquisition of French Tense, Aspect, Mood and Modality
by Dalila Ayoun

The Second Language Acquisition of French Tense, Aspect, Mood and Modality

Dalila Ayoun
University of Arizona

John Benjamins Publishing Company

Amsterdam / Philadelphia

The paper used in this publication meets the minimum requirements of
the American National Standard for Information Sciences – Permanence
of Paper for Printed Library Materials, ANSI z39.48-1984.

Library of Congress Cataloging-in-Publication Data

Ayoun, Dalila, 1963-
The second language acquisition of French tense, aspect, mood and modality / Dalila
    Ayoun.
p.   cm. (AILA Applied Linguistics Series, ISSN 1875-1113 ; v. 10)
Includes bibliographical references and index.
1. French language--Study and teaching--English speakers. 2. French language--
    Grammar--Study and teaching. 3. Second language acquisition. 4. Cohesion
    (Linguistics) I. Title.
PC2065.A96   2013
448.0071--dc23   2013014950
ISBN 978 90 272 0526 1   (Hb ; alk. paper)
ISBN 978 90 272 7178 5   (Eb)

John Benjamins Publishing Co. · P.O. Box 36224 · 1020 ME Amsterdam · The Netherlands
John Benjamins North America · P.O. Box 27519 · Philadelphia PA 19118-0519 · USA

Erros

My latest found, my sakesbelieve,
this nakeshift *is*--
my ownly
$$l=u=n=g=u=a=g=e.$$

Table of contents

Preface

"...aspect is expressed in English by all kinds of idiomatic turns, rather than by a consistently worked out set of grammatical forms".

Sapir (1921:108)

The study of tense, aspect and mood/modality has been a very productive area of research from a variety of theoretical and applied perspectives because, as noted elsewhere (e.g. Ayoun & Salaberry 2005; de Saussure, Moeschler & Puskás 2009; Salaberry 2008), it is relevant to so many areas of inquiry – syntax, morphology, semantics, discourse/pragmatics – as well as to the integration of information across the interfaces formed by each one of these domains. Temporal-aspectual systems have thus a great potential of informing our understanding of the developing competence of second language (L2) learners. However, the vast majority of empirical studies investigating L2 acquisition have largely focused on past temporality (e.g. Ayoun 2001, 2004, 2005a; Bardovi-Harlig 2000; Granda 2004; Salaberry 2008), neglecting the acquisition of the expression of the present and future temporalities with rare exceptions (e.g. Benati 2001; Wiberg 2002 for L2 Italian) aside from ESL (English as a second language) learners (e.g. Bardovi-Harlig 2004a, 2004b, 2005; Salsbury 2000), leaving unanswered the question of how the investigation of different types of temporality may inform our understanding of the acquisition of temporal, aspectual and mood systems as a whole.

Investigating the L2 acquisition of different temporalities adds another dimension because their expressions also encompass the various modalities such as the deontic and epistemic modalities. Thus, investigating how L2 learners express various temporalities (past, present, future), aspects (perfective, imperfective, progressive) and moods (indicative, subjunctive, conditional) will expand the empirical inquiry from the domain of tense-aspectual systems to the tense-aspect-mood/modality (TAM) systems, providing a much more complete picture of the developing competence of L2 learners.

Although the concepts of tense-aspect and mood/modality are presented in different chapters for ease of exposition, as it will become clear, some overlap will be unavoidable since these concepts are inextricably linked.

This monograph is organized as follows: Chapters 1 and 2 present a descriptive account of TAM in French and English from a Minimalist perspective; Chapter 3 introduces the current theoretical assumptions for the acquisition of TAM systems from a generative/minimalist perspective, while Chapter 4 is a non-exhaustive review of the generative and non-generative literature in the acquisition of TAM systems in French; new empirical data from English-speaking learners of French in an instructed setting are presented in Chapter 5; pedagogical applications based on our empirical findings are proposed in Chapter 6, while Chapter 7 summarizes the contents of each chapter and suggests directions for future research.

Although no single monograph could address all current empirical and theoretical questions in L2 acquisition, the objective of the present monograph is threefold: (a) to contribute to the already impressive body of research in the L2 acquisition of tense, aspect and mood/modality from a generative perspective, and in so doing to present a more complete picture of the processes of L2 acquisition in general; (b) to bridge the gap between linguistic theory and L2 acquisition; (c) to make empirical findings more accessible to language instructors by proposing concrete pedagogical applications.

Acknowledgments

My most sincere thanks and appreciation go to my colleagues Gladys Jean, Kevin McManus, Geoff Poole, Robert Reichle and Sylvia Reed who served as external reviewers, providing insightful comments and invaluable suggestions. I would also like to thank the undergraduate and graduate students from my FRE 467/567 (Topics in French Linguistics; Fall 2012) who took the time to read, comment and evaluate individual chapters. The final version of this monograph greatly benefitted from their input as well. All remaining errors are mine. They are Allison Akmajian, Jordan Bartlett, Kelsey Cockerill, Charlène Gilbert, Laura Hook, Christophe Moller and Andra Soria.

I am grateful to Continuum Press for allowing the rephrasing of a few pages of Ayoun (2003).

Sincere thanks also go to Rosa M. Manchón as the editor of the AILA Applied Linguistics Series (AALS) series. Last, but not least, I very much appreciated how prompt, professional and reliable Kees Vaes was, as always.

CHAPTER 1

Tense, temporality and aspect

Le temps a-t-il seulement un sens, n'est-ce pas plutôt une durée qui, elle, cerne le temps, l'immobilise et lui apporte une valeur?

Jacques Lamarche

1.1 Introduction: The concepts of time, tense and aspect

From a linguistic perspective, the concept of time is expressed with the two distinct grammatical categories of tense and aspect. It is interesting to note that in French, both the concept of time and the grammatical category of tense are expressed with the same word *le temps*; the contrast between the singular and plural forms of determiners (e.g. *le vs. les* 'the') is necessary to distinguish between the concepts of time (*le temps*) and tense (*les temps*).

Tense is a deictic category that "relates the time of the situation referred to some other time, usually to the moment of speaking" (Comrie 1976: 1–2), whereas aspect represents the "different ways of viewing the internal temporal constituency of a situation" (Comrie 1976: 3). Thus, tense orders events along a timeline, situating them in reference to others (i.e. past, present, future, or before, at the same time or later), whereas aspect reflects the speaker's internal perspective on a given situation, which is why it is also referred to as viewpoint (i.e. perfective for completed, imperfective for incomplete, and progressive for an event which is still in progress).[1] As a verbal inflection, tense is a morphological category, but it is also an important syntactic category, particularly within the framework of generative grammar adopted in this monograph.

As illustrated by Figure 1.1, aspect is further divided into two distinct categories: grammatical aspect and lexical aspect.

Grammatical aspect is concerned with the internal temporal constituency of a given situation, not with its external temporal points of reference. It is expressed through morphological markers. For instance, the main aspectual distinction that French makes between perfective aspect and imperfective aspect is realized

---

1. Perfective comes from Latin *perfectus* 'accomplished'.

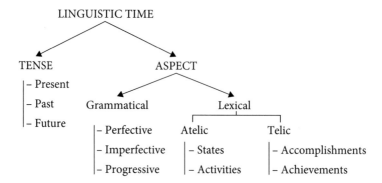

Figure 1.1. Grammatical and lexical aspects

through the inflectional morphology of the *passé composé/passé simple* and the *imparfait*, respectively (e.g. Smith 1991/1997). The perfective aspect focuses on the beginning and the end of a situation, while the imperfective aspect focuses on the situation from within, without definite temporal boundaries, as illustrated by the following sentences:

(1) a. *Paul a écrit   une lettre à ses parents.*
         Paul write-PERF a   letter to his parents
         'Paul wrote a letter to his parents'

     b. *Paul écrivait   une lettre à ses parents.*
         Paul write-IMP a   letter to his parents
         'Paul was writing a letter to his parents'

As we will see below in greater details, (1a, b) illustrate two different past tense markings: the same predicate *écrire* 'to write' is encoded with the *passé composé* in (1a) to indicate that the action of writing a letter is viewed as completed (i.e. Paul started to write a letter and was able to finish writing it within a specific temporal frame such as the afternoon); whereas in (1b), encoding the predicate with the *imparfait* conveys that the action is viewed as incomplete (i.e. Paul started to write a letter but did not finish writing it for some reason: he was interrupted by someone or stopped to attend to another task). Thus, Langacker (1982:274) contends that "a perfective predicate describes the change of a configuration through time", whereas "an imperfective predicate describes the constancy of configuration through time". Similarly, Caudal and Roussarie (2005:267–268) argue that the perfective focuses on changes of state, whereas the imperfective addresses the permanence of the state in the world.

English is said to be limited to two tense forms: past and present (or past and nonpast referring to present and future time) and its main aspectual distinction is between the perfective and the progressive, although a more detailed account would include four aspects: simple (or imperfective), perfect (or perfective), progressive and perfect progressive as shown in Table 1.1 (adapted from Celce-Murcia & Larsen-Freeman 1999:110):

Table 1.1. The English tense-aspect system

		Aspect		
		Simple	Perfective	Progressive	Perfect progressive
Tense	past	talked	had talked	was/were talking	had been talking
	present	talk/talks	has/have talked	is/are talking	has/have been talking
	future	will talk	will have talked	will be talking	will have been talking

Table 1.1 includes future in the tense axis to present a complete picture of the various tense-aspect combinations in English.

Lexical aspect or *Aktionsart*[2] refers to the inherent semantic property of the verb phrase or predicate. Most of the literature on tense-aspect has adopted Andersen's (1991) description of the well-known Vendler-Mourelatos hierarchy (Mourelatos 1978; Vendler 1967) to propose the following aspectual categories: (1) prototypical states refer to situations which do not involve change over time, do not have salient endpoints or gaps, are non-volitional, and do not require any input of energy (cf. Binnick 1991; Comrie 1985) (e.g. 'to know something'); (2) Activities are dynamic situations which involve change over time, but lack a specific endpoint (e.g. 'to swim'); (3) Accomplishments are dynamic situations which have a certain duration and include an end result (e.g. 'to paint the house'); (4) Achievements refer to dynamic situations which involve an instantaneous change (e.g. 'to realize something').

Achievements and accomplishments are also said to be telic to convey that they have an inherent outcome or endstate, whereas states and activities are said to be atelic to indicate that they lack such an inherent outcome or endstate. Two additional lexical aspectual distinctions oppose stative (states) to dynamic (activities), and punctual (achievements) to durative (accomplishments) (e.g. Andersen 1991). The semantic features of these aspectual distinctions in association with lexical aspectual values are summarized in Table 1.2.

---

2.   The word *Aktionsart* means literally 'kind of action'. Its origins are traced back to Aristotle who distinguished between *enérgeia* (incomplete movement) and *kíne:sis* (complete movement) as referring to the two basic types of situation found in our natural environment (Verkuyl 1993:43).

Table 1.2. Semantic features of aspectual categories

	States	Activities	Accomplishments	Achievements
punctual	–	–	–	+
telic	–	–	+	+
dynamic	–	+	+	+

Table 1.2 shows that aspectual classes can be distinguished by a single semantic feature: activities and accomplishments are distinguished by the [±telic] feature, while the distinction between accomplishments and achievements is established by the [±punctual] feature, and the [±dynamic] feature separates states and activities.

Some researchers distinguish more lexical classes, whereas others recognize fewer. Thus, semelfactives (activity verbs denoting single action events such as *wink, wave, jump* or *knock*) are added by combining the feature [+instantaneous] with the feature [+telic] in the classification proposed by Smith (1991/1997), while eliminating durativity as a relevant semantic feature combines accomplishments and achievements into a single class (Dowty 1986; Mourelatos 1981; Ramsay 1990; Salaberry 1998, 2000a).

The use of lexical aspectual classes as a theoretical framework to analyze the development of verbal morphology among second language (L2) learners was pioneered in Andersen (1986, 1991) and became known as the Aspect Hypothesis.[3] As we will see in Chapter 4, the Aspect hypothesis is the theoretical proposal that has generated the largest body of L2 empirical research among instructed learners so far.

1.2   Past temporality and aspect

French and English exhibit two different tense and aspectual systems: French relies on tense, periphrastic tenses and time adverbials, while English uses tense, modals, *have* and time adverbials.[4] Thus, both languages use morphological means (tense marking), lexical means (time adverbials plus modals in English) and syntactic means (periphrastic tenses) to express past temporality.

---

3.   The Aspect hypothesis is also known as the Lexical Aspect hypothesis, the Primacy of Aspect hypothesis (e.g. Robison 1990, 1995), or the Redundant Marking Hypothesis (e.g. Shirai & Kurono 1998); there are no principled differences between these terms, Aspect hypothesis is used in this monograph.

4.   A periphrastic form is composed of an auxiliary and past participle as opposed to a single form bearing a verbal inflection (e.g. *j'aurais voulu* 'I would have like' *vs je voudrais* 'I would like').

The main past tenses in French are the *passé composé* (or indefinite past), *passé simple* (or definite past), *imparfait* and *plus-que-parfait*, as illustrated respectively by the following examples:

(2) a. *Estelle   a   acheté   des   livres.*
         Estelle   has   bought-PERF   some   books
         'Estelle bought books'

     b. *Sophie   acheta   des   livres.*
         Sophie   bought-PERF   some   books
         'Sophie bought books'

     c. *Marie   achetait   des   livres.*
         Marie   bought-IMP   some   books
         'Marie bought/was buying/would buy books'

     d. *Anne   avait   acheté   des   livres.*
         Anne   had   bought-PERF   some   books
         'Anne had bought some books'

Both the *passé composé* in (2a) and the *passé simple* in (2b) are perfective past tenses, but the latter is more rare and typically limited to written contexts, to more elevated registers, or to refer to the historic past in oral contexts. The *passé simple* can express a punctual event as in (3a), an iterative event as in (3b) or a durative event as in (3c):

(3) a. *Paul   sonna   et   entra   sans   attendre   de   réponse.*
         Paul   ring-PERF   and   walk   in-PERF   without   wait   answer
         'Paul rang the bell and walked in without waiting for an answer'.

     b. *Pour   gagner   sa   vie,   avant   d'être   célèbre,   ce   photographe*
         To   win   his   life,   before   be   famous,   this   photographer

         vendit   des   cartes   postales.
         sold-PERF   postcards

         'To make a living, before he became famous, this photographer was selling postcards'.

     c. *Ne   pouvant   y   croire,   je   demeurai   prostré   dans*
         Not   can   it   believe,   I   stayed-PERF   prostrate   in

         mon   fauteuil.
         my   armchair

         'I couldn't believe it, so I stayed prostrated in my armchair'.

The *plus-que-parfait* in (1d) is also a perfective past tense that always refers to a point further back in time than a predicate encoded at the *passé composé* or the *imparfait*. The *imparfait* in (1c) is an imperfective past tense that also expresses iterative and durative semantic aspectual values (see Ayoun 2004 for an empirically-based distinction, following Kaplan 1987), whereas the *passé composé* embodies only the perfective. By definition, the imperfective is understood as being nonperfective as in (4b):

(4)   a.   *Attila   a   choisi   les   meilleures   photos.*
Attila   has   selected   the   best   photos
'Attila selected the best photos'.

b.   *Attila   choisissait   les   meilleures   photos.*
Attila   select-IMP   the   best   photos
'Attila selected the best photos'.

The action of selecting photos was completed in (4a), while it was still ongoing in (4b) and never completed. The iterative expresses habituality as in (5a, b):

(5)   a.   *Le   samedi   matin,   ma grand-mère   allait*
The   Saturday   morning,   my   grand-mother   go-IMP

au marché.
to   the market
'On Saturday mornings, my grand-mother would go to the market'.

b.   *Charlotte   voyageait   toujours   seule.*
Charlotte   travel-IMP   always   alone
'Charlotte would always travel by herself'.

Note that it is the phrase *le samedi matin* that expresses habituality in (5a); its omission would give the predicate a perfective reading and the verb would have to be encoded at the *passé composé* (*samedi matin, ma grand-mère est allée au marché*).

On other hand, the durative is most often used with stative or activity predicates as in (6):

(6)   a.   *Nous   ne   voulions   pas   partir parce   qu'il pleuvait*
We   neg   want-IMP   NEG   leave   because   it   rain-IMP

très   fort.
very   strong
'We did not want to leave because it was raining very hard'.

b.   *Elle   dansait   et   adorait   cela.*
She   dance-IMP   and   love-IMP   this
'She danced/was dancing and loved it'

The examples in (5) and (6) show that the *imparfait* may correspond to various forms in English such as the simple past or the past progressive. As a matter of fact, L2 learners have a tendency to erroneously equate the *imparfait* with the progressive in English which typically appears with non-stative predicates which is not true for the *imparfait*, as illustrated with the following examples in (7a, b):

(7) a. *Marthe   a   vécu   à   Paris.*
         Martha   has   lived   at   Paris
         'Martha lived in Paris'

     b. *Marthe   vivait   à   Paris.*
         Martha   lived-IMP   at   Paris
         'Martha was living in Paris'

According to Smith (1997: 200), the example in (7a) presents a closed situation, in contrast with the example in (7b) which introduces a situation that may or may not still be open, whereas the *imparfait* in (6b) does not have or imply any type of activity or temporary status.

Standard English main past tenses are the simple past, the past progressive, and the past perfect as illustrated in (8a), (8b) and (8c), respectively:

(8) a. The players practiced all week.
     b. The players were practicing all week.
     c. The players had practiced all week.

The main past tense forms in French and English are summarized in Tables 1.3 and 1.4.

Table 1.3. Past Tense morphology in French

Tense	Morphological encoding	Example
passé composé. (PC)	auxiliary *avoir/être* present + past participle	*j'ai, tu as, il/elle/on a, nous avons, vous avez, ils/elles ont travaillé*
passé simple. (PS)	verb + inflectional endings	*je travaillai, tu travaillas, il/elle/on travailla, nous travaillâmes, vous travaillâtes, ils/elles travaillèrent*
imparfait. (IMP)	verb + inflectional endings	*je travaillais, tu travaillais, il/elle/on travaillait, nous travaillions, vous travailliez, ils/elles travaillaient*
plus-que-parfait. (PQP)	auxiliary *avoir/être* imparfait + past participle	*j'avais, tu avais, il/elle/on avait, nous avions, vous aviez, ils/elles avaient travaillé*
past progressive. (PastProg)	auxiliary *être* + en train de + nonfinite verb	*j'étais en train de travailler*
passé antérieur	auxiliary *avoir/être passé simple* + past participle	*quand j'eus fini de travailler, je m'offris un cigare*

As illustrated with the examples above in (1a) and (1c), French distinguishes between the perfective aspect and the imperfective aspect as realized through

Table 1.4. Past Tense morphology in English

Tense	Morphological encoding	Example
simple past	verb + -ed	I worked
present perfect	has/have + verb + -(e)d	I have worked, he has worked
past perfect	had + verb + -(e)d	I had worked
past progressive	verb + - ing	I was working/you, they were working
past perfect progressive	had been + verb + -ing	I had been looking forward to it

the inflectional morphology of the *passé composé* and the *imparfait*, respectively, whereas English contrasts the perfective with the progressive, as realized through the inflectional morphology of the simple past and the periphrastic expression *to be + -ing*. This aspectual distinction is not expressed grammatically in French, but lexically with the idiomatic, periphrastic expression *être en train de* ('to be in the middle of'), as shown in (9):

(9)   a.   The children were playing outside.
      b.   *Les enfants étaient en train de jouer dehors.*
           The children were in the middle of to play outside

The progressive aspect can also be expressed with *aller* ('to go') followed by the present participle as in (10a, b) or *être en voie de* as in (11a):

(10) a.   *La   crise   économique   va   s'aggravant.*
           The   economic   crisis   goes worsening
           'The economic crisis is worsening'

      b.   *Ses difficultés personnelles allaient grandissantes.*
           His difficulties personal   went-IMP growing
           'His personal difficulties were increasing'

(11) a.   *Avatar est en voie de détrôner Titanic au   box-office.*
           Avatar is on way to dethrown Titanic at the box-office
           'Avatar is about to replace Titanic at the box-office'.

However, the structure in (10) is becoming increasingly rare, while the structure in (11) is not very common.

Although English distinguishes between the perfective and the imperfective aspects as well, it does not exhibit a strict correspondence between morphological forms and aspectual values contrary to French: the simple past expresses the perfective aspect as in (12a), the non progressive aspect as in (12b), and the habitual aspect as in (12d):

(12) a. Dad took care of all the paperwork.
      b. We understood their arguments.
      c. *I was understanding their arguments, I just did not agree.
      d. We went/used to go windsurfing when we lived in Florida.

The example in (12c) shows that typically the progressive is ungrammatical with a stative predicate in English, while it is perfectly acceptable in French (*nous comprenions leurs raisons*).

Both the habitual and the nonprogressive are imperfective. Thus, a single morphological form, the simple past in English expresses three different aspectual values from the perfective to the imperfective which lead Giorgi and Pianesi (1997), among others, to propose that English eventive verbs are inherently [+perfective], in contrast with Romance languages such as French or Spanish in which verbs are classified as either perfective or imperfective, not at the predicate level, but at the Aspectual Phrase level.

The main aspectual distinctions in French and English are summarized in Figure 1.2.

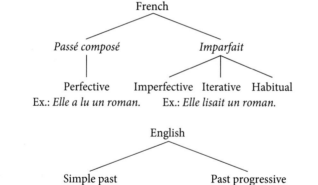

Figure 1.2. Aspectual distinctions in French and English (from Ayoun & Salaberry 2008)

Past tense can be hypothetical instead of expressing past temporality in both languages with if-clauses as in:

(13) a. *Si j'avais su, je n'aurais rien dit.*
          If I know-PQP, I nothing say-CondPast
      b. If I had known, I would not have said anything.

In addition, while English distinguishes between the indefinite past expressed by the present perfect as in (14a), and the definite past conveyed by the simple past as in (14b), only the *passé composé* is available in French to express both as shown in (14c):

(14)   a.   They have proposed new solutions.
       b.   They proposed new solutions.
       c.   *Ils ont proposé de nouvelles solutions.*

As its name indicates, the present perfect has the particularity to be anchored both in the past and the present; it refers to an event anterior to the present which may or may not continue into the present (Celce-Murcia & Larsen-Freeman 1999):

(15)   a.   The event continues into the present: 'we've lived here for years', *nous vivons ici depuis des années*. French uses the present because the event is still true at the time of the discourse.
       b.   The event was completed before the time of the discourse: 'she has rented the house for years', *elle a loué la maison pendant des années*. In French, the perfective aspect indicates that indeed the event was completed in the past.
       c.   The event was recently completely: 'Paul has just won his match', *Paul vient de gagner son match*. The recent past is conveyed by the lexical expression *venir de* + infinitive in French, but the main verb *venir* is in the present.
       d.   The event occurs in the past but still has present relevance: 'She has already tried on this dress', *elle a déjà essayé cette robe*. In French, there is no difference between this situation and the situation in (b): in both cases, the perfective is used to indicate that the event was completed in the past. *Déjà* is not compatible with the recent past of the lexical expression *venir de* as in (c).
       e.   With verbs in subordinate clauses of time or condition: 'If you've eaten all your vegetables, you can have a cookie', *si tu as fini tous tes légumes, tu peux avoir un biscuit*. 'When you've finished the summary, you can start on the reading', *quand tu finiras/auras fini le* résumé, *tu pourras commencer la lecture*.[5]

In other words, the English present perfect can be expressed in French as a present (including the recent past with *venir de* encoded with the present), *passé composé* and future or *futur antérieur*.

To sum up, when they arrive at their adult mature grammar, the past temporality system of French native speakers exhibits both tense and aspect with rich morphological forms, along with semantic and pragmatic features. The past temporality

---

5.   'When you finish-FUT/FUT ANT the summary, you can-FUT start the reading'

system of English native speakers also includes semantic and pragmatic features to convey tense and aspect; its predicates are characterized by a poorer verbal morphology which nonetheless offers many irregular paradigms (e.g. 'spoke', 'brought', 'took', 'did', 'sang') along with -ed for the regular past form. Moreover, the main aspectual distinction in French is between the perfective (*passé composé*) and the imperfective (*imparfait*), whereas in English, it is between perfective (simple past) and progressive (-ing), which is lexicalized but not grammaticalized in French. English distinguishes between indefinite past (present perfect) and definite past (simple past), whereas French does not, but its perfective form (*passé composé*) is structurally identical to the present perfect to which it is also sometimes identical aspectually, but not always.

1.3   Present temporality and aspect

1.3.1   The simple present or indicative present

An event encoded with the simple present in French is simultaneous with the time of discourse (Speech = Reference = Event) to convey "immediate factuality" (Lewis 1986), but it can also evoke: (a) an event in progress or unfolding; (b) an immediate past event; (c) a future event deemed certain at the moment of discourse; (d) a series of past events one wishes to represent more dramatically (*présent historique*). On the other hand, the English simple present only has two functions: (a) to make an event more punctual or more real; (b) to evoke a static or fixed reality.

The main functions of the simple present are as follows:

1.   To make an event more punctual or more real. This is a common function of the present in French (e.g.: *je lance la balle et je la frappe de toutes mes forces* 'I throw the ball and hit it as hard as I can'), but only in certain contexts in English such as to add a dramatic effect to a sportcast (e.g.: 'the biathlete aims, shoots, scores and skies away') or in an historical narrative (*présent historique*) which is a common in both French and English, as well as when the event and expressing it are simultaneous (e.g.: 'I quit!' *je démissionne!*).
2.   To evoke a static or fixed reality.
     –   state verbs (although more so in French than in English): *cette voiture appartient à mes parents*, 'this car belongs to my parents'; *je sais que c'est possible*, 'I know it's possible'.
     –   verbs expressing feelings or thoughts: 'she just loves winter', *elle adore l'hiver*; 'I suppose it's possible', *je suppose que c'est possible*. Some of these English verbs can be encoded both at the present and the present progressive, but take on a different meaning: 'I feel sad' vs 'I'm feeling silly'; 'am I hearing you correctly?' vs 'I hear his flight was cancelled'.

- expression of habituality: *je joue au tennis le dimanche*, 'I play tennis on Sundays' vs 'I'm playing tennis Sunday morning' which indicates a single or new occurrence. Similarly, *je travaille en ville* 'I work downtown' vs 'I'm working in the downtown office tomorrow morning'.
- general timeless truths such as physical laws: *la terre tourne autour du soleil*, 'the earth revolves around the sun'.

3. To express a future certainty, usually with a future-adverbial: 'they retire next year' *ils prennent leur retraite l'année prochaine*. The present progressive is also possible here, but with a greater emphasis on the future.

4. To express an immediate past: 'we come to honor his memory' *nous venons honorer son souvenir*.

5. *Venir de* also expresses an immediate past in French as in *elle vient de partir*, but it corresponds to the simple past in English with the expression 'just + verb': 'she just left'. On the other hand, *je viens vous parler de notre projet* is conveyed by the present perfect 'I've come to talk to you about our project'.

6. Adverbials *depuis, il y a, voilà…que/cela fait…que*. With these adverbials, the simple present in French clearly has a global aspect that views the situation from its beginning to the moment of speech:
   - *je le connais depuis cinq ans* 'I've known him for five years'.
   - *cela fait cinq ans que nous travaillons ensemble* 'we've been working together for five years'.
   In contrast, English uses the present progressive (to indicate an ongoing event) or the present perfect (to indicate that the event is anchored in the past).

7. In the subordinate clauses of condition when the main clause contains a future-time verb in both English and French: 'If I have time, I will give her a call', *si j'ai le temps, je lui téléphonerai;* but the two languages differ for subordinates of time as we will see below: 'I will give her a call when I have time', *je lui téléphonerai quand j'aurai le temps*.

In addition to the present indicative, and contrary to French for which it is the only tense to express present temporality and refer to events at the moment of discourse, English also has:

1. the present progressive: the children are playing tennis
2. an emphatic present with 'do': the children do play tennis
3. the present perfect: the children have played tennis

The various morphological forms are summarized in Tables 1.5 and 1.6.

Table 1.5. Present temporality in English

English tenses	Morphological encoding	Example
simple present	verb + -s/Ø	I, you, we, you, they work/(s)he works
present progressive	present 'be' + -ing	I'm reading a new novel
emphatic present	'do' + predicate	I do believe the show starts at 8pm
present perfect	'have' + past participle	I have started a new project

Table 1.6. Present temporality in French

French tenses	Morphological encoding	Example
simple present	verb + inflectional endings	*je travaille, tu travailles, il/elle/on travaille, nous travaillons, vous travaillez, ils/elles travaillent*
present progressive	lexical expressions	*je suis en train de lire; elle est en voie de réussir; ses difficultés vont grandissant*

When describing reality as a present truth, the simple present indicative forms of French and English convey the global aspect.

If-then clauses in French require specific tense concordances, as shown in (16):

(16) a. *Si je gagne,   je pars   en vacances.*
          if I   win-IndPres, I go-IndPres on vacation
          'If I win, I'm going on vacation'

      b. *Si je gagne,   je partirai en vacances.*
          if I   win-IndPres, I go-Fut on vacation
          If I win, I will go on vacation

      c. *Si je gagne,   partons   en vacances.*
          if I   win-IndPres, go-Imper   on vacation
          If I win, let us go on vacation

      d. *Si je gagne,   nous partons   en vacances!*
          if I   win-IndPres, we   go-IndPres on vacation
          'If I win, let's go on vacation!'

      e. **Si je gagne,   je suis   en train   de partir*
          if I   win-IndPres, I go-IndPres in the middle of leave-Inf

          en vacances.
          on vacation
          'If I win, I'm going on vacation"

Si clauses are used to express a possibility or hypothesis: the simple present can be followed by the present, future or imperative in the main clause. The present is clearly taken in its global aspect because it does not have a present reference, but at best a near future reference. The present renders the situation more real for the speaker.

In English, the present of the if clause can be followed by the present progressive, the future or the imperative.

(17)   a.   If I win, I'm taking a vacation
      b.   If I win, I'll take a vacation
      c.   If I win, let's take a vacation
      d.   If I do win, I will/am taking a vacation

The lexical expressions for the present progressive are not possible in French in these cases because the main clause is hypothetical, not actually conveying an event in progress as in (15e) above.

When adverbials clauses are used to express future temporality, projecting ahead to anticipate an event, both the subordinate and the main clauses require the future in French as in (18):

(18)   a.   *Nous sortirons quand il fera beau.*
      b.   **Nous sortirons quand il fait beau*
      c.   We will go out when it's nice.
      d.   *We will go out when it will be nice

Thus, in English a simple present can express a probable future in the subordinate clause even when the main clause is encoded with a probable or certain future. In contrast, French gives the same degree of probability to both clauses.

1.3.2   The present progressive

The present progressive is used in English to express:
    An activity or change in progress:

(19)   a.   The children are playing soccer
         Les enfants jouent au football

      b.   They are becoming more and more like their father
         Ils ressemblent de plus en plus à leur père

A temporary situation:

(20)   She's driving a rental car on her trip
      Elle conduit une voiture de location

A repetition or reiteration of similar ongoing actions:

(21)   Paul is focusing, aiming and shooting calmly
      Paul se concentre, vise et tire calmement

An extended present without the permanence of the simple present:

(22)   My niece is studying at Harvard
        Ma nièce fait des études à Harvard

The translations show that French uses the simple present for all these situations.

The present progressive in English has at least four aspectual values:

–   punctual: 'She's dropping out of school', *elle arrête ses études*
–   durative: 'They are working downtown', *ils travaillent en ville*
–   static: 'The children are sleeping peacefully', *les enfants dorment paisiblement*
–   habitual: 'The trains are always arriving late', *les trains sont toujours en retard*

The present progressive can be used readily with activity verbs to stress the duration:

(23)   a.   My brother is swimming.
              Mon frère nage.

        b.   I always enjoy reading mysteries.
              J'aime toujours lire des mystères.

The progressive adds the meaning of iteration as in (24) or inception of an event as in (25) to achievement verbs:

(24)   We are building houses for Habitat.
        Nous construisons des maisons pour Habitat.

(25)   She is winning the race.
        Elle gagne la course.

As noted above, the present progressive is used more rarely with stative verbs because of the inherent semantic contradiction between the grammatical aspect of the progressive and the lexical aspect of states, but Celce-Murcia and Larsen-Freeman (1999: 121) list the following cases which show how "progressive statives" can be used to express the following (the examples are partially adapted):

(26)   a.   A greater emotion: 'I'm hating this assignment', *Je déteste ce devoir;* 'I'm loving it', *j'adore.*

        b.   A current behavior as opposed to a general characteristic: 'They are being difficult' ≠ 'they are difficult', *Ils se montrent difficiles ≠ ils sont difficiles;* 'they are being silly ≠ they are silly, *ils sont bêtes /font les bêtes ≠ ils sont bêtes.*

        c.   A change in states by stressing differences in degrees: 'I'm understanding this less and less', *je comprends de moins en moins.*

Celce-Murcia and Larsen-Freeman (1999:121) also cite Gavis (1997) for the additional following uses of progressive statives (examples partially adapted):[6]

> d. To show limited duration: 'are you understanding this?', *comprenez-vous?*; 'I'm not getting this', *je ne comprends pas.*
>
> e. To stress a voluntary state: 'what we are seeing is a red star', *ce que nous voyons est une étoile rouge.*
>
> f. To increase the intensity: 'I'm hearing the wind howling', *j'entends le vent hurler.*
>
> g. To be polite: 'are you enjoying it?' ≠ 'do you enjoy it', *est-ce que cela vous plait? or vous aimez?'*
>
> h. To attenuate criticism: 'I like the beginning, but I'm not liking it toward the end', *j'aime le début mais je n'aime pas trop la fin.*

1.4   Future temporality and aspect

The future can be represented as speech time preceding event time, that is, Speech < Event (Reichenbach 1947). It is sometimes argued that the future is not marked as consistently as past time reference (Dahl 1985:109). The future stands out from the past and the present in encompassing both temporality and modality, as opposed to the past and the present which only express temporality.

The modal readings of the future include possibility, probability, intention and desire or volition (Bybee 1985), with intentionality usually assumed to be the most common reading (Bybee 1985; Bybee, Perkins & Pagliuca 1994). Bybee et al. (1994) also propose that the future expresses two main modalities in desire and obligation, and two minor modalities in ability and attempt, while Larreya (2000:120) suggests that 'will' expresses a "particular type of necessity, which is *necessary consequence*". [original emphasis].

English has a variety of ways to express future temporality as listed in (27):

(27) a. Lexical futures: semantically future predicates (e.g. *want, hope, have to*)
      b. Adverbials (e.g. *tomorrow, next week, soon*)
      c. *About to* (e.g. *she's about to sing*)
      d. *Will* + predicate (e.g. *she will sing*)
      e. Periphrastic future: *going to* + predicate (e.g. *she's going to sing*)

---

6. To avoid imposition with the example 'I was just wanting to invite you to a gathering' is an expression of politeness as in (g) and more likely to be used in the past progressive than in the present progressive.

    f.   Present + adverbial *(e.g. she sings tomorrow)*
    g.   Present progressive *(e.g. she's singing)*
    h.   Future perfect *(e.g. she will have left by the time you arrive)*

'Will' is one the several modal auxiliaries English has (e.g. 'might, may, can, could, will, would, should'; Coates 1983; Palmer 1990); a modal being defined as a pragmatic/semantic device to express a speaker's opinion or feeling about a proposition.

    French has the following means of expressing future temporality as enumerated in (28):

(28)   a.   Present tense morphology *(praesens pro futuro)* + time adverbial: *je pars ce soir* 'I leave tonight' (Mellet 2000)

          b.   Periphrastic future *(futur proche* for imminent or immediate future) (Vet 1993): *je vais partir demain/*dans dix ans* 'I am leaving tomorrow/ in ten years'

          c.   Synthetic future *(futur simple)* or inflected future: *je partirai ce soir/ dans dix ans* 'I will leave tonight/in ten year'

          d.   *Futur antérieur: dès que/aussitôt que vous aurez enregistré vos bagages, vous pourrez embarquer* 'as you as you will have checked your luggage, you will be able to board'

As Bonami (2002: 34) points out, the future tense is aspectually neutral, contrary to past tenses which express perfectivity *(passé composé)* or imperfectivity *(imparfait)* (see above and e.g. Andrews 1992; Ayoun 2005b), as illustrated by the fact that it combines equally well with both telic and atelic predicates in their basic interpretation. Thus, both (29) and (30) are grammatical, although the predicate in (29) is combined with an atelic description, while the predicate in (30) is combined with a telic description (examples from Bonami 2002: 34):

(29)   a.   *Paul dormira*
            Paul sleep-FUT
            'Paul will sleep'

(30)   a.   *Paul ira   à la plage*
            Paul go-FUT to the beach
            'Paul will go to the beach'

However, as in past tense morphology, the future can express the progressive aspect with the lexical expression être en train de 'to be in the middle of' as in *Paul sera en train de travailler quand on arrivera* 'Paul will be working when we arrive'.

The main ways of expressing futurity in French and English are summarized in Table 1.7:

Table 1.7. Futurity in English and French

English	French
I will dance	*Je danserai*
I want to dance	*Je veux danser*
I'm going to dance	*Je vais danser*
I will do it if I have time	*Je le ferai si j'ai le temps*
I will do it when I have time	*Je le ferai **quand j'aurai** le temps*
I will do it as soon as I get there	*Je le ferai **dès que je serai** arrivé*
She will have left by the time you arrive	*Elle sera partie quand tu arriveras*

Table 1.7 shows that the two languages share three morphological forms: The simple future ('I will dance'/ *je danserai*), the lexical future ('I want to dance'/*je veux danser*), and the periphrastic future ('I'm going to dance'/*je vais danser*). However, they are not necessarily equivalent in English to French and vice-versa. Thus, it is generally agreed that 'will' is an expression of modality, whereas the simple future in French expresses mostly temporality (but see e.g. Larreya 1996, 2000, for arguments against a purely temporal meaning of the French *future simple*). Both English 'will' and simple future in French express volition or have a predictive value (Larreya 2000). Moreover, English 'will' often corresponds to the French periphrastic future which expresses a more immediate future.[7]

Larreya (2000) argues that the French immediate future *aller* + predicate has a wider range of uses than 'be going to', and focuses on five of these uses as illustrated in (30) (the examples are from *ibid*: 116–119):

(31)   a.   Facts linked to a condition
             Ne touche pas l'assiette, tu vas te brûler les doigts/?tu te brûleras.
             Don't touch the plate, you will burn your fingers/*are going to burn
             your fingers

        b.   Intention/decision
             Donne-moi cette boîte, je vais te l'ouvrir/??je te l'ouvrirai.
             Give me this box, I will open it for you/??am going to open it for you

---

7.   English is also known for 'futurates' or sentences without an obvious way of referring to the future, but still convey a future eventuality as planned or determined such as 'The surfing contest starts/is starting tomorrow' (e.g. Binnick 1991; Copley 2009).

c. Characteristic behavior
En Amérique, c'est pas pareil, surtout sur la côte ouest. Une femme se mettra du maquillage et s'habillera bien pour elle-même, pas pour les autres/va se mettre, se met du maquillage.
A woman will make herself up and dress elegantly for herself/makes herself up/*is going to make herself up

In the case of characteristic behaviors, both English and French can use present, as well as simple future, and French also allows the use of periphrastic future, in contrast to English.

d. Conjecture
That will be Amelia/?is going to be
Ça sera sûrement Amélie

e. Directive uses
Linda, vous m'appellerez ce numéro s'il vous plaît/appelez/allez appeler
Linda, will you get me this number please/?are going to/?you get me

Praesens pro futuro is more common in French than in English (Le Goffic & Lab 2001) which tends to use a present progressive instead: *je pars demain soir*/'I'm leaving tomorrow night'. In other words, similarities between the two languages are only at the surface level. Similar morphological forms yield different semantic expressions that L2 learners have to acquire.

The last four examples in Table 1.1 illustrate another similarity between the two languages for the 'if'/*si* clauses which are followed by the present when the future is used in the main clause in French. But it also shows two differences between French and English, namely: (a) *quand* is followed by the future in French, but by the present in English when the main clause is in the future; (b) *futur antérieur* (future perfect) is generally not required in English, whereas it is not always, but usually required in French.

Futur antérieur is considered as a complex form with primary temporal and aspectual functions, or a "compound tense-aspect" (Waugh 1987: 12). In its temporal meaning, the event takes place after the speech point (Speech < Event < Reference). In other words, it is a past relative to the future. It is one of the rare forms that French, which unlike English does not have clearly marked modal auxiliaries, may rely on to indicate epistemic modality (Palmer 1986: 35–36). *Futur antérieur* has three main modal meanings: probability in the past as exemplified in (32a), eventuality in the future as in (32b), and indignation as in (32c):

(32) a. *Paul n'est pas encore arrivé?   Il   se sera   perdu.*
Paul is   not yet   arrived? He be-FUT lost-PP
'Paul hasn't arrived yet? He probably got lost'

b. *Quand elles auront   trouvé ce   qu'elles   cherchent, elles*
    When   they   have-FUT   find-PP what they look for-PRES,   they

    nous le diront.
    us   it tell-FUT
    'When they find what they are looking for, they will tell us'

c. *Elle aura   encore menti!*
    She   have-FUT   again   lie-PP
    'She lied again'

Gobert and Maisier (1995: 1006–08) list eighteen modal uses of *futur antérieur* from their analysis of a written corpus of *L'Express*, but explain that in twelve cases, the *futur antérieur* is being used instead of the *passé composé*, that is, to express a perfective, as in the example in (33) (*L'Express*, n. d., *ibid*: 1007):

(33)   *Jamais, depuis sa nomination, M. Rocard n'aura subi pareille disgrâce dans l'opinion.*
       'Never since his nomination, M. Rocard has suffered such disgrace in public opinion'

However, L2 French learners in instructed settings are unlikely to come across such examples until a very advanced stage of their instruction, and corpus data show that the *futur antérieur* has a very low frequency; in fact, it is outnumbered by all other tenses (Engel 2001).

1.5   Summary

This chapter has highlighted similarities and differences between English and French regarding the central concepts of time and temporality, lexical and grammatical aspect as well as morphological forms. Both languages use lexical, morphological, pragmatic and syntactic means to express past, present and future temporality, but differently. Thus, perfective *vs.* imperfective is the main aspectual opposition in French whereas it is perfective *vs.* progressive in English which is characterized by a poorer verbal morphology than French which nonetheless offers many irregular paradigms. The two languages also differ when it comes to tense concordances with a partial overlap for 'if' clauses. Finally, a past tense form does not necessarily imply a past reference the same way a present tense form does not necessarily imply a present reference, illustrating the complexity and subtleties of TAM systems.

CHAPTER 2

Mood and modality

Les hommes vivent dans un monde où ce sont les mots et non les actes qui ont du pouvoir, où la compétence ultime, c'est la maîtrise du langage.

Muriel Barbery

2.1 Introduction

In the introduction to his review of several works on modality, Hoye (2005:1297) notes that "'modality', as a unique and challenging field of enquiry into human thought and language, has truly come of age having now achieved a status in linguistics scholarship along with tense and aspect". Hoye goes on to explain how central to human thought and expression are the modal concepts of *possibility*, *certainty*, *probability* and *necessity*.

> As Perkins (1983:6) has argued, the human attitudes and behavior from which such concepts are extrapolated can be understood in terms of a marked human tendency to conceive of things as they might be, may or must have been or could be, should or ought to have been. This desire to conceive of things being otherwise "constitutes an essential part of the fabric of our everyday lives".
>
> (Hoye 2005:1298)

Modality thus embodies a crucial property of natural languages, displacement. Contrary to animal communication systems, human beings are not limited to reality – the here and now – modality allows us to express a vast range of emotions, thoughts and dreams.

Modality has also been defined as "the grammaticalization of the speakers' (subjective) attitudes and opinions" (Palmer 1986:16), while "modality selection is determined by the evaluation of the status of the conceptualized event with respect to reality" (Achard 2002:197). It is the speaker's choice, and is thus entirely subjective.

Modality has also come of age in that it is now considered to be a fully-fledged grammatical category on a par with tense and aspect – it was initially classified as a semantic term (e.g. Palmer 1979), then later as a grammatical category (Palmer 1986, 2001) – and TAM, as the acronym for tense, aspect, mood/modality, is now well known and widely recognized.

Modality differs from tense and aspect in that it does not directly refer to the event itself, but rather to the status of the proposition. Let us consider the following examples:

(1)   a.   It may be Paul's birthday tomorrow.
      b.   It should be Paul's birthday tomorrow.
      c.   It can't be Paul's birthday tomorrow.

The example in (1a) expresses the possibility that Paul's birthday is tomorrow, but more as an uncertainty than as a possibility. In (1b), the speaker expresses a tentative belief based on a deduction or reasoning: I know that Paul's birthday comes soon after Lisa's and her birthday was two days ago so Paul's birthday should be tomorrow. Finally, in (1c), the speaker is making the stronger assertion that by deduction or personal knowledge, Paul's birthday cannot be tomorrow because it comes soon after Lisa's who has not had her birthday yet.[1] On the other hand, all the examples in (2) refer directly to the event, be it in the past, future or present:

(2)   a.   Paul's birthday was two days ago.
      b.   Paul's birthday will be in a week.
      c.   Paul's birthday is in the spring.

The literature traditionally establishes a clear basic distinction between *mood*, *modality* and *modal system*, with modality being defined as the main grammatical category, while mood and modal system are being viewed as two grammatical sub-categories. Most languages appear to either have a modal system such as English, or a mood system such as the Romance languages. Thus, mood is principally exemplified by the contrast between indicative and subjunctive in French, also referred to as realis and irrealis in other languages such as Native American languages (Palmer 2003).

However, a modal system and mood may co-exist in languages whose modal verbs have not been fully grammaticalized and/or where the subjunctive is losing ground, as in French or Italian (e.g. Palmer 2001). Palmer (2003: 3) even contends that "the two types of modality are mutually exclusive: languages have either mood or modality, but not both".

Thus, the English modal system has developed – and continues to develop with the emergence of new modal forms as we will see below – while the subjunctive has dwindled down to the point that some even argue that the subjunctive can no longer be referred to as a mood in English (e.g. James 1986).

---

1.   Lyons (1977:797) makes a distinction of "some theoretical interest" between objective and subjective modality while noting it cannot "be drawn sharply in the everyday use of the language; and its epistemological justification is, to say the least, uncertain".

In contrast, French is still very much a 'mood language' because it clearly instantiates the traditional five moods: indicative, subjunctive, imperative, conditional and infinitive. In English, only the indicative, imperative and infinitive can still be classified as moods. However, since conjugated French verbs combine tense, aspect and mood into a single form, it is not always clear whether a given verbal form represents a tense or a mood, an ambiguity that English avoids with distinct modal auxiliaries and lexical verbs.

Following the logician von Wright (1951: 1–2), it is generally agreed that there are three main types of modality: epistemic, deontic and dynamic.[2] Epistemic modality expresses the speaker's attitude regarding the status of the proposition (i.e. its truth value, what is known and what is believed about the proposition), whereas the potentiality of the event is expressed by the proposition in both deontic and dynamic modalities; in the former, the event is controlled by circumstances external to the subject of the sentence, whereas in the latter, the control is internal to the subject, as in the following examples:

(3) a. The children may be in school.   epistemic modality
     b. The children can come in now.   deontic modality
     c. The children can run very fast.   dynamic modality

These examples also illustrate that deontic and dynamic modalities are directive in that they both enable the subject to act, but the deontic modality gives permission to the subject to do so, whereas the dynamic modality comes from the subject's ability to perform action, in this case, to run very fast.

Some languages display a fourth kind of modality – evidential modality – in which the speaker provides evidence for the truth value of the proposition (see e.g. Aikhenvald 2004, for a study of grammatical evidentials). The epistemic and evidential modalities are also said to be propositional, while the deontic and dynamic modalities are said to be evidential. The essential feature of modality is that of assertion expressed by the indicative – when the veracity or factuality of the proposition is clearly established – versus non-assertion expressed by the subjunctive – when the veracity of the proposition is in doubt or the proposition is

---

2. Palmer (2001) has replaced the fundamental "epistemic" vs. "deontic" notions with propositional vs. event modality, with propositional being further divided into evidentiality and epistemicity, and event modality being further divided into deontic and dynamic modality. See also Gotti, Dossena, Dury, Facchinetti and Lima (2002) for detailed subcategories of deontic modality (into volition, necessity, possibility), epistemic modality (into possibility, inference, necessity) and dynamic modality (into ability, possibility, prediction, necessity, habit).

unrealized or presupposed (Lunn 1995:430). Evidential modality is also referred to as aletheutic (or alethic from the Greek word for 'truth') modality.

Although evidential modality is not very common in English, 'must' and 'will' exhibit some of its characteristics (Palmer 2003:8), and it appears that French has a few means of expressing grammatical and lexical modality (Dendale & Van Bogaert 2007), although it is argued to lack both morphological evidentials (Lazard 2001:360) and grammatical v (Aikhenvald 2004:17) (cited in Dendale & Van Bogaert 2007:66).

2.2   Mood in French and English

2.2.1   Overview

According to the traditional dictionary definition, a verbal mood conveys what the speaker wishes to express from a fact (indicative mood), a command (imperative mood), a question (interrogative mood), to conditionality (subjunctive mood). It also includes verbal inflections for languages which exhibit rich morphology such as the Romance languages.

Matte (1989:1) contends that "[w]hat distinguishes one verb mood from another is the kind of mental process each reflects, the level of abstraction above concrete tangible reality at which each mood operates". Matte goes on to classify the five moods from the lowest to the highest level of abstraction in terms of the mental process they require as follows: indicative, imperative, subjunctive, conditional and infinitive. Moods are also classified as personal (i.e. indicative, imperative, subjunctive, conditional) and impersonal (infinitive, participle).

French still uses all five moods, whereas English essentially uses only the indicative, imperative and infinitive. The subjunctive in English has dwindled down to the point that it is no longer considered a mood, while the conditional is expressed by modals. One may also refer to sentence moods as opposed to just predicates which gives English three main moods (declarative or indicative, interrogative, imperative) as well as two minor moods (exclamatory and subjunctive) (Celce-Murcia & Larsen-Freeman 1999).

The indicative mood represents temporal reality at the lowest level of abstraction; it allows the speaker to indicate where and how he or she situates the event in time (past, present, future) (Matte 1989:166). In expressing the speaker's volition at the moment of the discourse, the imperative is closer to the atemporal moods (subjunctive, conditional and infinitive) than to the clearly temporal indicative. One may say that the imperative acts as a bridge between the indicative and the subjunctive, not only because of its level of abstraction, but also because it borrows verb forms from both moods, in French as well as in English. Thus, the French imperative uses the present subjunctive endings for several verbs such as *avoir, être, savoir* and *vouloir* and all the forms for the indirect imperative are drawn from the present subjunctive [suppletive imperative]. This is also true for the imperative forms of 'to be' in English where 'be' is the sole form for both moods.

With the subjunctive mood, we reach a higher level of abstraction than expressed by the indicative and the imperative. Both the imperative and the subjunctive express volition, but the subjunctive has a much greater variety of modalities or attitudes which can be roughly divided in three categories: volition (commands, wishes, requirements, requests, etc.), subjectivity (in judgment, opinion, belief, etc.) and doubt, all of which only exist in the mind of the speaker at the moment of the discourse.

Finally, the infinitive form of a verb is its uninflected form, that is, its base form. It is sometimes called the nominalized form of the verb because it "attaches labels to states of being, to events or to actions to indicate the type of verb processed involved" (Matte 1989: 173). Incidentally, very few verbs have indeed been nominalized such as *le boire* 'drinks, drinking', *le manger* 'food, eating', *le rire* 'laugh'. We will also consider past and present participles.

2.2.2   The indicative and subjunctive alternation in French

The indicative mood is the most common realis mood used to express the factuality of an opinion (e.g. *je pense que vous avez raison* 'I think you are right'), state a fact (e.g. *le président Kennedy a été assassiné* 'President Kennedy was assassinated'), or ask a question (e.g. *savez-vous si la pièce a déjà commencé?* 'do you know if the play has already started?'). It is probably the mood with which learners are most familiar because it is introduced very early on in the curriculum of instructed foreign languages and because indicative morphological forms (i.e. tenses) convey all three temporalities: past, present, future. Moreover, the indicative is considered as the default mood, while the subjunctive is viewed as a marked mood because it must be triggered and occurs in fewer contexts, syntactically.[3]

Morphologically, French exhibits simple tenses (present, *imparfait*, future, *passé simple*), compound tenses (*passé composé, plus-que-parfait, futur antérieur*), as well as lexical expressions (*être en train de* and *aller* en + present participle, *venir de, aller* + infinitive, to express the progressive, a recent past, and a near future, respectively).

If the indicative mood expresses certainty, then the subjunctive mood expresses uncertainty as well as subjectivity in many different cases (superlatives, emotion,

---

3.   The word *subjonctif* comes from Latin *subjungere* which means 'to place under the dependance of'.

doubt, (im)probability, (im)possibility), volition and judgment (e.g. desire, wishes, commands, regrets), as contrasted in (4):

(4)   a.   *Il   est en   retard parce   qu'il*
          he   is-IndPres late   because he

          s'est   perdu.   indicative, *passé composé*
          get-PC   lost

          'He's late because he got lost'

      b.   *J'ai   peur qu'il*
          I have-IndPres fear   that

          se   perde.   present subjunctive
          he get-SubjPres lost

          'I'm afraid he'll get lost'

      c.   *Lisa réussit   toujours dans ce*
          Lisa succeed-IndPres always   in   what

          qu'elle entreprend.   indicative, present
          she   undertakes-IndPres

          'Lisa is always successful in her undertakings'

      d.   *Je suis   contente qu'elle*
          I   be-IndPres happy   that

          ait   réussi.   past subjunctive
          she   succeed-PastSubj

          'I'm happy she succeeded'

It is the predicate in the main clause that determines whether the predicate in the subordinate (or embedded) clause will be encoded with a tense of the indicative mood as in (4a, c) or the subjunctive mood as in (4b, d). More specifically, the predicate in the main clause expresses certainty or uncertainty/subjectivity as far as the event in the subordinate clause occurring or not.[4]

The distinction between semantic contexts triggering the subjunctive or not can be quite subtle. Thus, lexical expressions of doubt, possibility, impossibility and improbability trigger the subjunctive but lexical expression of probability do not, as illustrated in (5):

(5)   a.   *Il n'est pas impossible qu'il   pleuve.*   (impossibility)
          it is   not impossible that it rain-SubjPres
          'It is not impossible that it rains'.

---

4.   See any traditional grammar for a complete list of contexts which require the use of the subjunctive.

b.   *Il se peut   qu'elle n'ait   plus   confiance*
     it is possible that   she have-SubjPres no more trust

     en eux.   (possibility)
     in them

     'It could be that she no longer trusts them'.

c.   *Il est improbable que ce*
     it is unlikely   that this

     document soit authentique.   (improbability)
     document is-SubjPres

     'This document is probably not authentic'.

d.   *Il est probable que notre équipe perdra/?perde.*   (probability)
     it is probable that our   team   lose-Fut/?SubjPres
     'Our team is likely to lose'.

However, as indicated in (5d), anecdotal evidence suggests that some French native speakers may extend the use of the subjunctive to expressions of probability as well.

Similarly, one may wonder why only certain verbs expressing an opinion trigger the subjunctive, while others do not depending on the context. Thus, if the predicate in the main clause expresses a statement (e.g. *dire* 'to say', *affirmer* 'to assert', *annoncer* 'to announce', *déclarer* 'to declare'), the subjunctive will be triggered in the subordinate clause typically only in the case of a negative principal clause as shown in (6):

(6)   a.   *Je n'ai pas   dit vous ayez/?avez tort.*   (negative)
           I not say-PC that you have-SubjPres/?IndPres
           'I did not say you were wrong'.

    b.   *J'affirme que c'est faux.*   (affirmative)
           I assert that it is-SubjPres false
           'I'm asserting that this is false'

    c.   *Déclarez-vous que cela est/?soit faux?*   (informative)
           declare you   that this is-IndPres/?SubjPres false
           'Are you saying it's wrong?'

The subjunctive in French thus generally appears in a subordinate clause, contrary to English. If only the subordinate clause is used, it is necessarily introduced by the complementizer *que* as illustrated in (7):

(7)   a.   *Qu'il   vienne!*
           that he come-SubjPres
           'Let him come'.

b.   *Que Dieu t'entende.*
     that God   you hear-SubjPres
     'May God hear you'.

c.   *Qu'à cela ne   tienne.*
     that to   this hold-SubjPres
     'If that's the only problem, it's fine'.

Although French exhibits a *subjonctif présent* and a *subjonctif passé*, the present/
past distinction is not temporal in that it does not necessarily refer to a past event;
thus, although the example in (8a) indicates the anteriority of the event expressed
by the predicate in the subordinate clause, the examples in (8b, c) do not:[5]

(8)   a.   *Elsa est heureuse que vous ayez chanté.*
           Elsa is happy   that you sing-SubjPast
           'Elsa is happy that you sang'

      b.   *Elsa est heureuse que vous chantiez.*
           Elsa is happy   that you sing-SubjPres
           'Elsa is happy that you are singing'

      c.   *Elsa est triste que vous n'ayez pas chanté.*
           Elsa is sad   that you sing-SubjPast not
           'Elsa is sad that you didn't sing'

In all three sentences, Elsa is happy or sad in the present, but the event of singing
is anterior in (8a) and (8c), whereas in (8b) it corresponds, or is posterior, to Elsa
being happy. However, singing never took place in (8c) and is indeterminate in
(8b), which may be confusing for L2 language learners.

    The following examples show that the choice of present versus past subjunctive
is independent of the tense used in the main clause:

(9)   a.   *Je voulais   qu'elle   vienne   avec moi.*
           I   want-IMP that she come-SubjPres with me
           'I wanted her to come with me'

      b.   **Je voulais   qu'elle soit venue   avec moi*
           I   want-IMP that   she come-PastSubj with me
           'I wanted her to come with me'

---

5.   The *imparfait du subjonctif* has fallen into disuse (see e.g. Wagner & Pinchon 1991 for a
description of its morphology and contextual uses. And example would be: *je craignais qu'il ne
vînt pas* 'I feared he wouldn't come'. The *plus-que parfait du subjonctif* is no longer used either
and an example would be: *j'aurais préféré qu'il n'eût eu de père* 'I would have preferred he had
never had a father'.

    c.   *Je suis/étais   contente qu'elle soit venue   avec moi*
        I am-IndPres/IMP happy   that   she come-PastSubj with me
        'I am/was happy that she is coming/came with me'

    d.   *Je serai/s contente   qu'elle   vienne   avec moi.*
        I am-Fut/CondPres that she come-SubjPres with me
        'I will/would be happy if she came with me'

    e.   *J'étais contente   qu'elle   vienne   avec moi.*
        I   am-IMP happy that she come-SubjPres with me
        'I was happy that she came with me'

    f.   *J'étais contente   qu'elle soit venue   avec moi.*
        I   am-IMP happy that   she come-SubjPast with me
        'I was happy that she came with me'

The subjective attitude of happiness in the main clause can be in the past, present or future; however, the event in the subordinate clause remains in the present subjunctive except in (9b) to express the anteriority of the event in the subordinate clause.

    Although the indicative and the subjunctive moods are usually mutually exclusive, they do alternate with verbs of opinion, such as *penser* 'to think', *croire* 'to believe', *supposer* 'to suppose', *estimer* 'consider', *trouver* 'think/find', in negative as well as in interrogative contexts, but not in affirmative contexts as follows:[6]

(10) a.   *Marc pense   que Lisa est/*soit   intelligente.*
         Marc think-IndPres that Lisa is-IndPres/*SubjPres intelligent
         'Marc thinks that Lisa is intelligent'

      b.   *Marc croit-il   que Lisa est/soit   intelligente?*
         Marc believes-IndPres that Lisa is-IndPres/SubjPres intelligent
         'Does Marc believe that Lisa is intelligent?'

      c.   *Marc ne considère   pas que Lisa*
         Marc considers-IndPres not that Lisa

         est/soit   intelligente.
         is-IndPres/SubjPres intelligent

         'Marc doesn't consider Lisa to be intelligent'

The indicative competes with the subjunctive when following some superlative and restrictive expressions as in (11):

(11) a.   *C'est le   meilleur film que j'aie jamais vu/ai jamais vu.*
         it   is-IndPres the best film that I   ever   see-PastSubj/PC
         'It's the best film I've ever seen'

---

6. See also Abouda (2002).

b.   *Lisa est   la   seule   qui*
     Lisa is-IndPres the only one who

     me comprenne/comprend.
     me understand-PresSubj/PresInd

     'Lisa is the only who understands me'

The indicative is more factual while the subjunctive is more subjective, maybe even emotional, in these cases.

Similarly, the subjunctive competes with both the indicative and the conditional in specific relative clause constructions such as in (12):

(12)   a.   *Marc cherche   un secrétaire qui*
            Marc look-IndPres a   secretary that

            sache/sait/saurait   parler arabe.
            know SubjPres/IndPres/CondPres speak Arabic

            'Marc is looking for a secretary who can speak Arabic'

       b.   *Lisa aimerait travailler avec   des   collègues   qui*
            Lisa like-CondPres   work-Inf with colleagues that

            la   comprennent/comprendraient.
            her understand-SubjPres/IndPres/CondPres

            'Lisa would like to work with colleagues who would understand her'

Contrary to French, Modern English is a modal rather than a mood language; consequently, the remnants of the subjunctive are quite marked.[7] The few instances of subjunctive left in Standard English (from Palmer 2003: 4) are shown in (13).

(13)   a.   Long live the King!
       b.   I propose that they be excluded.
       c.   May he rest in peace.
       d.   I'm surprised that Anne should think that.
       e.   If I were you.

The examples in (13a) and (13c) are more like frozen expressions; (13a) and (13b) exhibit uninflected verbal forms; (13d) and (13c) use modal verbs, while the form of 'be' in the last example remains the same in person and number and is always in the past tense form.

---

7. The loss of the subjunctive in English is due to phonological changes (Visser 1963–73: 789, cited in Roberts 1985: 41) which eliminated distinctions between the indicative and the subjunctive.

When it occurs in embedded clauses, the verb does not vary, it is never inflected for person regardless of time reference as shown in the following examples from Celce-Murcia and Larsen-Freeman (1999: 632–647):

(14) a. They insist that all the students sign up for a counselor.
      b. They insist that this student sign up for a counselor

(15) a. The customer is demanding that the stores return his money.
      b. The customer demanded that the store return his money

(16) a. We insist that he be the one to make the call.
      b. The customer demanded that his money be returned.

The subjunctive in English is also visible in negative embedded clauses in which the negation 'not' appears alone, without a 'do' operator, before the verb: a negation element is always placed directly before the main verb rather than after an auxiliary verb; thus, no addition of the 'do' operator is impossible:

(17) a. We insist that he not make the telephone call.
      b. *We insist that he do/does make the telephone call.

According to Celce-Murcia and Larsen-Freeman (1999: 633), verbs of urging and advice such as 'ask, request, prefer, propose, recommend' also trigger the use of the subjunctive in the embedded clause, as well as certain main-clause adjectives such as 'important, imperative, vital':

(18) a. It is important that she be given another chance.
      b. It was imperative that she act immediately.
      c. What is vital is that he not be/get overly anxious.

Thus, the subjunctive mood does survive in Standard English in specific contexts, but it is definitely a less frequent occurrence and a more marked form than it is in French. Furthermore, it occurs exclusively in specific contexts in English, whereas the subjunctive in French can compete with the indicative and the conditional to which we now turn.

2.2.3   The conditional mood

Although the conditional is sometimes considered as an indicative tense with both temporal and modal aspects (e.g. Wilmet 1997: 289), it is more often classified as a mood that expresses irrealis, that is the hypothetical aspect, since the ideas conveyed are abstract. Thus, contrary to the indicative that is firmly anchored in reality, the conditional indicates that the event is construed as an alternative to reality. Moreover, it is an atemporal mood because the events it refers to cannot be reliably placed in the past, present or future, but they do suggest it, as exemplified in (19):

(19) a.   *Il   a promis   qu'il le   ferait.*
           He   promise-PC that he it do-CondPres
           'He promised he would do it' [later: future reference]

      b.   *Il   le ferait   mais il   a été   retenu.*
           He   it do-CondPres but   he hold-PassPC up
           'He would do it' [now: present reference], but he was held up.

      c.   *Il   l'aurait fait   mais il   a été   retenu.*
           He   it   do-CondPast but   he hold-PassPC up
           He would have done it [past reference] but he was held up.

In some cases, the event expressed by the present conditional or past conditional implies that it did in fact take place depending on the predicate used in the main clause, as shown in (20):

(20) a.   *Paul espérait   que sa lettre arriverait   le lendemain.*
           Paul hope-IMP that his letter arrive-CondPres the next day
           'Paul was hoping that his letter would arrive the next day'.

      b.   *Paul savait   que sa lettre arriverait   le lendemain.*
           Paul know-IMP that his letter arrive-CondPres the next day
           'Paul knew that his letter would arrive the next day'.

      c.   *J'avais   bien prédit   que les socialistes*
           I have-IMP well predict-PastPart that the socialists

           obtiendraient   la majorité.
           obtain-CondPres the majority

           'I did predict that the socialist would win'.

      d.   *Tu n'aurais   pas dû lui   dire ça!*
           you not have-Cond neg should-PastPart him/her tell this
           'You should not have told him/her that!'

In (20a) we did not know whether the letter arrived the next day, whereas (20b) implies that it did. In (20c), the socialists did win, whereas the example in (20d), which expresses a reproach implies that someone did say something that he or she should not have said, according to the speaker.

   French always uses the same inflectional endings (future stems with imperfect endings, *-ais, -ais, -ait, -ions, -iez, -aient*),[8] whereas English can express the

---

8.   Because of its morphological form of the future plus the imperfect endings, it is sometimes referred to as *futur du passé* 'future of the past' (e.g. Gosselin 1996; Vuillaume 2001; Wilmet 2001; but see Caudal &Vetters 2005, or Achard 2002, for a different perspective).

conditional mood with two modals, 'would' as seen in the above examples, and 'could' as in the following examples:

(21) a. Marc could answer your questions.
          Marc pourrait répondre à vos questions.

      b. The children could play outside.
          Les enfants pourraient jouer dehors.

      c. We could take an earlier flight.
          Nous pourrions prendre un vol plus tôt.

The conditional is commonly used in counterfactual constructions with *si* 'if', in which the main clause introduces an event that did not, and may never, take place whether the point of reference is in the present or future as in (22a), or in the past as in (22b):

(22) a. *Si j'avais   le   temps, je ferais les   courses.*
          if I have-Imp the time, I do-CondPres shopping
          'If I had time, I would go shopping'

      b. *Si j'avais eu   le   temps, j'aurais fait les courses.*
          if I have-PQP the time,   I do-CondPast
          'If I had had time, I would have gone shopping'.

The conditional is also appropriately used following lexical expressions such as *au cas où* 'just in case' or *selon* 'according to' expressing irrealis as in (23):

(23) a. *Prends   ton parapluie au cas où il pleuvrait.*
          take-Imper your umbrella in case it   rain-CondPres
          'Take your umbrella in case it rains'.

      b. *Selon   la   presse, le Président se serait rendu en Afrique.*
          according to the press, the president go-CondPast in Africa
          'According to the press, the President would have gone to Africa'.

Finally, the conditional attenuates the illocutionary force of the indicative as in (24):

(24) a. *Je vous demande   de ne pas fumer.*
          I   you ask-IndPres to not   smoke
          'I'm asking you not to smoke'.

      b. *Je vous demanderais   de ne pas fumer.*
          I   you ask-CondPres to not   smoke
          'I would ask you not to smoke'.

      c. *Je veux   que vous m'aidiez.*
          I   want-IndPres that you   me help-SubjPres
          'I want you to help me'

    d. *Je voudrais*   *que vous m'aidiez.*
       I   want-CondPres that you   me help-SubjPres
       'I would like you to help me'

As the alternative translations 'would you please not smoke' for (24b) and 'would you please help me' for (24d) indicate, when used as an attenuating mood, the conditional allows the speaker to be more polite. The conditional inflectional endings apply to all lexical and auxiliary verbs in French, whereas English uses the modals 'could' and 'would'.

2.2.4   The imperative mood

The imperative mood expresses the speaker's volition at the time of the discourse. As such, it implies an immediate or more distant future time and resembles the atemporal subjunctive, conditional and infinitive moods.

Contrary to English which only allows the 2nd person single pronoun 'you' with imperative forms (e.g. 'you be quiet!', 'don't you forget to pick her up!'), French exhibits a full paradigm as shown in (4) with *sortir* 'to go out':

(25) *Que je   sorte!*
     that I-1st SG go out
     'let me go out!'

     Sors!
     go out-2nd SG
     'go out!'

     Qu'il/elle/on   sorte!
     that he/she/one go out-3rd SG
     'let him/her go out!'

     Sortons!
     'go out-1st-PL'
     'let us go out!'

     Sortez!
     go out-2nd PL
     'go out!'

     Qu'ils/elles   sortent!
     that they-msc-PL/they-FEM-PL go out
     'let them go out!'

The context indicates whether the predicates conveys an immediate future as in (26a, b) or a more distant future as in (26c, d):

(26) a. *Prends   ton parapluie en sortant. Il pleut.*
       take-2nd SG your umbrella in going.   It rains
       'Take your umbrella when you go out, it's raining'

b. *Ne   jette pas le   journal,   je vais le lire.*
Throw-2nd sg   not the newspaper, I go it read'
'Don't throw away the newspaper, I'm going to read it'

c. *N'oubliez   pas   d'appeler quand vous serez   arrivés.*
forget-2nd pl not to call   when you will be arrived
'Do not forget to call when you arrive'

d. *Revenez   nous   voir à Noël*
come-2nd pl back us   see   at Christmas
'Come back to see us at Christmas'

The three traditional forms or forms used most often (i.e. second singular and plural, first plural) are typically the same forms as the indicative present, while the other forms (i.e. first singular, third singular and plural, those of the so-called indirect imperative because the speaker is not directly addressing anyone) are the same forms as the subjunctive present and are introduced by the complementizer *que*. There is thus some morphological overlap between the subjunctive present and the imperative. There is also some overlap between the imperative and the infinitive since the infinitive base forms of verbs can be used in specific contexts such as giving instructions or recipes, as illustrated in (27):

(27) a. *A conserver   au frais.*
to keep-INF   at the cool
'Keep refrigerated'

b. *Saisir   vos   données personnelles.*
enter-INF your data   personal
'Enter your personal information'

c. *Laisser mijoter   quelques minutes.*
let-INF stew-INF few   minutes
'Let stew for a few minutes'

In that case, the imperative is more neutral and impersonal in that there is no specific interlocutor. The example in (27a) could be found on a food item, the sentence in (27b) could be read by someone performing a task online and the last example in (27c) would be encountered in a cook book that could read by anyone.

English exhibits an imperative as in (28) and a progressive imperative as in (29):

(28) *Leave! Get   out!*
Let   them come in!
Let us be happy!

(29) Don't be sleeping when I come back.
Be working on that project until it's done.

Since French does not grammaticalize the progressive, it is not surprising that anecdotal evidence indicates that possible equivalents for the examples in (29a, b) shown in (30) range from slightly to completely unacceptable for French native speakers:

(30) a. ?*Ne   sois   pas en train   de dormir   quand*
        Not be-SubjPres in   the process of sleep-INF when

        je   reviendrai.
        I come back-Fut

        'Don't be sleeping when I come back'.

    b. **Sois   en   train   d'étudier   jusqu'à l'heure*
        Be-SubjPres in the process of study-INF until   the hour

        de dîner.
        of eat-INF

        'Be studying until dinner time'.

    c. **Ne soyez   pas en train   de lire n'importe quoi.*
        Not be-SubjPres in   the process of read-INF   whatever
        'Don't be reading nonsense'.

Dominik (2002) notes that there are also non-verbal imperatives with the same illocutionary force of verbal imperatives as follows:

(31) a. *Tout le   monde sur le   quai!   Au   lit!*
        all   the world on the platform! To the bed!

        A   table!   (prepositional)
        To table

        'Everybody on the platform! Bedtime! Dinner is ready!'

    b. *Vite! Tout de suite!*   (adverbial)
        'Quickly! Right away!'

    c. *Attention! Du calme! Pas de panique!*   (nominal)
        'Watch out! Be calm! Let's not panic!'

    d. *Les lèvres Plus rouges! Pas rouges!*   (adjectival)
        "The lips! More red! Not red!'

2.2.5   The infinitive, present and past participles

Although neither the infinitive or present and past participle forms are considered to be traditional moods because they do not carry mood (or tense, aspect, voice) inflectional markers, they are included here because they are very common verbal forms with a variety of uses.

The nonfinite form in French expresses temporality by ordering events along a timeline as shown in (32) which contrasts a simple infinitive form in (32a, b) with a past infinitive (auxiliary + past participle) in (32c, d):

(32)　a.　*Les enfants   veulent   jouer.*
　　　　　The children want-IndPres play-INF
　　　　　'The children want to play'.

　　　　b.　*Elle préfère   voyager   de nuit.*
　　　　　she prefer-IndPres travel-INF of night
　　　　　'She prefers to travel by night'.

　　　　c.　*Il   ne peut   pas avoir   déjà   fini.*
　　　　　He not can-IndPres neg have-INF already finished-PastPart
　　　　　'He can't possibly be done already'.

　　　　d.　*Après avoir   déjeuné,   ils   pourront aller   jouer.*
　　　　　after have-INF eat-PastPart they can-Fut go-INF play-INF
　　　　　'They can go play after eating lunch'.

The simple infinitives are infinitives used as complements of other verbs when they share the same subject:

(33)　a.　*Kent$_i$ veut$_i$ sortir$_i$ avec nous ce soir.*
　　　　　'Kent wants to go out with us tonight'.

　　　　b.　*Les chercheurs$_i$ préfèrent$_i$ travailler$_i$ dans leur laboratoire.*
　　　　　'Researchers prefer to work in their lab'.

　　　　c.　*Je$_i$ sais$_i$ nager$_i$ mais je$_i$ n'aime$_i$ pas plonger$_i$.*
　　　　　'I can swim but I don't like diving'.

Infinitives also appear in lexical phrases as in shown in the examples in (34):

(34)　a.　*Attendre sous la pluie, ce n'est jamais drôle.*
　　　　　'It's never fun to be waiting in the rain'.

　　　　b.　*Grignoter à toute heure fait grossir.*
　　　　　'Munching all day long leads to weight gain'.

　　　　c.　*Chiner aux puces le dimanche, quel plaisir!*
　　　　　'It's a real pleasure to hunt for bargains at the flea market on Sundays'.

A few common verbs are used as nominals (e.g. *le boire* 'drinking', *le manger* 'eating', *le rire* 'laughter).

As seen above and reproduced here, the infinitive can be used as an imperative:

(35)　a.　*A conserver au frais.*
　　　　　to keep-INF at the cool
　　　　　'Keep refrigerated'

b. *Saisir   vos   données personnelles.*
    enter-INF your data   personal
    'Enter your personal information'

c. *Laisser mijoter   quelques minutes.*
    let-INF   stew-INF few   minutes
    'Let stew for a few minutes'

The French present participle in *en* +verb-*ant* is used to express two simultaneous actions by the same subject as in (36):[9]

(36)   a. *Ne   téléphonez pas en   conduisant,   c'est   dangereux.*
           not call-IMP   neg prep drive-PresPart, it is-IND dangerous
           'Don't use your phone while driving, it's dangerous'.

       b. *Elle s'est présentée tout en sachant   qu'elle ne   serait*
           she present-PC   all   know-PresPart that she not   be-COND

           pas élue.
           neg elected

           'She ran while knowing she would not be elected'.

       c. *Etant   vacciné   contre la grippe, j'ai*
           be-PartPres vaccinate-PastPart against the flu,   I have

           pu   voyager.
           can-PP travel-INF

           'Being vaccinated against the flu, I was able to travel'.

Adding '*tout*' in front of the present participle as in (36b) expresses that the two events are contradictory. And a present participle can be followed by a past participle as in (36c) to situate the event further back in the past.

There are some striking differences between French and English regarding the use of the infinitive and the present participle as illustrated in (37):

(37)   a. *J'ai entendu les   oiseaux chanter*
           I   hear-PC the birds   sing-INF
           'I heard the birds singing'

       b. *Paul a vu   l'homme voler   l'argent*
           Paul see-PC the man steal-INF the money
           'Paul saw the man steal the money'

       c. Don't forget to turn off the lights before leaving.
           N'oubliez pas d'éteindre les lumières avant de partir.

---

9.   Traditional grammarians distinguish between the gerund (*en* +verb-*ant*) and the present participle (verb-*ant*).

    d. He answered quickly without thinking.
        Il a répondu rapidement sans réfléchir.

    e. Smoking is bad for you.
        Fumer est mauvais pour la santé.

Thus an infinitive in French can be expressed by an English gerund (37a, c, d, e) or a bare infinitive (37b).[10]

2.3   Modality in French and English

2.3.1   Expressing modality in English

Both French and English have various means of expressing modality which include adjectives (e.g. *possible* 'possible', *probable* 'likely', *nécessaire* 'necessary', *essentiel* 'essential'), adverbs (e.g. *peut-être* 'perhaps/possibly', *nécessairement* 'necessarily'), lexical verbs (e.g. *insister* 'insist', *permettre* 'permit', *exiger* 'demand') and nouns (e.g. *possibilité* 'possibility', *nécessité* 'necessity', *permission* 'permission').

    English also uses a large number of auxiliaries (e.g. 'may', 'can', 'might') as well as infinitival constructions (e.g. 'I'm to pick him at the airport'), whereas according to Achard (1998), French is limited to three main modal verbs – *pouvoir* 'can', *devoir* 'must' and *savoir* in its capability sense of 'to know how to' – although *vouloir* is also sometimes classified as a modal verb (e.g. L'Huillier 1999), while other lexical verbs can be considered as expressing a type of modality as well: *compter* 'to expect', *désirer* 'to desire', *faillir* 'to (only just) fail to', *falloir* (impersonal) 'to be necessary to', *oser* 'to dare to', *paraître* 'to appear to', *sembler* 'to seem to', and *(mieux) valoir* (impersonal) 'to be preferable to', *trouver* 'to find', *avoir l'impression* 'to feel'. Cervoni (1987) refers to other verbs which take an infinitival complements such *croire* 'to believe' or *espérer* 'to hope' as "semi-auxiliaries of modality".

    In additional to the traditional full modal auxiliaries – 'can', 'may', 'must', 'will', 'shall', 'could', 'might', 'should' and 'would' – Modern English has three semi-modals (following the terminology of Biber, Finegan, Atkinson, Beck, Burges & Burges 1999): 'have to', 'be able to' and 'be willing to', which appear to fill the gaps created by the deficient morphosyntax of the modals as we will see below. Thus, 'have to' is a substitute for 'must', 'be able to' for 'can' and 'be willing to' for 'will'. Modern English also has so-called emerging modal auxiliaries (see edited volume by Krug 2000). The modal expressions in English are summarized in Table 2.1.

---

10. A reviewer notes that the -ing form in (37a, c, d) could be referred to as a present participle, but gerund seems to be used just as often.

Table 2.1. Modal expressions in English (adapted from Quirk, Greenbaun, Leech & Svartvik 1985: 137)

central modals	can, could, may, might, shall, should, will, would, must
marginal modals	dare to, need to, ought to, used to
modal idioms	had better, would rather/sooner, be to, have got to, etc.
semi-auxiliaries	have to, be about to, be able to, be bound to, be going to, be obliged to, be supposed to, be willing to, etc.
catenatives	appear to, happen to, seem to, get + -ed past participle, keep + -ing participle, etc.
main verb + nonfinite clause	hope to + infinitive, begin + -ing participle, etc.

Modal auxiliaries differ not only from lexical verbs, but also from the auxiliaries 'have' and 'be' in exhibiting what Huddleston (1976: 333) labeled the NICE properties referring to their occurrence with negation (e.g. she couldn't sleep'), inversion (e.g. 'should I answer?', 'code' (e.g. 'they can run and so can we') and emphatic affirmation (e.g. 'I will get there on time'). Contrary to 'have' and 'be', modal auxiliaries exhibit the following features:

a. They do not co-occur: *would could swim, *may must leave vs 'she may have been sick'
b. They are not inflected for the third person singular: *she mays write vs he has left
c. They lack non-finite forms
d. They lack imperative forms
e. Not all modals have morphologically past tense forms
f. They lack suppletive negative forms
g. "There are formal differences between the modal verbs, in their epistemic and deontic senses, in terms of negation and tense" (Palmer 2001: 101, vii).

Modal auxiliaries do not co-occur, but they can be combined with lexical verbs which exhibit a modal value as in 'it may suggest that...', 'one would think that...'.

The main modals have past tense forms – 'may/might', 'can/could', 'shall/should', 'will/would' – to express past time reference, though not exclusively and they have taken on different meanings to the point that they are no longer considered past tense forms (e.g. Larreya 2003; Pinker 1999/2000) as shown in (38):

(38) a. I could work out but I am too lazy.
     b. Shouldn't you be studying right now?
     c. Would you please help me pick a color?
     d. Scheduling might be able to squeeze you in later in the week.

The modal system of English exemplifies the three main modalities as shown in (39):

(39)   a.   They may be in the office   epistemic
        b.   They may/can come now   deontic
        c.   They can run very fast   dynamic

All modals may be used to encode epistemic and deontic modality, however with clear formal distinctions as expressed by Palmer (2001:103): "(i) deontic 'must' has negative 'mustn't' and a suppletive 'needn't', but epistemic 'must' has no morphologically related negative; (ii) 'may not' negates the modality when deontic (no permission), but the proposition when epistemic ('it may be that it is not so'); (iii) 'may' and 'must' followed by 'have' are always epistemic, never deontic; (iv) 'may' is replaceable by 'can' only in the deontic use, though 'can't' may be epistemic".

Rather than being viewed as ambiguous because they express different modalities, modals can be viewed as being semantically polysemous (Sweetser 1990, but see Papafragou 1998 for potential caveats). Moreover, they may be viewed along a semantic scale that distinguishes between different interpretations. Thus, the epistemic scale can be represented as in Figure 2.1 (Wärnsby 2006:26):

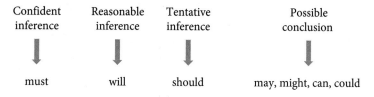

Figure 2.1. The scalar organization of English epistemic modals

Wärnsby (2006:33) suggests a deontic scale as shown in Figure 2.2:

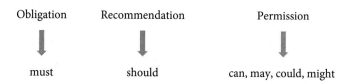

Figure 2.2. The scalar organization of English deontic modals

2.3.2   Expressing modality in French

In contrast to the rich English modal system, L2 French learners will only encounter the four main modal verbs listed above (*pouvoir* 'can', *devoir* 'must', *savoir* 'to know how', *vouloir* 'to want'), and with significant differences from the English auxiliary verbs. First, *pouvoir, devoir, savoir* and *vouloir* behave like lexical verbs in that they exhibit full paradigms for all moods and tenses, that is, they are not morphologically defective in a similar way to English modals. Second, French modal verbs are not structurally different from other verbs: they occur alone, they do need to be combined with auxiliaries or other lexical verbs, and they take infinitival and/or clausal complements. Last but not least, they are polysemous, as we will see below (e.g. Achard 1998; Benveniste 1974; Cervoni 1987; L'Huillier 1999).

The impersonal verb *falloir* 'to be necessary' is curiously missing from the main modal verbs typically listed, but it has a very high frequency of use among French native speakers as well as among L2 learners of French, it is thus included below.

The main modals, their meanings and French equivalent are presented in Table 2.2.

Table 2.2. French and English modals

Modal verb	meaning	French equivalent	Modality
can	ability	*pouvoir*	dynamic
	giving, asking permission	*pouvoir*	deontic
	general possibility	*pouvoir* *il se peut que*	epistemic
	skill	*savoir*	dynamic
could	ability	*pouvoir*	dynamic
	skill	*savoir*	dynamic
	reproach	*pouvoir, devoir*	deontic
	permission	*pouvoir*	deontic
	possibility	*pouvoir*	epistemic
may	permission	*pouvoir*	deontic
	possibility	*il se peut*	epistemic
might	permission	*pouvoir*	deontic
	possibility	*il se peut*	epistemic
shall	politeness	*vouloir*	deontic
	legality	*devoir*	deontic
should	obligation	*devoir*	deontic
	condition (if clause)	*imparfait*	deontic
will	polite request	*vouloir*	deontic
	wish	*vouloir*	deontic

(Continued)

Table 2.2. (Continued)

Modal verb	meaning	French equivalent	Modality
	prediction	*devoir*	epistemic
would	wish	*vouloir*	epistemic
	polite request	*vouloir*	deontic
	determination	*vouloir*	epistemic
	habitual event	*imparfait*	epistemic
	condition (if clause)	conditional	epistemic
	probability	conditional	epistemic
must/have to	necessity, obligation	*devoir* *il faut que*	deontic
must/have to	logical implication, supposition	*devoir*	epistemic

In addition to the main deontic and epistemic modalities, French scholars usually also refer to the alethic modality (most commonly referred to as evidential modality by Anglo-Saxon scholars as seen above) which is expressed with both grammatical – *devoir*, conjectural future, quotative conditional – and lexical means – a variety of expressions (e.g. *trouver* 'find' as in *trouver que* 'find that' to express direct evidence of a fact; *avoir l'impression* 'have the impression, feel', *penser* 'think' as markers of indirect evidence; and *paraître* 'appear', *sembler* 'seem' as modal markers by reference to another discourse (Authier-Revuz 2004) (Dendale & Van Bogaert 2007 following Ducrot 1975; Kronning 1996, 2001; Thuillier 2004).

Thus, Dendale and Van Bogaert (2007) cite several examples of alethic uses of *devoir* from Kronning (1996: 115–116):

(40)   a.   *Un nombre premier doit être impair.*
            'A prime number must be uneven.'

        b.   *Les candidats doivent avoir moins de 52 ans au moment de la nomination.*
            'Candidates must be under 52 years of age at the time of nomination.'

        c.   *Est-ce de la Galilée que le Christ doit venir?*
            'Is it from Galilee that Christ must come?'

According to Kronning (2001), the alethic use of *devoir* expresses necessity and differs from its epistemic use although it is not always easy to disambiguate between the two uses as in the example in (41) which "Dendale (1994: 34) had analyzed as an example of epistemic use, but which is interpreted by

Kronning (2001: 70) as an analytically true alethic use" (Dendale & Van Bogaert 2007: 81):

(41) *Cette figure doit être un cercle puisque la distance de chaque point de la circonférence au centre est identique.*
'That figure must be a circle as the distance to the centre is the same for every point on the circumference.'

Finally, "inferential *devoir* has often been semantically paired to the conjectural future, which can indeed have the same global effect of expressing inference or assumption", as in (42) (*ibid*: 83):

(42) a. *Il   n'est toujours pas là.   Il   aura   oublié*
       He is   still   not here. He will have forgotten

       le   rendez-vous.
       the   appointment
       'He is still not here. He has probably forgotten the appointment.'

      b. *Il n'est toujours pas là. Il a dû oublier le rendez-vous.*
       'He is still not here. He must have forgotten the appointment.'

Dendale and Van Bogaert (2007) argue that the conjectural future is more an "assertion marker or alethic marker (saying something about the truth value of the proposition)" (*ibid*: 84) than an evidential marker, but that distinction is not made by everyone (see e.g. Squartini 2001, 2004). It can be argued that there is no real difference between 'the truth in the world' (i.e. alethic) and 'the truth in an individual's mind' (i.e. epistemic).[11]

All modal verbs are polysemous and French verbs are no exception. Let us review the main meanings of the principal verbs *devoir, pouvoir, savoir, falloir* (following, e.g. Kronning 2001; L'Huillier 1999; Wilmet 1997), while keeping in mind that it is practically impossible to present an exhaustive account.

2.3.2.1 *Devoir*

Devoir expresses two main meanings: obligation or duty and probability (logical supposition). Obligation is exemplified in (43):

(43) a. *Paul ne pourra pas t'aider, il doit partir avant midi.*
       'Paul won't be able to help you, he has to leave before noon.'

---

11. To the best of my knowledge, not a single language formally distinguishes between the alethic and epistemic modalities with, for instance, a different grammatical mood. But all languages express modality in one way or another, and when no lexical means are employed, it is referred to as covert modality (Bhatt 2007).

b. *Les étudiants devront passer tous les examens.*
   'Students will have to take all the exams'.

As mentioned above, French modal verbs exhibit all moods and tenses yielding semantic differences as shown in (44):

(44) a. *Paul devait partir avec nous, mais il a dû rester pour aider Marc.*
        'Paul was supposed to leave with us, but he had to stay to help Marc'.

     b. *Paul aurait dû partir avec nous, maintenant il doit se débrouiller seul.*
        'Paul should have left with us, now he must manage on his own'.

     c. *Paul n'aurait pas dû le laisser seul.*
        'Paul should not have left him alone'.

In (44a), the *imparfait* indicates that the action did not happen, whereas it did with the *passé composé,* and the past conditional in (44b) expresses an opinion about an event that did not take place. It can also express reproach as in (44c).

The second meaning of *devoir,* probability (implying logical supposition), is exemplified in (45) again with various moods/tenses:

(45) a. *Tout est éteint, ça doit être fermé.*
        'All the lights are out, it must be closed'.

     b. *Marie n'a rien dit, elle ne devait pas être fâchée.*
        'Marie didn't say anything, she must not have been upset'.

     c. *L'équipe devrait obtenir de meilleurs résultats cette année avec un nouvel entraîneur.*
        'With a new coach, the team should get better results this year'.

     d. *Elle n'a pas dû le faire puisque rien n'a été touché.*
        'She must have not done it since nothing was touched'.

2.3.2.2 *Pouvoir*

Pouvoir is equally versatile, expressing dynamic, deontic and epistemic modalities. Dynamic *pouvoir* refers to the ability to do something as in (46):

(46) a. *Oui, je peux lire un livre en une heure, mais pas l'écrire!*
        'Yes, I can read a book in an hour, but not write one!'

     b. *Paul ne pourra jamais nager en plein océan.*
        'Paul will never be able to swim out in the ocean'.

     c. *Quand j'étais jeune, je pouvais courir des heures.*
        'When I was young, I could run for hours'.

     d. *Quand j'étais jeune, j'aurais pu apprendre à skier.*
        'When I was young, I could have learned to ski'.

Epistemic *pouvoir* refers to the possibility of doing something as shown in (47):

(47)   a.   *Il se peut qu'il pleuve, c'est très couvert.*
            'It could rain, it's very cloudy'.

       b.   *La cérémonie pourrait être annulée au dernier moment.*
            The ceremony could be cancelled at the last minute.

       c.   *Marc pouvait y aller, mais Paul n'a pas pu et l'a regretté.*
            'Marc was able to go, but not Paul, and he regretted it'.

Finally, deontic *pouvoir* expresses the granting or asking for permission (48a, b), a reproach (48c, d) or politeness as in (48e, f):

(48)   a.   *Les enfants pourront jouer tout l'après-midi.*
            'Children may play all afternoon long'.

       b.   *Vous ne pouvez pas emprunter les magazines.*
            'Magazines cannot be checked out'.

       c.   *Tu ne pouvais pas nous attendre quelques minutes?!*
            'Couldn't you wait for us for a few minutes?!'

       d.   *Paul aurait pu nous prévenir qu'il partait!*
            'Paul could have told us that he was leaving!'

       e.   *Puis-je vous m'accompagner?*
            'May I go with you?'

       f.   *Pourriez-vous me renseigner, je suis perdu.*
            'Would you please give me some directions, I'm lost'.

Again, *pouvoir*, as all modal verbs, is compatible with all moods/tenses, contrary to English modal auxiliaries.

2.3.2.3   *Savoir*

Savoir is essentially dynamic as 'to know how to do something' or 'to know something', as illustrated in (49):

(49)   a.   *Je ne sais rien cuisiner, mais j'adore manger.*
            'I'm a terrible cook but I love to eat'.

       b.   *Un mécanicien saurait changer cette roue en quelques secondes.*
            'A car mechanic would know how to change this tire in seconds'.

       c.   *Je ne savais pas où se trouve ce musée, alors nous sommes allés ailleurs.*
            'I didn't know where the museum was, so we went elsewhere'.

       d.   *L'étudiant n'a pas su répondre à la dernière question de l'examen.*
            'The student didn't know how to answer the last question on the exam'.

2.3.2.4   *Falloir*

The impersonal verb *falloir* expresses the deontic meaning of obligation as in (50):

(50)   a.   *Il faut que vous choisissiez une nouvelle couverture.*
       'You need to choose a new cover'.

       b.   *Il a fallu se dépêcher parce que nous étions en retard.*
       'We had to hurry up because we were late'.

       c.   *Il faudrait se dépêcher pour ne pas manquer l'avion.*
       'We should hurry up if we don't want to miss our flight'.

       d.   *Il faudra bien se décider tôt ou tard!*
       'We will have to decide soon or later!'

       e.   *Il fallait une accréditation, je n'en avais pas, il aurait fallu que je m'y prenne plus tôt.*
       'Credentials were required, I didn't have them, I should have applied for one earlier'.

As an impersonal verb, *falloir* is only used with third person singular pronoun *il* 'it', but it is not morphologically defective in that it may be used with all moods/tenses.

Again, this review of the uses and meanings of the French modal verbs does not have the ambition of being exhaustive, it is simply an illustration of the polysemy of these verbs. The literature displays an embarrassment of riches (e.g. Bres & Mellet 2009; Dendale & Van Der Auwera 2001; Foullioux 2003; Gosselin 2005, 2009), and in addition to studies focusing on modality, some scholars explore the modal uses of temporality (e.g. Declerck 2006 examines the modal uses of indicative forms, while Patard 2011 studies the epistemic uses of the English simple past and the French *imparfait*) blurring the traditional line between temporality and modality (see also Patard & Richard 2011 for a study of hedging in French simple tenses).

2.4   Summary

This chapter's overview of mood and modality in French and English illustrates that the lexical, grammatical and semantic means of expression are as complex, subtle and sophisticated as the speakers' thoughts they are designed to convey. The central concepts of possibility, certainty, probability and necessity are conveyed by nouns, adjectives, adverbials, auxiliaries and verbs. Morphologically and syntactically defective modal auxiliaries prevail in English, while morphologically and syntactically fully-fledged modal verbs predominate in French, which is traditionally described as a mood language, but is really a mix between modality and mood. Finally, mood/modality is not limited to modal auxiliaries and verbs, it also impacts temporality, blurring the lines between tense and modality.

CHAPTER 3

Tense, aspect, modality and the minimalist program

From syntactic theory to language acquisition

Il n'y a pas de langage innocent.
Roland Barthes

3.1 Introduction

In Ayoun (2003), I contended that modern linguistics started with Chomsky's (1959) seminal refutation of Skinner's stance that language was simply another form of behavior conditioned by positive and negative reinforcement. The discipline's major conceptual shifts of the 1950s through the 1960s transformed the investigation of language as cognitive representations and mental processes. Universal Grammar (henceforth UG) – an innate language faculty equipped with abstract principles of grammar and parameters to account for cross-linguistic variation – was offered as a possible answer and became known as the parameter-setting theory or as the principles-and-parameters theory (e.g. Chomsky 1981, 2006; see reviews in e.g. Ayoun 2003; Carroll 2001; Hyams 1986). From this perspective, language is viewed as an internal component of the mind/brain (i.e. I-language). It is a cognitive system that interacts with other cognitive systems.

Arguing that this initial definition of the language faculty was too general to be useful to empirical inquiries, Hauser, Chomsky and Fitch (2002) claim that it should be divided into a faculty of language in the broad sense (FLB) and a faculty of language in the narrow sense (FLN). The FLB would be composed of an internal computational system as well as two "organism-internal systems" – a sensory-motor system and a conceptual-intentional system (*ibid*: 1570–1571). Hauser et al. further assume that "a key component of FLN, is a computational system (narrow syntax) that generates internal representations and maps them into the sensory-motor interface by the phonological system, and into the conceptual-intentional interface by the (formal) semantic system", with recursion being a core property: "FLN take a finite number of elements and yields a potentially infinite array of discrete expressions [...] Each expression is [...] a pairing of sound and meaning" (*ibid*: 1571). Based on comparative data on animal communication systems, Hauser et al. also tentatively hypothesize that only the FLN is unique to the human species, while the cognitive and perceptual mechanisms that the FLB contains would be common to other species. This hypothesis generated a lively debate from a biolinguistic and evolution perspective (see exchanges in Fitch, Hauser & Chomsky 2005; Jackendoff & Pinker 2005; Pinker & Jackendoff 2005; and references therein) which shows that the question of what the faculty of language is exactly, and how it has evolved, is still far from settled.[1]

What most scholars appear to agree on is that the faculty of language includes a computational system and at least two other internal systems, the "sensory-motor" (phonetics/phonology) system and the "conceptual-intentional" (semantics/pragmatics) system (Hauser et al. 2002: 1570–1571). These two systems being interdependent, they are linked by an "interface", the same way the various components (or modules) of any given language are linked and interact, creating various interfaces which have become the locus of much of the current theoretical (see e.g. Adger & Ramchand 2005; Chomsky 2005) and applied research (see e.g. Sorace 2011).

3.2   From parameter-setting theory to current minimalist assumptions

How do we acquire the knowledge of a particular language and the ability to use it (see e.g. Chomsky 1999a, for a retrospective)? As stated above, the existence of a Universal Grammar (UG), an innate language faculty equipped with abstract principles of grammar and parameters, was offered as a possible answer, and became known as the parameter- setting theory or as the principles-and-parameters theory (P&P) (Chomsky 1981).

Early generative grammar (Chomsky 1965; Jackendoff 1977) used a formal evaluation metric with a general rule writing system. It was abandoned because it both lacked explanatory power and failed to put forth empirically testable claims regarding language acquisition (Williams 1987). It was first followed by the proposal of a "universal but parameterized rule" (Bach 1965), then by "substantive universals" (Chomsky 1965), which still amounted to fixed rules of grammar, but were part of a Universal Grammar defined as a set of linguistic principles and elements common to all natural languages.

---

1.   See Chomsky (2005) for an historical perspective on biolinguistics from Lenneberg (1967) to the current formulation of the Minimalist program as well as an updated list of relevant publications at ⟨http://www.wjh.harvard.edu/~mnkylab/publications/languagespeech.htm⟩. See also Di Sciullo and Boeckx (2011) for state-of-the-art articles on evolution, variation and computation.

Although Williams (1976, 1977a, 1977b, 1978) was the first to mention the concept of a parameterized theory "with head-position and presence vs. absence of the specifier and complement left open as parameters for each phrase" (Williams 1987: viii), it was Chomsky (1981) who really captured the attention of the theoretical and applied linguistic community.

Parameter-setting theory was suggested as a solution to three major problems: (1) the developmental problem of language acquisition or how to account for the process of its acquisition over time; (2) the logical problem of language acquisition or how children are able to acquire their first language (L1) so quickly and effortlessly in spite of the scant evidence available to them (i.e. the poverty of the stimulus), a problem which is compounded by the intricacies and subtleties of any language; (3) cross-linguistic variation: the fact that languages vary across well defined and constrained ranges means that seemingly different languages are actually related; this explains both their typological similarities and differences. Their differences are explained by their selection of one of (usually) two parameter settings. In Ayoun (2003), a standard parameter was defined as subsuming several apparently unrelated properties governed by a single abstract principle.

In the early 1990s, the Minimalist Program (Chomsky 1992, 1995, 1999b) maintained two important points: (1) languages were still assumed to be "based on simple principles that interact to form often intricate structures" (Chomsky 1993: 2) and Universal Grammar still "[provided] a fixed system of principles and a finite array of finitely valued parameters. The language-particular rules reduce to choice of values for these parameters" (Chomsky 1993: 4). However, an important change was that parameters were now assumed to be almost completely limited to the lexicon and the "strength" or "weakness" of functional elements, such as Agreement, Tense and Complementizer, following much earlier work. Thus, Borer (1984) suggested that all parameters could be reduced to the "inflectional system", while Fukui (1986, 1988), followed by Chomsky (1989), argued that parameters involved only functional categories (i.e. abstract lexical items) (see also Ouhalla 1991).

The Minimalist Program introduced in Chomsky (1993, 1994, 1995), and subsequently developed in Chomsky (2000, 2001) proposed that knowledge of language can be captured as a function defined by a small number of very general syntactic operations from sets of lexical items to meaning-sound pairs. The syntactic operations are universal and cross-linguistic variability is reduced to the specification of lexical items which are just considered to be bundles of morpho-phonological, semantic and syntactic features. In other words, current minimalist theoretical assumptions are entirely based on the concept of "features" and the literature now refers to syntax as being feature-based. But it is important to note that this is not exactly a new concept for the idea of a feature matrix goes back to the days of early generative syntax. In fact, more than forty years ago, Chomsky (1965) posited an N node branching into a feature matrix that contained the φ-features of gender, number and case. The features of the noun were assigned to the determiner (following Postal's 1966 analysis), which were then matched with lexical items (based on the work of Halle (1962) as well as Jakobson, Fant and Halle (1963) on phonological structure). In other words, one may say that traditional grammatical categories were simply turned into 'features', but that term will be used to conform to the present theoretical and applied literature.[2]

There are three categories of grammatical features (Chomsky 1995, 2001): phonological features, semantic features and formal or syntactic features. The sets of the semantic features and the formal features intersect, and the difference between these two categories of features is that formal features carry the value interpretable/uninterpretable – formalized as [uF]/[iF], following Pesetsky and Torrego (2001) – whereas the semantic features do not.

Formal or syntactic features are further categorized into features with a semantic interpretation (e.g. the feature [present]) – hence interpretable features – and features with a purely syntactic function (e.g. Case on Nouns or Agreement marking on verbs) – hence uninterpretable features. The uninterpretable features of a lexical item are the properties of a lexical item that do not make a semantic contribution such as the φ-features of verbs or the Case features of nouns. Examples of uninterpretable features are the nominative Case [uNom] on subject DPs (checked by a finite verb) or the uninterpretable person feature on AgrS that requires verb agreement, [upers].[3]

Uninterpretable features capture syntactic dependencies by having the following property: they must be checked (or valued, i.e. assigned a value) by a matching lexical element bearing the same feature (be it interpretable or not). This means that every syntactic dependency is triggered by a presence of an uninterpretable feature, and checking theory is essentially a matching theory. In other words, the Minimalist Program (Chomsky 1993, 1994, 1995) introduced a distinct morphological component from which lexical items emerge fully derived and inflected (e.g. with Case features, Agreement features), where they

---

2.   Other syntactic theories make extensive use of features as properties of lexical elements such as the generalized or head-driven phrase-structure grammar (Gazdar, Klein, Pullum & Sag 1985; Pollard & Sag 1994).

3.   The features person, number, gender, negation, tense, aspect, and possibly others, have interpretable and uninterpretable counterparts (iF, uF).

must be checked (or valued)[4] against the functional categories at Logical Form (LF) within their checking domain (i.e. usually the specifier-head relation).

Functional positions are posited to contain only morpho-syntactic features (φ-features) which are used in checking lexical output. Thus, checking relations are triggered by the uninterpretable features of a lexical item which must be checked off at the end of a syntactic derivation in order to meet the Legibility Conditions at the interfaces (particularly at the LF interface). As a result, the final representation received by the semantic component consists only of interpretable features since all uninterpretable features have been deleted, following the principle of Full Interpretation (Chomsky 1993, 1995).

The assumption of (un)interpretable features quickly evolved. In Chomsky (2002/2004: 113), the notion of uninterpretability is already reduced to valuation: one of the properties of an uninterpretable feature F is that it must be valued under Agree for the narrow syntax derivation D to converge. The difference between checking and valuation is that checking is an operation that deletes the uninterpretable feature out of two base generated features (e.g. *u*Tense and Tense) under an Agree relation, whereas valuation consists in a valueless feature being assigned a value by another element (e.g. agreement features are valued by the NP). However, checking and valuation both have the same end result: uninterpretable features are not allowed at LF.

Uninterpretable features are eliminated when they satisfy certain structural conditions:

> an uninterpretable feature of α must be in an appropriate relation to interpretable features of some β. Furthermore, β must be *complete*, with a full set of features. Nouns are always complete since their φ-features are always present (and interpretable); hence, nouns check the φ-features of agreeing categories. Participles are not complete (lacking person) and do not check Case. T may be complete or *defective*; if the latter, it does not check Case. Feature checking, then, resolves to pairs of heads ⟨H,H′⟩ where at least one is complete and they are in an appropriate relation. (Chomsky 2002/2004: 113)

Intuitively, the process of 'checking and valuation' may make more sense than the lexicalist approach of 'checking and deletion' because in the latter, a lexical item is fully inflected before making its way through syntax, whereas in the former, a lexical item is uninflected and the relevant features (e.g. aspect or phi-features for a verb) are added by the syntactic computations as needed as opposed to being deleted if not needed or allowed.

---

4.   I am grateful to Andrew Carnie for the clarification of this point (personal communication, October 2011).

Adger and Ramchand (2005: 172) follow Chomsky (2002/2004) in accepting that "checking is just valuation of an unvalued feature: uninterpretable features are actually just features that need to be valued before interpretation". However, they differ from Chomsky's stance in arguing that there are no inherently uninterpretable features because "either they are already interpretable at the interface, or they start off uninterpretable (unvalued) and become interpretable via valuation in the course of the derivation".[5]

Adger and Smith (2005: 150–151) illustrate how a simple sentence such as 'they bark' is derived. First, they assume that the sentence is headed by T, a syntactic element which bears the interpretable present tense feature [tense:pres], as well as the uninterpretable features [*u*case:nom] and [*u*num:pl], because nominative case in English is syntactically dependent on finite T, and because English verbs agree in number. Following previous work on English verbal morphology (e.g. Lasnik 1981; Bobaljik 1995), Adger and Smith (2005: 151) further assume that "the morphology of the main verb arises because a morphological operation has spelled out the tense and number features of T as a verbal suffix".

The sound pattern of the sentence 'they bark' is linked to its meaning by the following syntactic derivation:

(1)   a.   The relevant lexical items are selected: [*pronoun*[num:pl, *u*case:], *bark* [V], T(ense) [tense:pres, *u*case:nom, *u*num:]].

   b.   *Pronoun* and *bark* are grouped to create a VP constituent by the syntactic operation *Merge*.

   c.   Tense is merged with VP to create a T(ense)P(hrase)

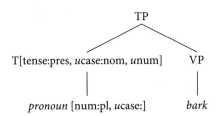

   d.   The checking relation *Agree* checks and values the uninterpretable case and number features on T and *pronoun*. Uninterpretable case features are marked with a strikethrough:

---

5.   Adger and Ramchand (2005) follow Pesetsky and Torrego (2004) and also cite Svenonius (2002). See also Adger and Smith (2005) as well as Adger (2003).

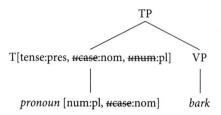

e. The operation *Move* takes the pronoun to the specifier of TP (a copy stays in the original position, as indicated with angled brackets.

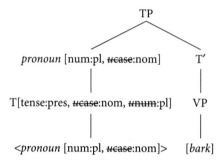

f. Morphemes are associated with these feature bundles. Thus, *they* will be the spell-out of *pronoun*[num:pl, ucase:nom]; note it would have been *them* if it has been valued as [accusative].

g. Further morphological operations may be triggered by the featural properties of lexical items. The most important operation being the one that "realizes the inflectional features on T as a suffix on V" (*ibid*).

h. Phonological operations are performed to derive the final surface phonetic representation 'they bark'.

However, (un)interpretable features present several issues. First, their motivation is purely theoretical at a very abstract level of syntactic computation. Second, there is little consensus among syntacticians about which features are (un)interpretable and how they function. For instance, some features can be interpretable on a given lexical item, but uninterpretable on another. Thus, the φ-features (person, number, gender) are interpretable on pronouns (e.g. 'he' and 'she' are distinguished by the gender feature while 'I' and 'we' are distinguished by the number and person features), but the gender feature is uninterpretable on auxiliaries; only the number and person features are interpretable since 'is' and 'are' have different meaning, for instance. As summarized by Travis (2008: 7–8), "[…] the details of not only the feature inventory, but also the uses made of features are not clear […] both shift from year to year and from researcher to researcher". We do not even know "*why* lexical items bear uninterpretable features" (Pesetsky & Torrego 2001: 358, original emphasis), assuming there even are "inherently uninterpretable features", as disputed by Adger and Ramchand (2005), and yet, as we will see below, SLA researchers have quickly embraced the concept of (un)interpretable features and use it to make learnability predictions.

Let us illustrate how the motivation for (un)interpretable features is strictly theory-internal. For instance, as Den Dikken (2000:9) puts it, "[e]liminating a feature under checking is tantamout to making it inaccessible to the mechanisms of the interpreting components", which means that it cannot be used for future syntactic operations, it becomes inactive. Thus, a pronoun which has been assigned case cannot be assigned another case, or to use the example given in Carnie (2010:289), example (15) adapted and reproduced in (2):

(2)   a.   They believe [*John* to be lying].
      b.   They believe *him* to be lying.
      c.   They believe [*John* is lying].
      d.   *They believe *him* is lying.

The sentences in (2a) and (2c) differ as follows: in (2a) *John* can receive exceptional accusative case marking from 'believe' – as shown by the morphological accusative case marking on the pronoun 'him' in (2b) – because it is not assigned any case within its bracketed clause, whereas in (2c) *John* receives nominative case from *is* within its own clause and is consequently unavailable for further case assignment, as illustrated in the ungrammatical form *him* in (2d).

Moreover, following Chomsky's Uniformity Principle, uninterpretable features are necessarily present in all languages without being necessarily realized phonetically. It follows that they are part of UG and as such do not need to be "triggered or activated", they are basic linguistic concepts, such as the genitive Case or gender features on nouns, or the tense feature on predicates.

Matching features are then projected onto functional categories which are viewed as bundles of morpho-syntactic and semantic features. The inventory of functional categories varies crosslinguistically, but most syntacticians agree that at least C, Agr_S, T, Agr_O and Asp(ect) are universal. Thus, agreement ϕ-features matching the ϕ-features on nominals are projected onto Agr_S and Agr_O, while tense features and the nominative case feature (associated with finite tense) are projected onto T (e.g. Adger 2003; Chomsky 1995; Giorgi & Pianesi 1997; Hegarty 2005). The way features can be bundled together onto functional categories is subjected to cross-linguistic variation as well. However, the bundles must respect the linear checking order in that a feature checked earlier than another cannot be bundled onto a functional category which is merged later (higher) in the phrase structure of the clause than the category on which another feature is bundled.

It bears repeating that a so-called 'feature-based syntax' is not new. It goes back to the early Minimalist proposals (Chomsky 1993, 1994, 1995) as illustrated by the verb movement phenomena which has been extensively researched by both theoretical and applied linguists. Verb movement was formalized as in (3):

(3)   A strong [+finite] lexical verb moves to Infl^0 before Spell-Out to check and erase its features.[6]

The principle of Full Interpretation required, as it still does, that no uninterpretable features be present at LF; thus Infl's strong morphological features had to be checked and erased before Spell-Out which meant that French finite lexical verbs had to move to Infl, hence triggering verb movement. French was described as a [±mvt] language, whereas English was described as a [-mvt] language and the verb-movement parameter was associated with a cluster of properties – placement of negation, adverbs, floating quantifiers and pronominal inversion (see e.g. Ayoun 2005a). It was also assumed that although English is a [-mvt] language, the auxiliaries *have* and *be* undergo V-to-T^0 raising (Battye & Roberts 1995). It was suggested that English auxiliaries were bundles of features moved as 'free riders' (i.e. features moved along with the feature triggering movement) with the overtly moved weak V-features.[7]

To sum up and as succinctly put by Shlonsky (2010: 424):

> Minimalism introduced a distinction between interpretable and uninterpretable features. The latter drive computations: movement or internal merge is triggered by the need to check and delete these features (Chomsky 2002/2004) or value them (Chomsky 2001). Interpretable features, on the other hand, are those that can be understood and exploited by the modules which interface with the computational system, semantics, pragmatics, and indirectly, the thought systems.

Let us now see how tense, aspect and mood/modality are viewed in Minimalist terms.

3.3   Minimalist assumptions for tense, aspect and mood/modality

The Minimalist program construes tense, aspect and mood/modality (TAM) as semantic features (e.g. Borer 2005; Giorgi & Pianesi 1997; Smith 1997). As such,

---

6.   "Infl^0 is used interchangeably with T for expository purposes. It stands for the Tense + Agr complex that inhabits T^0 in the current framework. Also, the most recent accounts have replaced feature strength with the suggestion that V-to-T movement must occur if a language has an affixal Infl, usually associated with distinct inflectional endings (Chomsky 2000, 2001, 2002) (Ayoun 2005a: 66 ff1).

7.   See Roberts (1998) and Lasnik (1999) for alternative accounts.

they are necessarily interpretable as discussed above, that is, they play a role in the semantic interpretation of the event, as illustrated in (4):

(4)   a.   Paul *is* writing/Paul *was* writing.
      b.   Paul *is* writing a letter/Paul *has* writt*en* a letter.
      c.   Paul *must* leave/Paul *may* leave.

In (4a) the tense feature on the auxiliary situates the event in the present or in the past, while in (4b) the choice of auxiliary changes the aspect of the event from progressive to perfect and finally in (4c), selecting the modal auxiliary 'must' instead of 'may' changes the interpretation of the event from an obligation to a permission.

3.3.1   Functional categories

Several functional categories have been posited to express TAM systems: AspP (Aspect Phrase) for the repository of aspect, AgrP (Agreement Phrase) for agreement, TP (Tense Phrase) for tense, and MoodP (Mood Phrase) for mood/modality. In addition, as argued in Ayoun (2005b), the other functional categories that account for the formation of a finite clause are just as important because L2 learners must first be able to produce a well-formed tensed clause before they can acquire subtle aspectual and semantic differences. The main functional categories are: Complementizer (Comp), Inflection (Infl or I) – which is split into Agreement (i.e. the functional head AgrP) and Tense (i.e. the functional head TP) following Pollock's (1989) seminal proposal – Negation, Determiner, and Number.

More specifically, Pollock (1989) suggested to split Infl into an Agr(eement) head (called Agr0 in Chomsky 1991) and a T(ense) head, both projecting their own phrases, in order to account for the fact that finite and nonfinite verbs differ in their inflectional features. In the 1990s, earlier minimalist assumptions posited two Agr heads with: (a) uninterpretable agreement features to be checked with the interpretable agreement features on argument DPs; (b) valued uninterpretable case features which check with uninterpretable case features on the DP. In more recent minimalist terms, this yields the following derivation (Adger 2006: 15):

(5)   a.   Agr[agr:,case:nom] ... DP[agr:3PL, case:] →
      b.   Agr[agr:3pl,case:nom] ... DP[agr:3PL, case:nom]

Being semantically uninterpretable, the Agr features on the Agr head are checked and deleted as are the case features (to be further interpreted morphologically once they are spelled out).

Pollock's (1989) split-Infl proposal was extended in Cinque (1999), creating an exploded functional structure above VP*, whereby each one of the verb's inflectional features is attributed its own functional head, which in turn projects a full phrase.

Each of the verb's inflectional features is checked against an initially non-specific F head which is merged above VP*. The verb raises to F^0, overtly or covertly. F heads are merged as needed to check the various inflectional features of the verb, resulting in a hierarchy of FPs above VP*.[8]

As pointed out by Shlonsky (2010), Cinque's work is part of the Cartographic research program within the Principles & Parameter theory that started in Italy in the late 90s and became known in the first three volumes of *The Cartography of Syntactic Structures* series (Belletti 2004; Cinque 2002; Rizzi 2004). However, the ground work was laid by Pollock's (1989) seminal argument that French verbs require not just one but two inflectional heads leading to a split-Infl: an Agr head and a T head (to accommodate finite and nonfinite verbs), opening the door to further research into functional categories. "The foundation of cartographic research was thus laid and although the term 'cartography' was only coined a decade later, research in the aftermath of Pollock's paper set upon the endeavor to discover new functional heads and study their hierarchical organization" (Shlonsky 2010:419).

Cinque's initial (1999) inflectional hierarchy evolved to the one presented in Cinque (2006):

(6)   Inflectional hierarchy
   $MoodP_{speech\ act}$ > $MoodP_{evaluative}$ > $MoodP_{evidential}$ > $ModP_{epistemic}$ > $TP\ (Past)$ > $TP\ (Future)$ > $MoodP_{irrealis}$ > $ModP_{alethic}$ > $AspP_{habitual}$ > $AspP_{delayed\ (or\ 'finally')}$ > $AspP_{predispositional}$ > $AspP_{repetitive(I)}$ > $AspP_{frequentative(I)}$ > $ModP_{volitional}$ > $AspP_{celerative(I)}$ > $TP\ (Anterior)$ > $AspP_{terminative}$ > $AspP_{continuative(I)}$ > $AspP_{perfect}$ > $AspP_{retrospective}$ > $AspP_{proximative}$ > $AspP_{durative}$ > $AspP_{progressive}$ > $AspP_{prospective}$ > $AspP_{inceptive(I)}$ > $ModP_{obligation}$ > $ModP_{ability}$ > $AspP_{frustrative/success}$ > $ModP_{permission/ability}$ > $AspP_{conative}$ > $AspP_{completive(I)}$ > $VoiceP$ > $PerceptionP$ > $CausativeP$ > $AspP_{inceptive(II)}$ > $(AspP_{continuative(II)})$ > $AndativeP$ > $AspP_{celerative(II)}$ > $AspP_{inceptive(II)}$ > $AspP_{completive\ (II)}$ > $AspP_{repetitive(II)}$ > $AspP_{frequentative(II)}$

There are no less than twenty three possibilities for AspP which may seem overwhelming, but were proposed to address an important issue, that is, how to account for adverb placement and word order. In contrast, the MoodP corresponds more closely to the traditional modality values (e.g. epistemic, irrealis, deontic). After examing several examples mostly from Turkish, Cinque (2006:183) concludes that "[f]unctional heads *are* rigidly fixed, though one and the same morpheme, by filling different heads (with concomitantly different functions) may give the

---

8.   The label IP*is used to refer to this exploded IP.

impression of changing places" [original emphasis]. An example of ordering of functional heads in English would be as in (7):

(7)   It has been raining all day.
       Pres Perf Prog

According to Rowlett (2007: 774, ex. 63a, b, produced here as 7a,b), Cinque's (2006) inflectional hierarchy works as follows for the modal verb *pouvoir* as an example:

(8)   a.   *Jean peut parler.*
       b.   [$_{IP*}$ ... [$_{ModPability}$ *pouvoir* ... [$_{VP*}$ *Jean parler*]]]

Rowlett makes the following assumptions: "*parler* bears an ability-modality feature when drawn from the lexicon; in order to check this feature, VP*merges with a F head hosting (a finite form of) pouvoir; *Jean* raises to SpecIP*for case licensing; (the finite form of) pouvoir raises to I^{*0} to check finiteness; *parler* raises out of VP*into IP*to check its infinitival morphology" (*ibid*). The sentence in (8a) is "the surface word order derived from an underlying structure along the lines of [(8b)]" (*ibid*). Another modal verb such as *vouloir* would be in ModPvolitional and so on. The lexical verb *faire* which bears several features – andative, causative, perception and modal – has them checked, in that specific order, by each of the functional projections which are headed by the corresponding verbs.

3.3.2   The aspect phrase

Several structural implementations of AspP have been proposed. Thus, Travis (1991, 1994) suggests that AspP is located within the expanded VP-shell, whereas Borer (1993) proposes that AspP is situated between TP and VP creating a [TP AspP VP] structure. Pereltsvaig (2002) proposes an OuterAspP category below TP, along with an InnerAspP category below VP to account for Slavic predicates which is similar to the Inner Aspect Phrase suggested by Travis (1991) for lexical aspect (i.e. lexical perfectivity or telicity), and the Outer Aspect Phrase suggested by Zagona (1994) for syntactic aspect (i.e. perfective vs imperfective).

Sanz (1999) contends that inherently telic predicates check their lexical telicity features in another projection, AktionsartP or AktP. The head of AktP is specified as [±telic] and it is located in the VP-shell,[9] while Sanz (2000) proposes an Event Phrase to encode features related to event type such as telicity and punctuality.

---

9.   Telicity is an interpretable feature: [+telic] events have an inherent endpoint whereas [-telic] events do not. States and activities are atelic, achievement and accomplishment predicates are telic (e.g. Smith 1997). The way telicity is encoded varies cross-linguistically.

I will adopt the [TP AspP VP] structure as in Borer (1993) and Giorgi and Pianesi (1997), among others, and assume that in French, as in the other Romance languages, aspect is instantiated in the functional category AspP, where the interpretable [±perfective] features are checked through overt aspect morphology. Thus, in French, AspP is associated with both [+perfective] and [−perfective]; grammatical aspect is expressed morpho-syntactically with the *passé composé* and the *imparfait*, respectively. By contrast, the [−perfective] value is irrelevant in English where the perfective-imperfective contrast is not grammaticalized. All eventive predicates (i.e. activities, achievements and accomplishments) are inherently associated with the [+perfective] value (Giorgi & Pianesi 1997), whereas French predicates lack an inherent aspectual value and must acquire their aspectual properties by checking the [±perfective] features in AspP through *passé composé* and *imparfait* morphology. English has an additional [+prog] value for the progressive aspect. This is summarized in Table 3.1 where M-paradigm refers to morphological paradigm, and F-features refer to formal features.

Table 3.1. French and English feature composition and AspP values

French AspP		English AspP	
F-features	M-paradigm	F-features	M-paradigm
[+perfective] [−perfective]	passé composé imparfait	[+perfective]	Simple past
Ø, progressive	Lexical idiom: être en train de + verb	[+progressive]	-ing

3.3.3   Cross-linguistic variation

Although all languages have ways of encoding TAM information, they do not all use the same means or use non-syntactic means altogether. Semantic features such as [±past], [±telic], [±mood], [±perfective] are presumably encoded in the lexicon of languages in different ways, leading to cross-linguistic differences. Thus, Benmamoun (2000), citing verbless sentences in Hebrew and Arabic, argues that although tense is a universal projection – as part of a universal clause schema as suggested by Cinque (1999) – it does not necessarily occur with a verbal head.

Another well known example is the fact that Chinese is a tenseless language in that it does not encode tense overtly (i.e. its verbs lack overt morphological markers). Instead, according to Lin (2003, 2006), tense is expressed with temporal adverbials (*zuotian* 'yesterday'), discourse pragmatics and tense-aspectual particles or markers such as the perfective/imperfective marker *le*, the durative marker zhe, or the progressive marker *zai*, while future temporality is expressed with the modal verb *hui*.[10] The resulting syntactic structure exhibits AspP above VP but without a TP.[11]

Other languages analyzed as tenseless include the Eskimo-Aleut language Kalaallisut (aka West Greenlandic) (Bittner 2005, 2008; Shaer 2003), the Mayan language Yucatec Maya (Bohnemeyer 2002), Lakhota and Chamorro (Chung & Timberlake 1985), or Burmese and Dyirbal (Comrie 1985), Blackfoot (Algonquian) and Halkomelem (Salish) (Ritter & Wiltschko 2004), as well as the coordination constructions in Japanese and Korean, although matrix clauses are tensed (Lee & Tonhauser 2010).

For instance, Lee and Tonhauser's (2011) semantic analysis suggests, following others (e.g. Bohnemeyer 2002; Bittner 2008), that tense, temporal adverbs, *Aktionsart*, as well as the discourse context, come into play for the temporal interpretation of Korean and Japanese matrix clauses; non-final conjuncts in Korean and Japanese coordination constructions are similarly affected by the discourse context and *Aktionsart*, but they are tenseless.

Bittner (2005) also concludes that the inflectional system of Kalaallisut is tenseless in that it does not contain any type of tense inflection at all. She suggests that "Kalaallisut verbal inflections form a mood system, fused with aspect and centering, which contrasts facts, nonfacts, prospects, and circumstances: factual moods: indicative (IND), interrogative (QUE), factive (FCT); nonfactual moods: irrealis (IRR), non-factual (NON); prospective moods: optative (OPT), imperative (IMP), hypothetical (HYP); circumstantial moods: elaborating (ELA), habitual (HAB)"(*ibid*: 348).

3.4   From theoretical assumptions to language acquisition theory

The early Minimalist Program (Chomsky 1992, 1995, 1999b) maintained basic assumptions for language acquisition: first, "languages are based on simple principles that interact to form often intricate structures" (Chomsky 1993: 2); second, Universal Grammar still "[provides] a fixed system of principles and a finite array of finitely valued parameters. The language-particular rules reduce to choice of values for these parameters" (Chomsky 1993: 4).

---

10. See Lin (2006: 2) for a complete illustrated list of devices that Chinese uses to convey temporal information.

11. However see Sybesma (2007) for arguments in favor of a syntactic T node in Chinese and Dutch as well as counter-arguments in Lin (2010).

However, a notable change was that parameters were then assumed to be almost entirely limited to the lexicon and the "strength" or "weakness" of functional elements, such as Agreement, Tense and Complementizer. Consequently, experimental studies started to focus on the more subtle and complex properties of the functional category system (e.g. Ayoun 1999; Paradis, Le Corre & Genesee 1998).

From an oversimplified Minimalist perspective, language acquisition remains a process of setting parameters to the appropriate value for the language being acquired. Parameters are thus set or valued from a genetically determined initial state S_o, leading to "the familiar idealization: S_o (=LAD) maps primary linguistic data (PLD) to L" (Chomsky 2002/2004: 104). The initial state S_o also determines the set of properties (i.e. features) available to a given language. Thus, since features are at the heart of the most recent Minimalist assumptions in syntactic theory, they are also at the heart of language variation and language acquisition research: it appears that both first and second language acquisition research boil down to feature acquisition, but not without questions.

First, the switch metaphor of parameters initially proposed in the Government and Binding framework (Chomsky 1981) is now viewed as each feature equipped with its switchboard consisting of several binary options, begging the question of whether the very concept of parameter setting remains relevant. Readers will recall that parameter-setting theory was proposed as a solution to two major problems of language acquisition: (1) the developmental problem (i.e. how to explain the process of acquisition over time based on the learner's linguistic experience); (2) the logical problem: how can the acquisition of a first language with all its complexities and subtleties proceed so quickly and effortlessly given the meager, and sometimes ambiguous, evidence available to children? Parameter-setting theory also addressed the problem of cross-linguistic variation: the differences between languages were explained by their selection of one of the available parameter settings.[12]

Cross-linguistic variation is still accounted for: cross-linguistic parametric differences are now understood as variation in the inventory of features for specific grammars. But what about the developmental problem and logical problem of language acquisition? The assumption was that the acquisition of a single property among all the properties subsumed under a given parameter would trigger the almost instantaneous acquisition of the remaining properties.

---

12. The fact that languages vary across well-defined and constrained ranges led to the assumption that seemingly different languages are closely related, explaining both their typological similarities and differences.

However, it is now assumed that L1 learners have to assemble bundles of features for each lexical item, and that the task of L2 learners consists in "appropriately re-configuring or re-assembling the formal and/or semantic feature bundles in the L2 grammar, and determining the specific conditions under which their properties may or must be morpho-phonologically expressed" (Lardiere 2007: 236). If correct, that approach which amounts to reducing parameter setting to the selection of features from a universal inventory seems to eliminate its descriptive and explanatory power, and sends us back to square one in solving the developmental problem and logical problem of language acquisition.

I would thus agree with Travis (2008: 44) that caution is in order:

> For acquisitionists who strive to use current theoretical tools to lead their research, in some ways it is unfortunate that the dust has not yet settled. There are many competing views on what features there are, how they are organized, and what they can do. To a certain extent, features have simply provided a new list of terms to describe already noted language difference (a strong feature or a feature bundled with EPP simply means that the movement is overt). As long as this is true, the movement to a system of features should have no perceptible impact on the field of acquisition. At the point where the feature system begins to package phenomena in a different way, however, new ways of approaching acquisition data should emerge.

Putting a new label on an old problem does not solve it. Whether we are using the terms 'grammatical categories', 'properties' or 'features', be they 'interpretable' or 'uninterpretable', as applied linguists, we still have to explain how learners acquire (and why they fail to do so, if it is the case) additional languages.

We now turn to current L2 acquisition theory and learnability predictions.

3.5   Current second language acquisition theory

3.5.1   Introduction: From one end of the spectrum to the other

The current minimalist literature offers two completely different views on adult second language acquisition (SLA) which comes down to the acquisition of functional categories and their features.[13] At one end of the spectrum is the view that functional categories simply cannot be acquired because UG is either no longer available to adult learners as it is to children (e.g. Meisel 1999, 2000) or, if it is, it

---

13. This section is partially reproduced and adapted from Ayoun (2007: 144–145) with permission from John Benjamins Publishing.

is subjected to a critical period which severely constrains it. At the other end of the spectrum is the perspective that adult SLA remains constrained by UG which implies that functional categories and their features can be acquired, leading to successful adult SLA. An intermediary position contends that the L2 acquisition of functional categories and features is either limited to the features already available in the L1 (e.g. Hawkins & Chan's 1997 Failed Feature Hypothesis), or is impaired because the features remain "valueless" or "inert" (e.g. Beck 1998). Another limitation would be that functional categories are part of a sub-module of UG subjected to a critical period, preventing their representation in the L2 when they are not already present in the L1 (e.g. Franceschina 2005; Tsimpli & Roussou 1991; Smith & Tsimpli 1995).[14] This position is similar to the No Access/Partial Access hypotheses proposed earlier for L2 acquisition in general (e.g. Clahsen & Muysken 1986).

The Full Access Hypothesis (e.g. Epstein, Flynn & Martohardjono 1996; Schwartz & Sprouse 1994, 1996) and the Full Functional Hypothesis (Gess & Herschensohn 2001) were two of the initial hypotheses allowing for successful acquisition of functional categories and their features although there is still some disagreement as to the initial representation of the functional categories: are they present from the very beginning, or do they develop in stagelike fashion? Generally, child L2 acquisition research suggests that functional categories are present and operative from the very beginning (e.g. Grondin & White 1993; Haznedar 2003; Lakshmanan & Selinker 1994), but others argue that functional categories are initially absent in interlanguage grammars, and gradually develop in discrete stages on the basis of input.

Thus, according to the Minimal Trees Hypothesis proposed by Vainikka and Young-Scholten (1994, 1996a, 1996b, 1998), only lexical categories are available to adult L2 learners from the beginning, and they project the relevant functional categories progressively, starting with a bare-VP stage. Similarly, Eubank's Weak Transfer/Valueless Features (1993/1994, 1996) Hypothesis contends that there is partial transfer from the L1, and that the L2 initial state is incomplete. An alternative approach, the Missing Surface Inflection hypothesis, (e.g. Haznedar & Schwartz 1997; Haznedar 2001; Lardiere 1998a, 1998b, 2000; Prévost & White 2000b), assumes that abstract functional categories and

---

14.   It is important to point out that Smith and Tsimpli's (1995) claims are based on the data collected with Christopher, a person who was clearly impaired cognitively, at least partially, but who nevertheless seemed to be able to acquire several languages. Based on their analyses, Smith and Tsimpli concluded that parameter resetting was not possible when the L1 and L2 settings differed, but that Christopher's L2 grammar appeared to be constrained by UG principles anyway. It seems that generalizing Christopher's pathological case to non-cognitively impaired language learners is unwarranted.

features are present in L2 grammars, but that the difficulty lies in mapping the abstract features to their morpho-phonological forms on surface morphology. A study by Duffield, White, Bruhn de Garavito, Montrul and Prévost (2003) also challenges impairment hypotheses with empirical evidence from Spanish-speaking and English-speaking L2 learners of French. The Spanish native speakers' grammar has clitic projections, while the English native speakers' grammar does not. The results of a sentence matching task indicated that L2 learners can indeed acquire clitic projections which are not present in their L1, as well as reset feature values from weak to strong.

3.5.2   Impairment hypotheses

The first 'impairment hypotheses' in adult SLA were initially proposed by R. Hawkins and his colleagues based on ideas developed by Tsimpli and Smith (1991) as well as Smith and Tsimpli (1995) in an effort to account for empirical data indicating that adult L2 learners may not have full access to UG, but only to subparts of it, a possibility articulated early on in the literature (e.g. Bley-Vroman, Felix & Ioup 1988). Using longitudinal data from Christopher, a cognitively impaired but linguistically gifted man (i.e. a 'savant', born in 1962),[15] Smith and Tsimpli (1995) propose that the features of functional categories are no longer accessible in adult SLA because of maturational constraints which would imply a critical period for ultimate attainment in adult SLA. Thus, Smith and Tsimpli (1995: 24) "maintain that the set of functional categories constitutes a submodule of UG, namely the UG lexicon", but it is another assumption that one may take issue with: "[...] if we assume that the critical period hypothesis is correct, maturational constraints on the functional module can be interpreted as entailing its complete inaccessibility after the end of this period. The importance of this suggestion in the current context is that it has implications for adult second language learning: UG may still be available but parameter setting can not be" (*ibid* 24–25). Moreover, the modularity of the brain would explain how autonomous parts of it can be "selectively impaired" without affecting others (*ibid*: 40). Smith and Tsimpli (1995: 78) also acknowledge that "processing difficulties which involve the interaction of his modular, linguistic faculty with central system operations" rather than a "deficit in his grammar" may account for Christopher's less than optimal performance. Another important point is that "Christopher appeared to produce spontaneously

---

15.   Christopher, who was born with brain damage, exhibits a remarkable aptitude for languages. He knows about 20 languages, albeit to various degrees, and his L1 linguistic competence is "as rich and as sophisticated as that of any native speaker" (Smith & Tsimpli 1995: 78).

configurations which are allowed by UG even though there was no direct evidence for them in the input" (*ibid*: 152).

Hawkins and his colleagues further investigated the possibility of partial impairment with normal adult L2 learners. Thus, the Failed Functional Features Hypothesis was suggested to account for findings indicating that Chinese ESL (English as a second language) learners do not reach native-like knowledge of English restrictive relative clauses because they cannot reset a parameter involving a *wh*-movement operator "beyond *some* critical period" (Hawkins & Chan 1997: 199)[emphasis mine]. No details regarding such a critical period are provided in spite of how powerful it is assumed to be since it precludes parameter resetting as well as further presuming that "[s]ome other operation which is not parameter resetting must be involved in producing the observed restructuring of the learner's grammar away from the L1 and towards the L2" (*ibid*: 200). But given the performance of the French participants as a control group that was not significantly different from the English native speakers on extractions from *wh*-islands or complex-NPs, Hawkins and Chan (1997: 214) are forced to admit that "the advanced French speakers appear to acquire the appropriate syntactic representations. It would be a counter-example to the claim that the features of functional categories are no longer accessible to adult L2 learners", but they do not pursue it. Even the Chinese participants' performance improves with proficiency on some ungrammatical sentences particularly with [CP...gap] constructions in restrictive relative clauses, but Hawkins and Chan maintain that the Chinese learners' mental representations are not nativelike. However, it is unclear how such a claim can be maintained with such mixed findings whose reliability could be questioned since they were obtained with a single elicitation task on a single syntactic phenomenon.[16]

Hawkins and Liszka (2003) set out to test the claim that the apparent residual optionality in L2 tense marking is due to a mapping problem at the interface between syntax and morphology by comparing the oral production of Chinese-, Japanese- and German-speakers of L2 English (e.g. Lardiere 2000) in the retelling of an extract of *Modern Times* and the recounting of a personal experience. As seen above, Chinese exhibits a syntactic [±finite] feature but lacks a [±Tense] feature (Li 1990: 18, cited in Hawkins & Liszka 2003) contrary to English that has both, leading Hawkins and Liszka to predict that Chinese learners will be unable to assign that feature in English.[17] Participants first completed a morphology test (Prasada & Pinker 1993) to determine whether they could inflect existing

---

16.   Hawkins (2005) revisits Hawkins and Chan (1997).

17.   Both Japanese and German grammaticalize Tense as well.

and nonce verbs with the appropriate past tense form. Findings showed that "the morphological component is operating similarly in these speakers to the way it operates in natives" (Hawkins & Liszka 2003: 29); however, the results of the two oral tasks revealed that the Chinese participants (n = 2) performed significantly differently from both the Japanese (n = 5) and the German (n = 5) participants, while the Chinese learners' performance was inconsistent (only 62.5% accuracy on inflected regular verbs but 84.2% on irregular verbs and 100% accuracy on inflected past participles). Moreover, the findings cannot be generalized because of the small sample size. Hawkins and Liszka account for their results by suggesting that features such as [±past] which are absent in the L1 are inaccessible later in L2 acquisition, and that past participles have a different morphological status than verbs, which seems speculative at best.

In light of more recent developments in syntactic theory (e.g. Adger 2003), Hawkins (2005) proposes that only uninterpretable features are subject to a critical period (following Tsimpli 2003), as a modification of the Failed Functional Features hypothesis (Hawkins & Chan 1997). It is argued that there may be cases when "target-like performance conceals non-target-like underlying competence (Hawkins 2005: 135). Such an argument is based on a syntactic reanalysis with several assumptions and there is still no explanation or motivation for the demise of an uninterpretable feature such as [*u*tense] past a vaguely defined critical period.

The same claim for the unavailability of uninterpretable features in adult L2 if they are not present in the L1 is made in Hawkins et al. (2008) with the uninterpretable feature [*u*Infl] associated with *v* in English.[18] Chinese appears to lack the interpretable features [present] and [past] as well as [*u*Infl], whereas Japanese exhibits [present] and [past], but not [*u*Infl] either. Acquiring the [*u*Infl] feature would allow L2 learners to correctly interpret the habitual/generic interpretation of verbs in the past and simple present, and learning that [*u*Infl:*] is strong would allow them to acquire the Progressive with an event-in-progress/existential interpretation (*ibid*: 333, 335). Participants were administered an acceptability judgment task (60 contexts with pairs of continuation sentences in order to choose either the habitual/generic interpretation or the event-in-progress/existential interpretation, both in the present and in the past). Again, the sample sizes were relatively small (NSs = 10, Chinese L2 learners = 8, Japanese L2 learners = 10, various L1s group = 10) preventing a reliable generalization of the findings. It was found that L2 learners' grammars appropriately distinguish between the two types

---

18.   The so-called little *v* is a silent light verb which functions as a second predicate to assign an external thematic role (Chomsky 1995) (see e.g. Horvath & Siloni 2002; Kiparsky 1997 for critiques).

of semantic contexts, but there was also a group effect, mostly with the Chinese and Japanese learners behaving differently, which Hawkins et al. explain as their failure to acquire uninterpretable [*u*Infl] on v. Once again, the findings are mixed with some clear native-like performance on the part of all L2 learners, but also significantly different performance from some of the L2 learners.

Similar hypotheses to the Failed (uninterpretable) Functional Features hypothesis were proposed such as the "Representational Deficit or Interpretability hypotheses" (Hawkins 2001, 2003; Hawkins & Hattori 2006; Tsimpli & Dimitrakopoulou 2007) and the Contextual Complexity hypothesis (Hawkins & Casillas 2008). The latter is based on the assumption that native speakers and L2 learners do not store lexical items in the same way: for native speakers, "phonological exponents have entries in the Vocabulary which specify their *contexts of insertion*" and "insertion occurs through feature-matching between the exponent and the terminal node" (Hawkins & Casillas 2008: 601; original emphasis). The difference would be in the "representation of entries for phonological components in the Vocabulary" (*ibid*: 602) in that for native speakers, "vocabulary items are specified in terms of bundles of features at the point of insertion (i.e. the terminal node), with limited context-sensitivity", whereas L2 learners "have Vocabulary entries for exponents realizing dependencies […] that are context-sensitive" (*ibid*: 602). Hawkins and Casillas further assume that, at least at first, L2 learners do not have access to uninterpretable features so the phonological properties which express dependencies as such 3rd person singular -s are not associated with syntactic features. Hence, the Contextual Complexity hypothesis which states that:

> The probability with which a Vocabulary item is retrieved during the derivation of a syntactic expression is a function of the number of sister terminal nodes required to specify the context in which it is inserted. The more sister nodes required to specify the context, the greater the probability that the entry will not be retrieved (*ibid*: 603).

This would account for non-targetlike forms such as *she's walks or *she's walked. Hawkins and Casillas argue that the performance of Chinese (n = 10) and Spanish (n = 10) L2 learners of English on a sentence completion task supports this hypothesis; but the participants were only at a lower intermediate proficiency level.

As noted by the researchers themselves, their assumptions are highly speculative. Although they argue that L2 learners cannot access uninterpretable features, Hawkins and Casillas still claim that if "they invoke a syntactic uninterpretable feature immediately and if the property turns out not to be a general case of agreement, retreat from overgeneralization becomes problematic" (*ibid*: 611).

Let us now revisit the critical period hypothesis since it is partly the basis for these impairment hypotheses.

3.5.3   The critical period hypothesis and ultimate attainment

3.5.3.1   *A neurological basis for the critical period hypothesis?*

According to the Critical Period hypothesis, in order to be successful, L1 acquisition must take place before a certain age, which varies from three-year-old to five-year-old for phonology, to early puberty for morpho-syntax.[19] The Critical Period Hypothesis was initially grounded in the claim that the lateralization of cerebral functions and the myelination[20] of the cortex progressively reduce the neuronal substrate necessary for language acquisition, as originally proposed by Penfield and Roberts (1959), later followed by Lenneberg (1967:176) who contends that "the limiting factors postulated are cerebral immaturity on the one end and termination of a state of organizational plasticity linked with lateralization of function at the other end of the critical period".

This view quickly became, and still is, extremely popular, in spite of its lack of supporting empirical data. First, lateralization is already present at birth, and there is no evidence for a sharp cut-off point at adolescence as there should be for a biologically-based critical period (Aitchison 1989; Krashen 1973).[21] In addition, neurological researchers are usually very careful when stating any possible conclusions after observing structural changes in the brain, merely suggesting that a "decrease in plasticity [is] thought to occur during late childhood and adolescence" (Jernigan et al. 1991:2047).

One should also take into account that our understanding of the brain is constantly evolving, so our interpretations of brain-based research for language

---

19.   There is little consensus about the age at which the window of opportunity for language acquisition would be: 5 (Krashen 1973), 6 (Pinker 1994), 12 (Lenneberg 1967) or even 15 as the age of puberty (Johnson & Newport 1989). See Singleton (2005:273).

20.   Myelination refers to the process in which neurons are progressively wrapped by glial cells which 'nourish' the neurons. Myelin are the substance contained in the glial cells. It is claimed that myelination reduced brain plasticity around the age of puberty leading to age effects in language acquisition (Pulvermüller & Schumann 1994; Schumann 2001).

21.   Penfield and Roberts (1959) examined individual cases exemplifying different types of aphasia, but their comments related to language learning are either impressionistic or do not appear to be based on empirical data, but rather on anecdotal observations and the diaries of Leopold (1939–1959) about a bilingual child. See Singleton (2005) for a recent detailed review.

acquisition should as well.[22] No one would deny that the adult brain undergoes cognitive aging, but recent research shows that "cognition in old age also reflects structural and functional brain plasticity" (Greenwood 2007:657). Moreover, "training alone can lead to plastic changes in the brain. Expert Braille readers show an enlarged hand area and smearing of finer representations. That this result was seen in expert, but not novice, Braille readers suggests that it was not the blindess, but the training, which led to the change in cortical representation (Sterr et al. 1998; Taub et al. 2002) (*ibid*: 660). It was also found that the benefits of training could be substantial and durable (Nyberg 2005, cited in Greenwood 2007).

In a review article on language and the aging brain, Wingfield and Grossman (2006) suggest that language comprehension is well preserved in spite of cognitive and neural changes because plasticity in neural recruitment contributes to the stability of language comprehension. In fact, "spared abilities that keep language among the best preserved of cognitive functions in normal aging" (*ibid*: 2831) and linguistic knowledge, and the procedural rules for implementing this knowledge, remain well preserved in normal aging (Wingfield & Stine-Morrow 2000). Indeed, in all but late-stage Alzheimer's disease, the formal qualities of speech production (syntactic form, melodic line) and the ability to comprehend at least the surface meaning of speech are maintained (Kempler 2005)" (*ibid*: 2832).

Wingfield and Grossman stress that functional imaging studies "have identified a large-scale neural network that is activated during the course of sentence processing" and steps in, so to speak, to compensate quite efficiently for age-related neuronal changes.[23] Compensatory activations are quite remarkable in maintaining a high level of linguistic performance contrary to other cognitive domains.

3.5.3.2 *The critical period hypothesis in second language acquisition*
The field of adult L2 acquisition also quickly assumed that learners were subjected to a critical period (e.g. Long 1990; Pulvermüller & Schumann 1994), first for phonetics and phonology (Dunkel & Pillet 1957; Fahtman 1975; Oyama 1976; Scovel 1988), then for innate linguistic components (e.g. Bley-Vroman 1989), or only

---

22. See Stowe and Sabourin (2005) for a summary of current neuroimaging methods and review of studies. One of the conclusions is that the empirical data about the effects of age of acquisition are contradictory, and that additional factors (e.g. type of linguistic information being processed, amount and start of input exposure, proficiency, L1–L2 pairs) should be considered.

23. Wingfield and Grossman (2006:2837) "characterize this network in terms of a core perisylvian sentence-processing component together with both left and right hemisphere extrasylvian cortical regions that support the executive and working-memory resources necessary to process complex sentences".

for non-innate elements (e.g. Flynn & Martohardjono 1995). As MacWhinney (1997: 136–137) put it:

> Our general picture of the adult L2 learner is one that emphasizes the extent to which language learning is no longer supported by the fresh, uncommitted neural hardware available to the child. In addition, the adult often does not have access to the rich system of social support that provides high quality language input to the child (Snow 1995). Without this natural system of support for language learning, the adult has to construct a system of *auto-support* that uses functional neural circuits and carefully recruited social contexts as ways of maximizing the outcome of language learning.

Weber-Fox and Neville (1999) argue that the results of ERPs (Event-Related Brain Potentials) and other neural imaging techniques indicate that late-learning bilinguals are slower than early-learning bilinguals in their processing of various grammatical aspects. Neville (1995) and Neville and Weber-Fox (1994) also show that the neurological organization of late L2 learners can be distinguished from the neurological organization of early L2 learners.

However, Bialystok and Hakuta (1999: 177) point out that "neural organization can reflect different kinds of experiences without being abnormal or supporting inferior performance (Elbert, Pantev, Wienbruch, Rockstroh & Taub 1995; Locke 1993; Merzenich, Nelson, Stryker, Cynader, Schoppman & Zook 1984). In other words, special experiences may influence neural organization without affecting performance".

Why would one insist on expecting similar results by comparing different learners? We do not expect young and older learners to be similar in other general cognitive abilities, so why do we expect adult L2 learners to be similar to children native speakers, or even early bilinguals to be similar to late bilinguals? Differences are bound to be found, but they should not necessarily be used to argue in favor of a critical period hypothesis. Linguistic access and processing may be slower in late bilinguals because they have not had as much time for automatization. Thus, the point that although the same neural substrates are used for both L1 and L2 phonetic processing, but that the amount of neural activation is not the same (e.g. Hasegawa, Carpenter & Just 2002), or that the neural substrates are not necessarily the same in the two languages (e.g. Callan, Jones, Callan & Akahane-Yamada 2004), is moot. The important point is that the brain can, and does, handle more than one language at a time, and it does make use of excellent compensatory strategies as noted above (e.g. Wingfield & Grossman 2006). We also need to recognize that the mental system of every individual is probably unique, as stressed by Lamb (1999), among others.

Bialystok and Hakuta (1999: 162) further argue that "there may well be correlation between age of initial learning and ultimate achievement, but it does not necessarily follow that age is a causal factor in that relation". They refer to general cognitive abilities, and less than optimal social circumstances for adult L2 learners. Normal cognitive aging is also cited as a plausible explanation for the linear decline in the English proficiency of 2.3 million Spanish- and Chinese-speaking immigrants in Hakuta, Bialystok and Wiley (2003) who analyzed their census data looking for a clear discontinuity (i.e. a sharp, statistically significant difference) or decline in proficiency as evidence for a critical period. They did not find evidence for such a decline, but suggested that other factors – "age of immigration, socioeconomic factors, and in particular the amount of formal education" (*ibid*: 37) – play an important part in explaining immigrants' proficiency in English. Chiswick and Miller (2008), who used the 2000 U.S. Census, did not find evidence of discontinuity among immigrants either. A similar conclusion is reached by Muñoz and Singleton (2011) after an extensive review of the literature.

Birdsong (1999) summarizes the arguments in favor of a Critical Period Hypothesis presented by Bever (1981), Hurford (1991) and Pinker (1994) from an evolutionary perspective, which may be summed up as a "use it then lose it" proposition. Bever (1981) argues that as long as language learning takes place, the critical period can be delayed, but once one stops, the production system and the perception system become dissociated, preventing or hindering further language learning. Hurford (1991) suggests that a language acquisition is no longer necessary or even wasteful once it has accomplished its purpose. Pinker (1994: 295) concurs and proposes that the language learning faculty should be "dismantled" because it appears to be no longer needed: "greedy neural tissue lying around beyond its point of usefulness is a good candidate for the recycling bin".

This evolutionary argument is problematic from several perspectives. First, it is not supported by empirical data which indicate instead that language is one of the best preserved cognitive functions; the brain does retain linguistic capacities because we never stop using them and is able to use compensatory strategies to make up for deficiencies due to aging or lesions. Second, it betrays a strong bias toward a monolingual view of the human brain. Why should the brain be limited to a single language? In a world where roughly 5,000 languages are spoken in only about 200 nations, the norm is clearly multilingualism or multi-competence, not monolingualism or monocompetence (e.g. Cenoz & Jessner 2000; Cook 1992; Romaine 2001). This multilingualism can be the result of several situations:

1. A truly multilingual society in which everyone speaks an official language and several languages or dialects as it is the case in many African countries. The speakers are best characterized as compound multilingual speakers (the various languages are acquired at the same time)

or coordinate multi-lingual speakers (the various languages are acquired one by one but all before puberty);

2. Non-European immigrants workers in Europe who learn the official language of their new country and English as a third language, for example, Turkish immigrants in the Netherlands (Cenoz & Jessner 2000);

3. Native speakers of a majority language who maintain regional languages and learn a foreign language in school, for instance, French speakers who are also native speakers of Breton and learn German or English in an instructional setting.

Third, as already pointed out earlier, for the Critical Period hypothesis to hold, if the loss of the language acquisition device is due to evolutionary processes, there cannot be a single exception: no adult L2 learner should be able to ever achieve native-like proficiency in an additional language past the age of puberty. The Critical Period hypothesis does not meet this condition as amply documented by the empirical findings summarized in Birdsong (1999) (and numerous references cited therein). There appears to be an overall native-like performance for 5% to 25% of what Birdsong referred to as the "relevant population" of learners: "to determine the proportion of native-like attainers, we should look only at those learners with exogenous circumstances favoring language acquisition, not at any and all who have had some exposure to an L2 or who have tried to learn a foreign language" (*ibid*: 14).

For example, in Birdsong (1992), 6 out of 20 native speakers of English who started learning French past the age of puberty scored within the range of French native speakers on a grammaticality judgment task illustrating a variety of parametric phenomena.

In Mayberry (1993), L2 learners of American Sign Language showed very little variation from native speakers. Van Wuijtswinkel (1994) used a variety of syntactic structures to test two groups of Dutch native speakers who started learning English after puberty: 30% (8 out of 26) of the participants in the first group and 85% (7 out of 8) of the participants in the second group exhibited native-like performance in a grammaticality judgment task. White and Genesee (1996) tested the French acquisition of *wh*-movement by English native speakers with the administration of a grammaticality judgment task. A non-negligible number (16 out of 45) of these post-pubertal learners were indistinguishable from native speakers.

Bialystok and Hakuta (1994) and Birdsong and Molis (1998) replicated the seminal Johnson and Newport (1989) study and both found strong age effects. It seems undeniable that earlier exposure is better, but some late learners' performance at, or above, 92% accuracy is a serious challenge to the critical period hypothesis.

Abrahamsson (2012) also found a negative correlation between age of onset (AO) and ultimate attainment among 200 Spanish-speaking learners of L2 Swedish on two measures (aural GJT and test of categorical perception of voice onset time). It was found that among the 30 participants who performed within NS range on both tasks, 55% had an AO of 1–5, (28% for AO 6–10 and 9% for AO 11–15), which means that the other participants were nativelike on one of the two tasks. It is notable that the GJT and VOT results were completely unrelated for both the NS control group and the late-learner group, making it impossible to determine whether children and adults take fundamentally different approaches (cognitively and/or neurally) in acquiring language.[24]

Even in phonetics and phonology, the area of language which appears to be most likely to be subjected to a critical period, there is evidence that late learners can achieve native-like proficiency. In the Bongaerts, Planken, van Summeren and Schils' (1995) study as well as the Bongaerts, Planken and Schils' (1997) study, native speakers of Dutch who had started to learn English past the age of puberty were indistinguishable from native speakers of English. Similar results were found with the Dutch native speakers who were tested in English and French as reported in Bongaerts (1999).

Van Boxtel (2005) targeted dummy subject constructions to investigate ultimate attainment among very advanced L2 French, German and Turkish learners of Dutch whose performance on a sentence preference task and a sentence imitation task was compared with the performance of Dutch native speakers on the same elicitation tasks. A total of 8 L2 learners (out of 39 with a mean age of arrival of 23) performed within native speaker range on the first task and 7 on the second task. It is concluded that late L2 learners whose L1 is typologically distant from the L2 can perform at native levels of proficiency, thus providing further evidence against the critical period hypothesis.

Bongaerts (2005), as the introductory article to a special issue of IRAL, reviews studies that focused on the discontinuity, or lack thereof, in the decline of proficiency of L2 learners towards the end of the critical period as well as the issue of ultimate attainment by late L2 learners. For pronunciation, no clear discontinuity was found, but rather "a continuing and substantial decline in the pronunciation ratings not only before, but also after the terminus of the critical period (see also

---

24. It is also interesting to note that the NS control group (n=20) is not as homogeneous as some researchers argue. On the GJT, the mean is 66 but SD is 6.81 with a 56–76 range. The SD is actually lower for the late L2 learner group (5.29) although the mean (45) and range (31–57) are lower.

Bongaerts 2003)" (Bongaerts 2005:260).[25] Birdsong (2004) did not find evidence of a sharp discontinuity either in several studies focusing on morpho-syntax.

Hopp (2010) conducted four experiments with fifty-nine L1 Dutch, Russian and English late learners of L2 German to test their ultimate attainment on morpho-syntax (gender concord, subject-verb agreement and case marking). A proficiency test classified the participants as either advanced or near-native who then performed three different types of tasks (self-paced reading, off-line and speeded grammaticality judgments). Findings indicate native-like performance on case and subject-verb agreement inflection across tasks, albeit with some L1 influence limiting processing efficiency, thereby disconfirming claims made by the critical period hypothesis as well.

It is interesting to consider the findings of another recent study, Reichle (2010), because it focuses on the interface between syntax and pragmatics by investigating information structure, that is, "the way in which a speaker uses cues from sentence structure to guide a hearer toward knowing what is more or less important in a sentence" (*ibid*: 53). End-state, low-proficiency and high-proficiency L2 French learners as well as two groups of French native speakers performed judgment tasks in two experiments. Reichle argues that his findings act as counter-evidence to the critical period hypothesis because of the extremely high level of native-like performance of the participants on the judgment tasks. There is marginal evidence of progressive decline of performance with age of arrival but well into adulthood as opposed to a sharp discontinuity (i.e. the "stretched Z" of an hypothesized critical period following a criterion proposed by Johnson & Newport 1989).

To sum up, the critical period hypothesis is seriously compromised from several standpoints. First, Singleton (2005:280) contends that it "cannot plausibly be considered as a scientific hypothesis" but "at best an extremely vague and promissory note", and that "the very fact that there are such manifold and mutually contradictory versions of the CPH of itself calls into serious question the notion of a CP" in language acquisition (*ibid*: 269). Hyltenstam and Abrahamsson (2003:122) simply refer to it as "*une chimère*".

Second, its basic premise, changes in the neuronal structures of the brain, has been questioned as seen above, and recent reviews reveal mixed findings in neuroimaging studies (e.g. Abutalebi, Cappa & Perani 2001; Stowe & Sabourin 2005). They also show that there is evidence "of considerable plasticity in the network that mediates language comprehension in the bilingual brain"

---

25. Patowski (1980, 1990) reported sharp discontinuity but it was challenged by a different statistical analysis (Harley & Wang 1997), it was not supported by other studies, and the age used, 15, is well beyond the critical age for pronunciation (cf. Footnote 15 above).

(Abutalebi et al. 2001: 186). Proficiency may be more influential in determining neural representation than the age of onset of L2 acquisition. Pallier et al. (2003: 160), who investigated brain plasticity and the effect of the L1, also conclude against the hypothesis that "a window of brain plasticity is open at birth and progressively closes as the brain networks for language become stabilized, under the possible influence of maturational and/or experiential factors".

It thus seems quite difficult to claim as Hawkins (2005: 124) does that "there is a critical period for availability after which unused features of a certain type are cleared from the cognitive architecture. This possibility in syntax is analogous to the claim in phonology that features that are unused for phonological contrasts in primary language acquisition disappear beyond a critical period (Brown 2000; Larson-Hall 2004)".

Indeed, if the human brain loses the capacity to acquire languages past puberty, then not a single individual should even come close to near-native proficiency. But too many studies reported near-native performance level for so many late adult learners that the evidence cannot be dismissed as anecdotal, nor the learners considered "peripheral". Staunch supporters of a critical period hypothesis would argue that adult learners who appear to have achieved native-like competence remain largely irrelevant, if one assumes variation along with evolution (see Hurford & Kirby 1999, and Eubank & Gregg 1999, for additional arguments) or would claim methodological problems with most studies (e.g. Long 2005 makes some valid and important points), but again, empirical data cannot be so easily dismissed.

3.5.4   Access to Universal Grammar hypotheses

We now consider the other end of the spectrum, that is, hypotheses stating that adult L2 learners still have access to Universal Grammar and that ultimate attainment is thus possible. Assuming that L2 grammars are constrained by Universal Grammar implies that functional categories and features are as a matter of principle acquirable (Ayoun 2003, 2005a, 2005b, 2007; Ayoun & Rothman 2013; Duffield et al. 2003; Franceschina 2005; Iverson & Rothman 2008). This assumption is supported by the findings reviewed above.[26]

The initial hypotheses were the Full Access Hypothesis (e.g. Epstein, Flynn & Martohardjono 1996; Schwartz & Sprouse 1994, 1996) and the Full Functional Hypothesis (Gess & Herschensohn 2001) which posited that functional

---

26. There are of course other differences between child L1 acquisition and adult L2 acquisition. For a review of the Fundamental Difference Hypothesis originally proposed by Bley-Vroman (1990) and updated in Bley-Vroman (2009), see Herschensohn (2009).

categories and their features could be successfully acquired. Then, the Missing Surface Inflection hypothesis, (e.g. Haznedar & Schwartz 1997; Haznedar 2001; Lardiere 1998a, 1998b, 2000, 2003, 2006a, b, 2008; Prévost & White 2000b) was proposed to explain why the performance of L2 learners is not always consistent: although abstract functional categories and features are present in their grammars, they have difficulties in mapping the abstract features to their morpho-phonological forms on surface morphology.

According to the Missing Surface Inflection Hypothesis (Prévost & White 2000a), L2 learners' performance may suffer from a variety of factors such as processing pressure. Their errors are not random but result instead from the competition for lexical insertion, between more of less specified forms, following the theory of Distributed Morphology (DM) (Halle & Marantz 1993) which is itself based on the Separation Hypothesis (Beard 1987).[27]

The MSIH extends and clarifies the Missing Inflection Hypothesis proposed by Haznedar and Schwartz (1997), who examined data from a Turkish child acquiring L2 English in relation to the proposal of optional infinitives in L2 acquisition. Although they found evidence of the use of both finite and non-finite verb forms, there was little evidence of other properties normally associated with optional infinitives in L1 acquisition, such as null subjects or accusative Case markings of subjects instead of nominative. They concluded that there was no evidence to support the belief that this child exhibited a syntactic deficit, but instead that the child's use of non-finite morphology was the effect of missing inflection. Thus the abstract categories were present, but the surface inflectional morphology was missing. Similarly, Lardiere (1998b, 2000) attributed her case study Patty's inconsistent tense marking to a breakdown in the morphological component responsible for the mapping from syntax to morpho-phonological forms.

According to the Prosodic Transfer Hypothesis (Goad, White & Steele 2003), although L2 learners have appropriate syntactic representations, their failure to consistently produce target-like overt morphology is at least partially related to the L1 and L2 prosodic structures. Goad et al. (2003) suggested that prosodic

---

27. In Distributed Morphology, the term 'distributed' refers to the separation of properties which in other theories may be collected together in the lexicon. DM suggests that each inflection is associated with a bundle of (syntactic and semantic) features which are without phonological form (e.g. number, gender for adjectival inflection in a Romance language). A process of late insertion matches the features of the terminal node to the features of the lexical item; the features of the lexical item may not be fully specified, contrary to those of the syntactic node. The features of the lexical items form a subset of the feature bundle required. When there is no exact match, there will be a competition between two potentially acceptable lexical items.

structure could be a factor in explaining the performance of Mandarin Chinese native speakers (n = 12) with L2 English tense and agreement inflectional morphology. The initial hypothesis stated that learners' L2 competence would always be constrained by the L1 prosodic representation. Goad and White (2006, 2008) proposed a slightly weaker version according to which L2 learners can adapt the L1 prosodic structure as required by the L2 as long as they respect L1 licensing relations in new positions.

The literature review presented in Chapter 4 will introduce other studies that specifically targeted the acquisition of tense, aspect and/or mood/modality.

3.6   Summary

From the feature matrix of the early days of generative syntax to a feature-based syntax in the current minimalist program, basic theoretical assumptions have been remarkably consistent, with few changes in terminology. Thus, the traditional grammatical categories that were referred to as features in the early feature matrix are now viewed as bundles of morpho-phonological, semantic and syntactic or formal features in a feature-based syntax. Sets of semantic and formal features intersect and the two are distinguished by the (un)interpretable features that the formal features, but not the semantic features, carry. SLA researchers did not wait for syntacticians to arrive at a consensus on (un)interpretable features to make learnability predictions, and the literature now asks whether L2 learners can (re) assemble bundles of features or acquire uninterpretable features which are claimed to be subjected to a critical period by impairment hypotheses. The Critical Period hypothesis was reviewed in light of the most recent empirical data to conclude that it is not sustainable. However, proponents of UG access, and hence successful ultimate attainment in adult L2 acquisition, face the difficult task of accounting for the inconsistent performance of L2 learners on various elicitation tasks.

CHAPTER 4

The second language acquisition of tense, mood and aspect

C'est le langage qui enseigne la définition de l'homme.
Roland Barthes

4.1 Introduction

This chapter focuses primarily on a literature review of empirical studies conducted with L2 French learners from two broadly defined perspectives: a non-generative perspective in Section 2 and a generative perspective in Section 3. The review of non-generative studies in instructed and immersion settings is organized by temporality type (past, present and future), and then moves on to mood and modality. Finally, Section 4 reviews generative studies conducted with L2 learners of other languages, mainly English, Spanish and Portuguese; it also includes a few studies conducted with heritage learners. A summary concludes each section.

4.2 Literature review of non-generative L2 French studies

As mentioned in Chapter 1, the use of lexical aspectual classes as a theoretical framework to analyze the development of verbal morphology among L2 learners was pioneered in Andersen (1986, 1991) and became known as the Aspect hypothesis. It has generated the largest body of L2 empirical research among instructed learners so far.

The Aspect hypothesis "attempts to explain the observed correlation between tense/aspect morphemes and lexical aspectual classes according to the Relevance Principle (i.e. aspect is more relevant to the meaning of the verb than tense, mood, or agreement are) and the Congruence Principle (i.e. learners choose the morpheme whose aspectual meaning is most congruent with the aspectual meaning of the verb)" (Salaberry & Ayoun 2005: 14). In a nutshell, the Aspect hypothesis claims that the early stages of L2 acquisition are characterized by a verbal morphology that encodes inherent aspectual distinctions rather than tense or grammatical aspect.

4.2.1   Past temporality and aspect

Harley (1989) reports that a common finding of earlier studies conducted with immersion students in Canada was a poor performance on verbal morphology indicating that they did not have a well constrasted system of tense and aspect (Allen, Cummins, Mougeon & Swain 1983; Harley 1985; Harley & Swain 1978, 1984; Swain & Lapkin 1982). It is in particular the aspectual contrast between the *imparfait* (IMP) and the *passé composé* (PC) that led to subsequent studies, most of which will be reviewed or cited here (see Appendix A for a more complete list).

Harley (1989) used a functional approach to teaching (focusing on input targeting a specific area)[1] during an 8 week treatment with grade 6 immersion students in Ontario (Canada) who were divided into experimental and control groups who wrote compositions, filled out cloze tests, and were interviewed. All the materials were then rated for accuracy in the use of the *imparfait* and the *passé composé*. Participants in the experimental condition made significant improvement in their use and understanding of the aspectual distinction between the two past tense morphological forms, but the gains were not maintained in a post-test administered 3 months later. Similarly, Harley (1992), who focused on children in early immersion classes, found that the *passé composé* was acquired earlier than the *imparfait* or the conditional, and that the inflectional verbal system was only partially mastered.

Bergström (1995, 1997)[2] set out to test the Aspect Hypothesis (Andersen 1986, 1991) by asking Anglophone college learners (n = 75 at three proficiency levels) to perform two elicitation tasks (a written narrative and a cloze test) and found statistical differences between learner groups in the use of *passé composé*, but not *imparfait*, on the cloze test; significant lexical class and group effects for the *passé composé* and *imparfait* on both elicitation tasks. The *passé composé* appears to be more robust across all lexical classes (particularly with dynamic verbs as found previously, e.g. Kihlstedt 1994; Schlyter 1994, as cited in *ibid*: 154) than the *imparfait* which emerges more slowly (and initially mostly with statives).

Schlyter (1996) investigated how young (3 to 7 year old) Swedish-French bilingual children (n = 4) acquire the *passé composé/imparfait* aspectual distinction

---

1. The teachers were given very detailed instructions to use instructional materials that included an introduction, linguistic background on the *passé composé/imparfait* distinction and weekly classroom activities designed to teach specific grammatical aspects of the these two tenses and their aspectual differences. This functional approach may thus be equated with explicit instruction.

2. Bardovi-Harlig and Bergström (1996) uses a subset of the data from Bergström (1995) and is not reviewed here.

which is not marked in Swedish which only uses a perfective past tense and does not grammaticalize the progressive. Recordings of spontaneous storytelling were transcribed to analyze possible correspondences in Swedish with the French aspectual distinction between its two past tenses. It was found that at about 4 years old, children were starting to use a combination of aspectual distinction (*passé composé* for foregrounding, *imparfait* for backgrounding) and temporal connectors which were followed by subject-verb inversion in Swedish.

In Salaberry (1998), Anglophone learners of L2 French completed a cloze test and wrote a narrative (retelling a short film excerpt) to investigate the use of the *passé composé* and *imparfait*. The data were analyzed for morphological marking and lexical class and showed that with both elicitation tasks, L2 learners and native speakers alike tend to follow a distributional bias (i.e. grammatical aspect follows lexical aspect), and were very similar in their selection of aspectual marking for all four lexical classes. But the cloze test data revealed a difference between L2 learners and the NS control group in their use of non-prototypical grammatical aspect (i.e. instances of incongruence between lexical aspectual class and grammatical aspect). Overall, however, L2 learners showed a stable and systematic use of aspectual morphology with mostly prototypical marking.

Using a pre-test, repeated exposure and post-test design, Ayoun (2001) investigated the effectiveness of implicit versus explicit feedback with three different treatments (traditional grammar instruction, modelling, and recasting) in the acquisition of the aspectual distinction between *passé composé* and *imparfait* by Anglophone L2 French learners in an academic setting. A pre-posttest comparison of the production task data revealed very high accuracy levels for the *passé composé*, but not for the *imparfait* (with a significant group effect). As a follow-up qualitative study, Ayoun (2004) was designed to investigate that differential outcome. Learners seemed to associate past tense morphology with lexical aspectual classes starting with statives, but moving on to accomplishments before activities – *contra* the hypothesized prototypical progression – while imperfective marking spread from statives to accomplishments. Learners generally appeared to be limited to a few, common predicates for both past tense forms, and the *imparfait* was almost always restricted to the durative (the imperfective and the iterative are the other two semantic values of the *imparfait*).[3]

Kihlstedt (2002) who drew on the longitudinal data of 4 participants from the InterFra corpus (i.e. oral data from 32 Swedish university students learning French; e.g. Bartning 1997) presented qualitative analyses showing that all 4 learners use both *passé composé* and *imparfait* (albeit with individual variation),

---

3.   Please see Chapter 6 for a more detailed account of Ayoun (2001, 2004).

but mostly with a few high frequency verbal tokens such as *avoir*, and that the *plus-que-parfait* was rare. Tokens encoded with the *imparfait* were almost exclusively prototypical states, with few instances of dynamic verbs, and expressed limited semantic values.

The Aspect Hypothesis' prediction of a development sequence for verbal morphology following lexical aspect (i.e. semantic prototypes) was also put to the test in Howard (2002) with the analysis of oral interviews conducted with Anglophone advanced instructed learners.[4] It was found that the *passé composé* was mostly used first with telic verbs (achievement, accomplishment), then with activities and finally with statives, while the order was reversed for the *imparfait*. The participants tended to avoid past tense marking in past tense contexts, and used the present to a great extent instead.

Howard (2005) used the same oral data to study the emergence of the *plus-que-parfait* (PQP) among these advanced instructed learners. The PQP is used to refer to an event that had to occur before another one (e.g. *quand Marc est arrivé, nous avions déjà déjeuné* 'when Marc arrived, we had already eaten'), it is thus a matter of indicating the appropriate chronological order of events. It was found that the participants' production increased with their proficiency level, but remained limited to about one third of the contexts where it would have been appropriate, indicating that it was not yet productive. The most commonly used form in lieu of the *plus-que-parfait* was the *passé composé*.

Labeau (2007) investigated the use of the *passé simple*[5] (a rarely used past tense form) in the written and oral narratives of three types of learners: adult L2 learners, bilinguals and native speakers. They were all asked to first read the fairy tale Cinderella before recording a retelling of it as well as providing a written version. A qualitative analysis indicates an increasing number of accurate *passé simple* forms from the L2 learner groups to the bilingual group and finally the NS group without any surprises. What is more interesting is that the bilingual group (n = 8, thus a small sample with great individual variation) produced as many instances of *passé simple* forms in the oral as in the written narratives. The *passé simple* is characteristic of fairy tales which are rarely part of the input of instructed learners who cannot be expected to use it productively.

---

4. All the studies by Howard (2002, 2005, 2008, 2012) use the same group of participants with the same data from oral interviews.

5. *Passé simple* as a perfective past morphological form has been largely replaced by *passé composé*. Labeau (2009), a recent corpus study based on five Parisian newspapers as well as the corpus data presented in two other studies (Do-Hurinville 2000; Herzog 1981), reports that the *passé simple* accounts for only 9.86% of finite forms. See also Labeau (2004) which found that *passé simple* accounted for 2.64% of finite forms.

Participants in Izquierdo (2008) were native speakers of Mexican-Spanish, a Romance language very similar to French regarding the main aspectual distinction between perfective and imperfective; its acquisition is nonetheless a challenging task for Hispanophone learners, just as it is for Anglophone learners (*ibid*: 74). This classroom-based study used two form-focused multimedia instruction types (prototypical and nonprototypical past tense contexts) to administer four different lessons targeting the aspectual difference between the *passé composé* and *imparfait*. Data collection included cloze, comprehension and listening preference tests with reaction times that were administered over a ten week period. Findings were mixed in that participants' performance improved from pre- to post-testing measures, but it depended on the task (e.g. there were absolutely no gains in the listening task), while the type of multimedia instruction was irrelevant.

4.2.2   Present temporality and aspect

To the best of my knowledge, no L2 studies have investigated the acquisition of present temporality in French. One may speculate that this may be because it is assumed that the indicative present is easily acquired along with its early introduction in instructed settings, particularly compared to the *passé composé*, *imparfait* or *plus-que-parfait*. Two studies targeting other languages suggest that this may be the case. First, Ramat Giacalone and Banfi (1990) found that the present appeared to function as a general unmarked imperfective in the interlanguage Chinese-speaking learners of Italian (small sample of 4 learners, aged 16 to 44). Second, Housen (1994) reports an early semantic distinction between past and present in the longitudinal case study of the Dutch interlanguage of a native-English-speaking adult learner. However, given that the present in French has at least six functions as described in Chapter 1, it would be interesting to investigate whether L2 learners do acquire all of them, how, and at what rate.

4.2.3   Future temporality and aspect

Schlyter (1990) compared the L1 and the L2 acquisition of French by 2 untutored Swedish adult learners and 3 German-French bilingual children by examining a corpus of oral data. She found that her adult participants seemed to acquire lexical future (e.g. *je veux danser* 'I want to dance') and simple future (e.g. *je danserai* 'I will dance') at the same time, while her children participants appeared to acquire lexical future before simple future. German-French bilingual children acquired modal + infinitive before *va* + infinitive to express futurity, whereas it has been established that in L1 French, periphrastic future is acquired before simple future (Fleischman 1982; Sabeau-Jouannet 1975).

In a longitudinal study, Moses (2002) collected oral (interviews) and written data (compositions, judgment tasks) from 24 college students at 4 different instructional levels. The results allowed him to observe three distinct stages in the development of futurity in instructed L2 learners: a pragmatic stage, a lexical stage, and a morphological stage characterized by the productive use of verbal constructions. The learners moved from the present to periphrastic future to simple future, and tended to over-use simple future while under-using present and periphrastic future. The latter tendency does not correspond to their classroom input which shows that 60% of future forms were encoded with periphrastic future. But as Ellis (1996) notes, "instructional input often does not reflect language use outside the classroom" (cited in Bardovi-Harlig 2002). Another finding in Moses (2002) was that the verb-to-adverb ratio significantly decreases over time in oral and written data as L2 learners gain a better mastery of morphological forms. Moses concludes that overall, the data showed a systematic and relatively uniform development of future expressions with a clear pragmatic-lexical-morphological path.

Nadasdi, Mougeon and Rehner (2003) collected oral data from recorded interviews on a variety of topics from 41 French immersion students in Canada (aged 13–18). They found a clear preference for the periphrastic future (used 67% of the time), followed by the simple future (10%) and the present (10%). Non target-like forms made up the remaining 14% of the corpus. It was also found that the use of adverbial expressions correlated with the use of the present. Moreover, it appeared that students who had spent time in other francophone countries tended to make a greater use of periphrastic future, and lesser use of simple future. A comparison with the *Québécois* and the Ontario French corpora identified three future forms: periphrastic future (73%), simple future (20%) and present (7%). Nadasdi et al. also found an L1 effect in that it appears that non-English or Romance speakers use periphrastic future more often than other speakers.

In Ayoun (2005c), instructed L2 learners at three different proficiency levels wrote a personal narrative and completed a cloze test to address three main research questions: (a) how do instructed learners express future temporality? Do they use all three future expressions with equal frequency, and in a way similar to NSs? Or do they overuse *aller*+ predicate? Or does their production reflect classroom input which tends to rely on *futur simple* (Moses 2002)?; (b) does their production exemplify complex clauses with the appropriate *concordance des temps*? Do they use *futur antérieur* at all?; (c) is there a decreasing reliance on adverbials as proficiency increases? The findings were mixed. First, all participants demonstrated an increasing ability to use a variety of morphological forms (e.g. present, futurate present, *futur simple*, periphrastic future). Second, the three main expressions of futurity (*futur simple*, periphrastic future, futurate present) were not used with equal frequency (based on the narratives), nor in a way similar to the NSs who used primarily *futur simple*. The L2 learners did not overuse the simple future while the periphrastic future was underused. The *futur antérieur* was very rarely used which is not surprising given its very low frequency in the input (Engel 2001). The participants produced few complex clauses that would have required *concordance des temps*. Finally, there was no evidence of adverb-to-verb ratio decreasing over time as measured across three different proficiency levels, but very few adverbs were used to begin with, indicating that these L2 learners were already relying on grammatical and morphological means to express futurity rather than pragmatic means.

4.2.4   Mood and modality

Focusing on the written and spoken sociolinguistic performance of Canadian immersion students enrolled in grade 10, Swain and Lapkin (1990) reports on two tasks – note writing task and a simulated job interview; only the former is relevant here as it was designed to elicit the use of the conditional in its hypothetical or attenuating functions. The early immersion group (n = 20) produced 15 tokens of conditions whereas the late immersion group (n = 11) produced only 5 and the Francophone group (n = 6) produced 6, but note the uneven number of participants in each group.

Day and Shapson (1991) used a functional, communicative approach to focus on the conditional following Harley and Swain (1984) who found "accuracy rates of 15%, 41% and 56% for Ontario immersion students in Grades 4, 6, and 10, respectively, compared to an accuracy rate of over 94% for native French-speaking students" (Day & Shapson 1991:28).[6] All experimental and control groups were administered a pre- and post-test as well as three different elicitation tasks (cloze test, written composition, oral interview). Findings showed that although all groups improved (albeit unevenly for the control group), the experimental groups' gains were significantly greater on the cloze test and written composition.

Bartning (2005) analyzed the production of advanced Swedish learners (n = 8) from the InterFra corpus. It appears that the subjunctive is a late emerging feature initially limited to *il faut que* 'it is necessary that' with a low accuracy rate of 24%, but that very advanced learners (i.e. doctoral students who are already teaching) reach an accuracy rate of 86% in five different required contexts.

Howard (2008) investigated the emergence of the subjunctive in the oral production (sociolinguistic interviews) of instructed L2 learners. The three groups varied in their years of study (two and three years for Group 1 and Group 2; three years plus a year abroad for Group 3). Although the groups were small (n = 6 in each

---

6.   Day and Shapson (1991:28) suggest that these low accuracy rates may be explained by the input these immersion students receive since Swain and Lapkin (1986) reported that "less than 4% of finite verbs used by Grades 3 and 6 immersion teachers were in the conditional".

group), 18 hours of recording produced only 100 contexts in which the subjunctive was appropriate and only 1 (Group 1), 3 (Group 3 by only two learners) and 5 (Group 2 by four learners) unambiguous subjunctive forms were produced with *falloir* as the main triggering expression as it was with Swedish L2 French learners (Bartning 2005), albeit with slightly more varied syntactic contexts. However, in Lealess (2005), Canadian immersion learners are reported to overwhelmingly favor *devoir* over *falloir* to express obligation (cited in Howard 2008).

Howard (2012) compared the frequency of use of three different forms – future, conditional and subjunctive – in the oral interviews conducted with three groups of advanced instructed learners (see Appendix A and above). For ease of exposition, the data are reproduced here (*ibid*: 213, Table 4.1). For the subjunctive, Table 4.1 only shows what Howard (2012: 213) refers to as "salient forms", that is, unambiguously subjunctive forms as opposed to indicative forms which were rare anyway (from 4 to 13%).

Table 4.1. Use of future, conditional and subjunctive forms (adapted from Howard 2012: 213)

	Future contexts			Subjunctive	Conditional	
	Present n%	Infl. Fut. n%	Per. Fut. n%	Subjunctive n%	Cond. n%	Cond. Ant. n%
group 1 (n = 6)	17–61%	8–28%	0–0%	1–4.5%	32–55%	–
group 2 (n = 6)	7–27%	10–38%	8–31%	3–16%	38–66%	4–44%
group 3 (n = 6)	20–32%	29–47%	5–8%	5–13%	81–74%	–

The data reveal a strong group effect as well as significant differences between morphological forms with the conditional being used the most productively in required contexts and the subjunctive the least. Howard also reports that tense concordancing with *si* clauses (*imparfait* + conditional) is frequent (54% to 72% accuracy). However, these findings should be considered with caution as the sample sizes are small (n = 6 per group) and the data are limited to one hour of oral interview.

4.2.5   Summary

This literature review (along with a few additional studies listed in Appendix A)[7] shows that the overwhelming majority of L2 French studies from a non-generative perspective have focused on past temporality and the aspectual distinction between

---

7.   For an overview of studies conducted with Swedish learners and suggested stages of development see Bartning (2012), Bartning and Schlyter (2004), Housen (2006).

the *passé composé* and the *imparfait*. It appears that the former emerges earlier and is more robust than the latter. Other past tense forms such as the *passé simple* and *plus-que-parfait* are rare in L2 learners' productions. Immersion students and instructed L2 learners use several morphological forms to express future temporality, but the conditional and *futur antérieur* are sporadic even in the interlanguage of advanced learners. The few studies that investigated the subjunctive show low rates of production or accuracy and were limited by small sample sizes, while it appears that present temporality and aspect has not yet been investigated. The prospection/present relevance of future seems to be easier than the perfective/imperfective aspectual opposition of past temporal morphology, however, in both cases, there is a clear improvement in performance with proficiency levels, suggesting that adult L2 learners can and do eventually acquire temporal systems successfully, however difficult the task may be.

4.3   Literature review of generative L2 French studies

Although the acquisition of TAM systems by adult L2 learners from a generative/minimalist perspective is a relatively recent line of empirical research since it only started in the early 2000s, it has been expanding quickly with several L2 languages, but there are still very few L2 French studies. They are reviewed in chronological order.[8] We will then see what the general findings are from studies conducted with other L2s.

The results of four different elicitation tasks – two written production tasks (a composition to elicit past tense morphology, a sentence completion task to elicit verbal agreement and adverbs) and two preference tasks (one to test for Case, finiteness and agreement and the second to test for adverb placement) – administered to beginning and advanced L2/L3 French learners (Vietnamese monolingual and Cantonese-English bilingual learners) in Leung (2002, 2005) show near-native-like performance on agreement, adverbs and finiteness indicating some L1 transfer at the initial stages, but also that features which are not present in the L1 are acquirable in the L2 *contra* the Failed Functional Features hypothesis and in support of the Full Access/Full Transfer hypothesis.

Ayoun (2005) investigated the acquisition of past temporality by instructed English-speaking learners of French (n = 37) at three different proficiency levels with NS controls. The personal narratives revealed that the L2 learners' interlanguage exhibited well-formed sentences with correctly inflected verbs for tense,

---

8.   See also Prévost (2009) for a brief review of the acquisition of inflectional morphology by L2 learners.

person and number, as well as appropriate negation and adverb placement as expected when projecting the appropriate functional categories associated with strong features; they also appear to have acquired semantic contrasts, but with varying degrees of mastery across the different lexical classes. However, the cloze test results revealed significant differences between groups across all aspectual classes. Thus, the results of the personal narratives are the only results that support the prediction that the participants would be successful in acquiring the semantic properties of AspP. They seem to have acquired target-like use of inflectional morphology and the appropriate feature strength of AspP as evidenced by their productive and accurate use of perfective and imperfective morphology. Moreover, the fact that almost all past participles and lexical verbs were properly inflected for tense, number and gender, with a few rare gender agreement errors indicates that the L2 learners were successful in the mapping of surface morphology. Even if the tense/aspect system of these L2 learners is not yet completely target-like, it is important to note that, as for the non-generative studies, the L2 learners' systems shows contrasts and systematicity in that they differentiate between past, present and future temporalities and within past temporality, for instance, they are aware of the aspectual distinction between the perfective and the imperfective expressed by the *passé composé* and the *imparfait*.

Herschensohn and Arteaga (2009) is the longitudinal study of three advanced Anglophone learners of L2 French.[9] Oral and written data and grammaticality judgements collected over several months show that all three learners use a variety of morphological forms including indicative present, *passé composé, imparfait* as well as present conditional, and that they do so with nearly perfect accuracy. They are also highly accurate with respect to the syntactic phenomena subsumed under the verb movement parameter (i.e. negation, adverbs and quantifiers placement)[10] indicating that they are using the L2 setting of that parameter. The authors thus conclude that their data provide evidence for access to UG and against impairment hypotheses, since these L2 learners appear to have acquired the uninterpretable features of Tense and AgrS.[11]

---

9.   See also Herschensohn (2001, 2003, 2004). The participants were rated as advanced following the *stade avancé supérieur* in Bartning and Schlyter (2004).

10.   The GJs indicate a difficulty with the floating quantifier *tout* 'all'.

11.   Following Herschensohn (2000), Herschensohn and Arteaga (2009: 309) "presume that parameter resetting is not exclusively driven by UG, but rather bootstrapped by a coalition of resources including cognitive strategies and lexical learning".

4.4   Literature review of generative L2 studies in other languages

Ayoun and Rothman (2013) provide an extensive review of L2 studies conducted in the generative/minimalist framework by targeted language focusing on the L2/L3 acquisition of lexical aspect (telicity), grammatical aspect and mood/modality, so this section will only summarize findings as they relate to the L2 acquisition questions raised in Chapter 3 that can be summed up by a single one: can adult L2 learners achieve ultimate attainment in the acquisition of TAM systems and thus in general as well? The studies are organized by their L2 target instead of by the type of temporality, aspect or mood/modality to avoid overlaps and repetitions.

4.4.1   L2 English

In Slabakova (2000, 2001), results indicated that the ability and consistency of Bulgarian-speaking learners of English in judging and distinguishing between telic and atelic sentences increased with their level of proficiency. In Slabakova (2000), the hypothesis of L1 transfer was supported by the results of an aspectual interpretation task showing that both the English NSs and the Spanish L2 learners recognized the contrast between telic and atelic sentences contrary to the Bulgarian L2 learners who seemed to initially transfer the L1 value of the aspectual parameter.

Slabakova (2003) found that Bulgarian-speaking L2 learners of English were able to acquire the functional category AspP with its semantic implications since the results of the production task revealed that learners had acquired the simple and progressive aspect inflectional morphology, while the results of the truth value judgment task indicated that they improved in mapping inflectional morphology to appropriate semantic contexts with increasing proficiency levels.

In Hawkins and Liszka (2003), Chinese (n = 2), Japanese (n = 5) and German (n = 5) NSs performed a retelling task from a short film extract and a personal recount of a happy experience. The Japanese and German NSs produced regular simple past tense morphology in over 90% of the obligatory contexts, while the Chinese NSs did so 62% of the time; however, they correctly inflected verbs with irregular simple past morphology in about 84% of the mandatory contexts. Hawkins and Liszka concluded that these findings support the Failed Functional Features hypothesis (Hawkins & Chan 1997) since only Chinese does not morpho-syntactically encode tense; however, their conclusion is weakened by the very small sample sizes (n = 2 to 5). Also, Campos (2009) suggested that their findings may be accounted for by L1 prosodic transfer because Chinese does not allow for complex codas.

Moreover, and althougth it was not conducted in a generative perspective, Yang and Yuan Huang (2004) provide contradictory evidence to Hawkins and Liszka (2003) by showing that 10 to 19 years old Chinese instructed ESL learners (n = 453 at 5 different levels of proficiency, a much larger, and hence reliable sample) who did not benefit from exposure to English outside the classroom, performed extremely well in marking past verbal morphology in the obligatory ontexts (90.6% to 99.5%) of personal narratives.

In Gabriele, Martohardjono and McClure (2005) (based on Gabriele 2005), Japanese NSs (n = 83) at three different proficiency levels in L2 English completed an interpretation task to investigate whether their interpretation of the English past progressive would interact with L1 lexical semantics. It was found that even advanced learners had more difficulties with the past progressive than with the simple past; they allowed a perfective reading for the English past progressive even when the L1 Japanese interpretation is progressive, prompting the authors to propose that the perfective is a default interpretation in the mental representation of *te-iru*.

Gabriele and Maekawa (2008) compared three groups of L2 English learners – native speakers of Chinese (n = 32) to native speakers of Korean (n = 18) and Japanese (n = 55) – at different proficiency levels. Japanese and Korean are two languages that encode tense morpho-syntactically whereas Chinese does not and may even lack and a Tense projection (Lin 2006). The participants were administered an interpretation task with short stories targeting the present and past progressive; regular and irregular past tense forms were used as distractors. The advanced, but not the intermediate, Chinese learners were able to distinguish the present from the past progressive, while the L1 Japanese and Korean learners met expectations. Gabriele and Maekawa's (2008) findings thus provide evidence against Hawkins and Liszka's (2003) claim of a permanent syntactic deficit in L2 acquisition when a feature such as [±past] is not already part of the learners' L1.

Gabriele (2009) obtained mixed findings with two different groups of learners: Japanese NSs as L2 English learners at low, intermediate, high proficiency levels (n = 101), and English NSs of L2 Japanese at low and high proficiency levels (n = 33). The L2 English learners completed a story compatibility task targeting telic predicates with present and past progressive morphology (simple past acted as a control), while the L2 Japanese learners performed the Japanese equivalent of the story interpretation task to investigate the acquisition of the simple past marker -*ta* and the progressive marker *te-iru* with telic predicates. Both L2 Japanese and L2 English learners did well on accomplishments with the progressive and on achievements with simple past, but not as well on achievements with the progressive -*ing* or imperfective marker *te-iru*. Moreover, all L2 English learners incorrectly accepted stimuli in which the present progressive was used with perfected events (i.e. preemption context). Gabriele (2009) attributed this finding to the complexity of the semantic computation and the lack of transparency of input cues making preemption so difficult.

Two studies by Liszka (2006, 2009) focused on the potential implications of a representational deficit approach on pragmatic processes from a Relevance theoretic perspective (Sperber & Wilson 1986/95) with French-speaking learners of L2 English who performed a written narrative to elicit events and states as well as two oral tasks (description of a video and picture clip to elicit states and ongoing events and a contextualized dialogue). These studies targeted the distributional and interpretational properties of the English present simple and present progressive (French does not grammatically express the latter). In Liszka (2006), a study with a small number of participants (n = 8), the production of the simple present and present progressive was native-like, but in the oral tasks, learners tended to overgeneralize the present simple to present progressive contexts. In Liszka (2009), the findings from a larger number of participants (n = 16) confirm their ability to achieve near perfect scores on present simple (100%) and progressive forms (92.7%) in the oral picture description task; however, in the video clip description and the contextualized dialogue tasks, the use of present progressive forms drops to 52.8% and 54.8% of mandatory contexts (present simple forms remain high at 94.4% and 94.2%, respectively). Such mixed findings cannot be explained by a stressful processing load due to the nature of the oral tasks. It appears that these learners have acquired the simple present, but not the present progressive.

4.4.2   L2 Spanish and Portuguese

In Schell (2000), Anglophone study abroad learners in Spain produced written data at regular intervals during nine months performed with high to perfect accuracy rates (85% to 100%), indicating that they were successful in acquiring past tense morphology. Although the sample size was small (n = 5), the findings are important for it is a rare longitudinal study.

A series of studies by Montrul and Slabakova targeted the interpretive properties of the preterit and imperfect in Spanish by Anglophone learners and generally found that the higher the proficiency level of the learners, the better they performed. Thus, in Slabakova and Montrul (2000), the advanced group showed great accuracy on a truth value judgment task while intermediate learners were significantly more accurate with the prototypical imperfect than with the non-prototypical preterite when using state verbs, suggesting that L2 learners can acquire properties that are usually not explicitly taught in foreign language settings. Similarly, in Slabakova and Montrul (2002), all advanced and some intermediate learners showed that they were able to differentiate between the perfective and imperfective aspects in performing a sentence conjunction judgment task.

The same elicitation task was used in Montrul and Slabakova (2002) to test the semantic implication of the Spanish preterite and imperfect. It was found that the L2 learners who had performed with at least 80% accuracy on a morphological endings test appeared to have acquired the semantic interpretations of the two past tenses, whereas the others struggled (especially with states and achievements). It was concluded that "the formal features associated with the functional category AspP are acquirable and 'unimpaired' in SLA"(*ibid:* 141), and that "the acquisition of morphology precedes the acquisition of semantics, and that both types of acquisition are gradual developments" (*ibid:* 140).

Montrul and Slabakova's (2003) study revealed a task effect in that near-native speakers were undistinguishable from native speakers on the sentence-conjunction judgment task, whereas on the truth-value judgment task, only the near-natives performed like native speakers in the generic restriction on the preterite and specific-generic ambiguity of the imperfect, the former being easier than the latter for the advanced learners. It was thus again concluded that L2 learners may achieve near-native competence in the domain of aspectual interpretations.

A truth-value judgment task with 80 story-sentence combinations designed to test the Spanish preterite and imperfect as well as the possible generic interpretation of pronominal subjects was administered to intermediate and advanced Anglophone learners of L2 Spanish in Slabakova and Montrul (2003).[12] Findings revealed a developmental trend from the intermediate to the advanced learners toward the successful acquisition of the semantic properties tested (preterite *vs* and imperfect, conditionals, negative constraint on the generic interpretation of the preterite).[13]

Another study, Borgovono and Prévost (2003), also found a gradual learning curve in the acquisition of the polarity subjunctive triggered by the presupposition/lack of presupposition contrast by francophone learners of L2 Spanish (n = 25).[14]

---

12. In Spanish, when the predicate is encoded with the imperfect, the subject pronoun can have two interpretations: a generic meaning (i.e. people in general) or a specific meaning (e.g. we); the subject pronoun cannot have a generic interpretation when the predicate is encoded with the preterite. This distinction is generally not explicitly taught in foreign language classrooms.

13. A habitual clause reading implies a generic pronominal subject.

14. In Spanish, "polarity subjunctive is licensed with epistemic, perception and communication verbs" whereas in French "only negated epistemics license polarity subjunctive in embedded clauses" (*ibid:* 153); however, the two languages have the same interpretations of the choice of mood.

The participants who were asked to complete a truth-value interpretation task with 48 short scenarios in French followed by a test sentence in Spanish in either the subjunctive or indicative, displayed a near-native accuracy.

Díaz, Bel and Bekiou (2007) asked L2 Spanish learners at intermediate and advanced proficiency levels (n = 70) from different L1 language background or type (Romance, Modern Greek, Chinese, Japanese, Slavic; but there was a variable number of participants per language group and proficiency level, from 5 to 12) to complete three written stories in the past to test the hypothesis that only L2 learners whose L1 encodes the [±perfective] aspectual distinction would be able to acquire it in Spanish. It was found that Romance and Greek learners were helped by their L1 [±perfective] feature, but mostly for intermediate level learners and with a lexical class effect; all advanced learners performed at the same level for states and achievements.

Hsien-jen Chin (2008) compared Chinese- and English-speaking learners to NSs of Spanish by administering a morphology test and an acceptability test. Chinese uses aspectual markers (e.g. durative, progressive, perfective) while English and Spanish exhibit overt tense morphology. Findings revealed an L1 and lexical class effects in that English L1 learners distinguished perfective/imperfective contrasts on telic predicates, but not on states, while none of the Chinese L1 learners made distinctions. The individual results show that actually only 2 out of 22 English L1 learners recognized the contrasts. The low proficiency level of the L2 learners may have negatively impacted the findings, and the Chinese-speaking participants were in fact L3 Spanish learners.

In Iverson and Rothman (2008), advanced English learners of L2 Portuguese (n = 17) were administered two sentence conjunction judgment tasks to assess their knowledge of [±accidental] interpretative nuances of preterite and imperfect adverbially quantified sentences. Advanced L2 learners displayed native-like performance in 10 out of 11 contexts, providing evidence against impairment hypotheses.

Rothman and Iverson (2008) administered interpretive tests – two sentence conjunction judgment tests and a sentence-matching test – to two groups of Anglophone learners of L2 Portuguese (one intermediate group and one advanced group) and a group of native speakers of Brasilian Portuguese as controls, to investigate their knowledge of accidental/non-accidental semantic entailment properties. The advanced L2 learners performed like the NS group on all tasks except for the stimuli items in the first task exemplifying a non-accidental reading with adverbially quantified sentences in the preterit. Moreover, it is argued that all groups differentiated between the preterit and the imperfect in all the contexts tested although they are not explicitly taught.

A grammaticality judgment task was used to test the acquisition of indicative and subjunctive complement clauses with volitional and negated epistemic predicates by Anglophone intermediate (n = 25) and advanced (n = 17) learners in Iverson, Kempchinsky and Rothman (2008). There were significant differences between groups on all sentence types, but none between the advanced learners and the NSs in any rating of categories; moreover, the intermediate learners did not differ significantly from the NS group in negated epistemics with subjunctive embedded clauses.

4.4.3   Heritage learners of Russian and Spanish

Heritage learners differ from adult L2 learners in that they are exposed to a native language in their home country before moving to another country as immigrants where their native language is now a minority language. Some are simultaneous bilinguals, while others are sequential bilinguals, but in both cases, by the time they become adults, their first language is no longer their dominant one.[15] We have only begun to start investigating the ways in which their linguistic competence may resemble or differ from not only the competence of native speakers, but also of L2 learners.[16] Generative studies with heritage learners center around Russian and Spanish.

Thus, Pereltsvaig (2002) investigated the differences between two varieties of Russian: Standard Russian and American Russian (a variety spoken by English dominant second-generation Russian-speaking immigrants living in the U.S.) and proposed that American Russian encodes lexical aspect rather than grammatical aspect based on the analysis of 150 predicates (part of a corpus compiled with M. Polinsky, University of California San Diego). The American Russian aspectual system does not appear to clearly prefer either the perfective or the imperfective aspect since most predicates are always encoded with the same aspectual form, leading Pereltsvaig to suggest that in American Russian, "aspectual marking encodes a lexical semantic property of the verb" (ibid: 7). Lexical aspect seems to be marked by aspectual morphology while grammatical aspect is not marked at all (i.e. OuterAspP is missing); moreover, tense is marked correctly, but subject-verb agreement is not. The loss of uninterpretable features is explained by L1 attrition, because English becomes the dominant language before these speakers reach puberty, and they are no longer exposed to Standard Russian, a language in which they are illiterate.

---

15.   For a more detailed account of heritage learners see for instance, Carreira (2004) or Montrul (2012), as well as the very useful annotated bibliography in Polinsky (2011).

16.   *Heritage Language Learner* is a recent journal (the first issue appeared in 2003) dedicated to issues surrounding heritage language learners.

Polinsky (1997, 2006) also investigated Russian heritage learners whose English is the dominant language. Polinsky (1995) offers a descriptive account of the American Russian of 20 heritage speakers who had left their home country at various ages (from 0 to 18) and thus had spent from 3 to 73 years outside a native Russian community (one may argue whether all of them qualify as heritage learners). She notes a gradual attrition of subject-verb agreement (marked from 30% to 66% of occurrences), verbal reflexives and subjunctive (replaced by the indicative), as well as what appears to be a restructuring of the aspectual system: the contrast between the imperfective and the perfective is lost and "most verbs become either lexicalized perfectives or lexicalized imperfectives" (*ibid*: 384) based on telicity.

Similarly, Polinsky (2006) compares various lexical and morphosyntactic features in the American Russian of heritage speakers (n = 21) with Full Russian (i.e. standard Russian). They represent a somewhat more homogeneous group than the speakers studied in Polinsky (1995), but still with wide ranges: they emigrated to the United States between the ages of 3 and 11, and were from 12 to 21 years-old at the time of the study. There are significant variations in the use of perfective/imperfective forms based on telicity, and analytical expressions are replacing synthetic aspectual verbs; out of the two standard Russian conditional forms, the analytical form is being replaced by the indicative and the synthetic form does not appear at all. The differences between Standard Russian and American Russian are clear, however these speakers may exemplify more a case of incomplete acquisition than attrition since some of them emigrated to the United States at a very young age and thus did not have the time to fully acquire Russian as a first language.[17]

Several studies by S. Montrul (e.g. Montrul 2002, 2007) focused on English-Spanish bilingual speakers for whom Spanish was a heritage language. Montrul (2002) set out to compare them with monolingual Spanish speakers to explore whether the age of onset of bilingualism impacts ultimate attainment. She investigated the following research question: are morphological and semantic features equally affected by language loss or do bilingual speakers display patterns of incomplete acquisition in the Spanish preterite/ imperfect contrast when performing an interpretation and production tasks? The findings show that bilingual and monolingual speakers performed significantly differently on achievement predicates encoded with the imperfect, and on stative verbs encoded with both the preterite

---

17. See also Romanova (2008) comparing native speakers, heritage and L2 learners of Russian, and Au, Knightly, Jun and Oh (2002) as well as Au, Knightly, Jun, Oh and Romo (2008) for studies comparing heritage and L2 learners of Russian.

and the imperfect, whereas the early child bilingual speakers differed from the monolingual speakers on stative verbs encoded with the preterite. There was thus a lexical class and morphological form effects. Montrul interpreted these findings as incomplete acquisition for the simultaneous bilinguals and some attrition for the early child bilinguals, mostly for stative verbs in the preterite, which is a nonprototypical use.

Montrul (2007) found that heritage language speakers, while mastering the subjunctive when it is required as complement of volitional predicates for instance, differ from native monolingual Spanish speakers in other ways. Thus, in contexts where either the indicative or subjunctive is possible, but where there would a subtle native pragmatic preference for one mood over the other, Montrul found that heritage speakers significantly differed from monolingual speakers.

Finally, Montrul and Perpiñan (2011) administered the same written morphology recognition tasks and sentence conjunction judgment tasks used previously (e.g. Montrul 2002) to Russian native speakers (n = 23), L2 learners (n = 60) and heritage learners (n = 60) of Russian at low, intermediate and advanced proficiency levels in order to investigate whether they are able to recognize TAM morphology and distinguish various semantic implications. Effects were found for task (better performance on the recognition tasks than the sentence conjunction tasks) and morphological forms (better performance on the preterit than on the imperfect, and on indicative than on subjunctive). Overall, the NS group differed from the L2 learners and HL speakers, with the former performing better than the latter.

4.4.4 Summary

The generative studies reviewed here provide another piece to the puzzle of the developmental route of L2 TAM acquisition even if most of them focus more on tense and aspect than on mood/modality. The only study (Hawkins & Liszka 2003) that claims to have found evidence in favor of impairment hypotheses is weakened by small sample sizes (n = 2 to 5) as well as by a plausible alternative account (i.e. L1 prosodic transfer as suggested by Campos 2009). Five other studies (Gabriele 2009; Gabriele et al. 2005; Hsien-jun Chin 2008; Liszka 2006, 2009) report mixed findings, while the remainder of the studies found evidence for successful L2 acquisition, with a progressive improvement in performance with proficiency, leading up to near-native performance. In other words, L2 learners eventually arrive at a TAM system with well established contrasts and systematicity, particularly for tense and aspect; mood/modality has not been sufficiently investigated yet. If adult L2 learners were permanently impaired and unable to acquire new or different features, their performance across various elicitation tasks would not show such high accuracy rates in required contexts as was found in most of the studies reviewed.[18] However, studies conducted with Russian and Spanish heritage speakers clearly show that TAM systems, in addition to being extremely complex and subtle, can undergo attrition and are vulnerable to incomplete acquisition.

---

18.   Ayoun and Rothman (2013) reach the same conclusion following an extensive review of L2 generative studies.

CHAPTER 5.1

Methodology and findings

Production tasks

Tous les moyens de l'esprit sont enfermés dans le langage; et qui n'a point réfléchi sur le langage, n'a point réfléchi du tout.

Alain

1. Introduction

This chapter reports on the study that was carried out to test the research questions listed below. Its main purpose was to gain a better and more complete perspective on the tense, aspect, mood/modality system that second language (L2) learners build as they progress along the continuum from the L2 initial state to the L2 end state, that is, ideally, successful ultimate attainment.

As the literature review of Chapter 4 revealed, most empirical studies have focused narrowly on tense and aspect or mood/modality. Tense-aspect studies tend to study past tense morphology, while the few mood/modality studies conducted to date looked mostly into the indicative-subjunctive alternation. To the best of my knowledge, there are no studies on the entire TAM system of L2 learners. Although the present study does not accomplish this ambitious goal either, it nevertheless opens a wider window into the L2 learners' TAM system by eliciting data on past and future temporalities, as well as mood and modality.

2. Research questions

The four main research questions to be investigated are:

1. Does the L2 learners' interlanguage grammar display contrasts and systematicity? Do they acquire aspectual, modal and mood contrasts (e.g. indicative vs subjunctive)?
2. Does the L2 learners' performance improve with their proficiency level eventually leading to near-native performance levels?

3.   Do the L2 learners acquire targetlike use of inflectional morphology?
4.   Will there be an elicitation task effect and will it vary with the proficiency level?

3.   Participants

The participants were Anglophone learners of L2 French in the instructed setting of a large North American university. The data collected with a background information questionnaire are summarized in Appendix B.

The Anglophone participants were recruited from the various classes of French as a foreign language in which they were enrolled at the time of the data collection. Some of the participants who were placed in the Advanced group following the proficiency test were no longer taking French classes, but were all involved in an academic setting as graduate students. There were slightly more female than male participants (n = 24 vs n = 18), all three groups display a similar age range and average, most of the participants in the Advanced group were graduate students but not all; a majority of the learners in the Intermediate and Advanced groups were French majors, but not all; the age at which they started to learn French as an L2 varied greatly across all three groups, however it was past the age of puberty for almost all of them and they started to learn French in an instructed setting; most of the participants in the Intermediate and Advanced groups had spent time in France or in another French-speaking country, but the length of their stay was negligible for most. The majority of the participants felt that not only they were still learning French, but that they were from extremely to very motivated to learn it.

4.   Elicitation tasks and data collection

The data collection took place once a week over 5 weeks as summarized in Table 1.

Table 1. Overview of data collection

	Task 1	Task 2
session 1	background info questionnaire	proficiency test (42 item-GJT)
session 2	production (subjunctive)	cloze test (future temporality)
session 3	production (future temporality)	sentence completion (subjunctive)
session 4	production (past temporality)	sentence completion (modals)
session 5	cloze test (past temporality)	cloze test (past temporality)

All sessions were computerized to facilitate data collection and avoid the pitfalls of missing or incomplete data (the advantages of computerized data collection are well known; see e.g. Ayoun 2000; Hulstijn 1997). The participants were invited to come to a computer lab once a week to perform two tasks per session. With the exception of the last session which consisted of two cloze tests, all sessions included two different types of tasks and targeted different linguistic forms (e.g. past temporality and modals).

Session 1 was comprised of a background information questionnaire and a pre-test as an independent measure of proficiency. It consisted of a grammaticality judgment task (GJT) with 42 stimuli (isolated complete sentences) targeting various morpho-syntactic elements (e.g. verb movement properties – adverb and negation placement, question formation – clitics, relative pronouns). In sessions 3 and 4, participants first wrote a personal narrative (production task), and then perfomed a sentence completion task by providing the appropriate morphological form of lexical verbs or modals. Finally, in the last session, participants wrote two personal narratives, both targeting past tense morphology. Each session included two different elicitation tasks and two different linguistic targets for two main reasons: first, to avoid the possibility that participants would use the linguistic information contained in the first task to perform the second task; second, to keep the sessions interesting by providing the participants with different tasks to perform, thereby avoiding monotony or fatigue that may affect their performance. The last session is the only exception as it included two cloze tests both targeting past temporality to add to previous mixed findings (e.g. Ayoun 2001, 2004). Since the two stories used in these cloze tests were quite different, it was assumed that the participants could not use one to inform their decisions while performing the second one. All elicitation tasks are described in more detail below.

Different elicitation tasks were used as it is well-known that several task-related factors ranging from procedural factors (e.g. the way the instructions are given, the order of presentation of the tasks and the randomization of the stimuli within each task) to stimulus factors (e.g. context, meaning, parsability), may result in judgment variability in experimental tasks with well-documented caveats (e.g. Cowart 1997; Duffield 2003; Hedgcock 1993; Mandell 1999; Schütze 1996; Sorace 1996; Tarone, Gass & Cohen 1994), leading to mixed findings (e.g. Ayoun 2005b). For instance, grammatical judgments, which are very demanding in terms of processing, are subject to variation and extra-linguistic factors as all decision-making and judgment behavior. Cloze tasks are more difficult than free or controlled production tasks as they require participants to process and understand a text without the benefit of predicates marked for tense as important indications of the storyline. Participants also have to adopt the narrator's particular viewpoint, and if they fail to correctly interpret the semantic value and viewpoint of a few predicates early on in the storyline, they are very likely to misunderstand the rest of the story and to continue making erroneous assumptions throughout the task.

Mixed findings are thus expected as different elicitation tasks present different challenges and difficulties even for native speakers, but data obtained from several elicitation tasks present a more reliable and complete picture of the participants' competence through their performance.[1]

5. Findings of the production tasks

The raw data collected over the five sessions were coded and analyzed with SPSS. Results are given by elicitation task and by linguistic target (i.e. past or future temporality, modals) within each task and will be referred to as session number and task number, such as session 1, task 2.[2]

First, the scores obtained on the proficiency test were used to determine the placement of the participants in one of three proficiency levels labelled as followed: Beginning (n = 14), Intermediate (n = 15) and Advanced (n = 13). The mean scores out of 42 are displayed in Table 2; a one-way ANOVA revealed a significant difference between the three groups (F (2, 39) = 109.395, $p < .001$).

Table 2. Proficiency test scores

Group	n	mean	SD
Beginning	14	23.29	2.730
Intermediate	15	29.80	1.971
Advanced	13	36.85	2.410

5.1 Production task: Session 2, task 1

The participants completed three production tasks (task 1 of sessions 2, 3, and 4) which consisted of personal narratives (in the sense that the participants wrote about something personal) with a different topic designed to elicit various temporalities and moods. The topics were written in English so as to avoid giving the participants any indication regarding temporality. The only part in French was the email written by a friend in session 2.

---

1. Oral data were avoided as they create new potential difficulties such as determining with accuracy which forms participants intended to use due to the homophony of a large number of tenses (e.g. infinitives, past participles and *imparfait* forms sound the same).

2. My deepest thanks and gratitude go to Mark Borgstrom for his patience and his invaluable and thorough work as my professional statistical consultant over the years.

The participants first read a friend's short email in which s/he was saying that s/he had decided to move to China without money or planning because s/he could not stand living at home anymore. The participants were asked to reply to their friend to keep him/her from making that mistake. Although that topic was designed to elicit a variety of tenses and moods such as the imperative, subjunctive and conditional, the indicative present is always an option.

A summary of how many words, tokens, types, morphological forms and errors produced by the participants in their respective groups is displayed in Table 3. The complete data by individuals within each group are in Appendix C.

Table 3. Production task summary by groups (session 2, task 1)

		Beginning	Intermediate	Advanced
Total number of words	average	112.64	93.27	134.46
	range	69–167	74–158	82–198
Verb tokens	average	18.07	16.07	20.84
	range	10–28	10–19	13–28
Verb types	average	12.57	11.27	15.77
	range	9–19	8–15	11–21
Morphological forms	average	4.21	5.31	5.31
	range	2–6	2–9	2–9
Morphological errors	average	1.78	1.07	1.0
	range	0–5	0–3	0–3

The data displayed in Table 3 reveal only small differences between groups: in general, the higher the proficiency level, the more words, verb tokens and verb types were produced, but with minor differences, and the verb token and verb type averages are greater for the Beginning group than for the Intermediate group. A more noticeable difference is in the average and range of morphological forms produced, which are greater for the Advanced group than for the other two lower proficiency groups. The number of errors is also smaller for the Advanced group, but the average of errors produced on verb tokens is very low for all three groups. Morphological errors were considered to be a non-target like choice given the context (e.g. *passé composé* instead of *imparfait*).

Tables 4 through 6 present the morphological forms used by the Beginning, Intermediate and Advanced groups, respectively. The 'correct' column refers to the total number of tokens a given form was used appropriately given its context; conversely, 'incorrect' column refers to the total number of tokens a given form was used inappropriately given its context; the 'total' column adds up the two, while the '% correct' column indicates the percentage of appropriately encoded tokens for each morphological form, therefore indicating the accuracy of use of each morphological form. Finally, the '% total correct' column refers to the percentage a given morphological form represents among all forms used.

Table 4. Beginning group – summary of morphological forms used (session 2, task 1)

Morphological form	Correct	Incorrect	Total	% Correct	% Total correct
indicative present	176	6	182	96.7%	74.6%
future	18	2	20	90.0%	7.62%
imperative	16	0	16	100%	6.78%
subjunctive present	10	2	12	83.3%	4.23%
conditional present	6	4	10	60.0%	2.54%
passé composé	4	0	4	100%	1.69%
futur proche	3	0	3	100%	1.27%
imparfait	2	1	3	66.7%	.08%
plus-que-parfait	0	2	2	0%	0%
progressive present	1	0	1	100%	.04%
infinitive	n/a	5	5	n/a	n/a
Total	236	22	258	91.47%	

Table 5. Intermediate group – summary of morphological forms used (session 2, task 1)

Morphological form	Correct	Incorrect	Total	% Correct	% Total correct
indicative present	161	7	168	95.8%	69.7%
imperative	22	0	22	100%	9.52%
future	13	0	13	100%	5.62%
subjunctive present	12	2	14	85.7%	5.19%
passé composé	8	0	8	100%	3.46%
futur proche	7	0	7	100%	3.03%
conditional present	6	1	7	85.7%	2.59%
imparfait	2	5	7	28.6%	.08%
infinitive	n/a	1	1	n/a	n/a
Total	231	16	247	93.52%	

Tables 4, 5 and 6 display the data by proficiency. Although the topic was designed to elicit a variety of moods such as the imperative, subjunctive and conditional, it is clear that the participants overwhelmingly encoded predicates with the indicative present (74.6%, 69.7%, 63.67% for the Beginning, Intermediate and Advanced group, respectively), then either the future, imperative, subjunctive or

Table 6. Advanced group – summary of morphological forms used (session 2, task 1)

Morphological form	Correct	Incorrect	Total	% Correct	% Total correct
indicative present	163	5	168	97.02%	63.67%
future	20	3	23	86.95%	7.81%
subjunctive present	17	1	18	94.44%	6.64%
imperative	16	0	16	100%	6.25%
futur proche	15	0	15	100%	5.86%
passé composé	13	0	13	100%	5.18%
conditional present	10	1	11	90.09%	3.91%
imparfait	2	0	2	100%	.07%
plus-que-parfait	0	1	1	0%	0%
infinitive	n/a	1	1	n/a	n/a
conditional past	1	1	2	50.0%	.03%
Total	256	13	269	95.16%	

conditional present with much less frequency (under 10% of the total), but almost always with very high accuracy (e.g. for the Beginning group: from 83.3% for the subjunctive to 100% for the imperative, except for the conditional which was accurate for only 60% of the tokens).

A one-way ANOVA run with all the morphological forms in this first production task does not reveal a significant effect between groups for the form used the most often, the indicative present (F (2, 39) = 1.332, p =.276).[3]

5.2 Production task: Session 3, task 1

Participants were asked to address the following topics to elicit future temporality and possibly the conditional: what will your life be like in 10 years? Where would you like to live? What will you be doing? What would you like to have accomplished between now and then?

A summary of how many words, tokens, types, morphological forms and errors produced by the participants in their respective groups is displayed in Table 7. The complete data by individuals within each group are in Appendix C.

---

3. A significant effect was found for the *passé composé* (F (2, 39) = 6.104, p =.005) and the *futur proche* (F (2, 39) = 3.730, p =.033) which account for a small percentage of the forms used. Post hoc Tukey tests indicate that the Advanced group's performance was significantly different from the performance of the Beginning and Intermediate groups for the *futur proche* and the *passé composé*.

Table 7. Production task summary by groups (session 3, task 1)

		Beginning	Intermediate	Advanced
Total number of words	average	116.71	112.73	130.31
	range	61–159	63–165	60–173
Verb tokens	average	15.71	14.87	15.62
	range	8–30	5–21	9–23
Verb types	average	10.521	9.33	11.23
	range	5–15	5–15	4–19
Morphological forms	average	3.78	4.44	4.46
	range	2–5	1–7	2–6
Morphological errors	average	1.42	1.33	0.54
	range	0–9	0–4	0–1

The summary displayed in Table 7 reveals little to no difference in the number of words written, the number of verb tokens, verb types or morphological forms used for these tokens, although the ranges can be rather large. The only small difference between the three proficiency levels is the average of errors in the choice of morphological forms (Beginning = 1.42, Intermediate = 1.33, Advanced = 0.54), but all groups have participants whose production was always on target and systematically used the appropriate morphological form.

Tables 8 through 10 display a summary of the morphological forms used by group.

Table 8. Beginning group – summary of morphological forms (session 3, task 1)

Morphological forms	Correct	Incorrect	Total	% Correct	% Overall
indicative present	108	9	117	92.31%	53.73%
future	54	2	56	96.43%	26.86%
conditional present	20	3	23	86.95%	9.95%
futur antérieur	14	0	14	100%	6.96%
futur proche	1	6	7	16.7%	.49%
past infinitive	2	0	2	100%	.09%
imperative	1	0	1	100%	.05%
participle present	1	0	1	100%	.05%
conditional past	0	2	2	0%	0%
subjunctive present	0	3	3	0%	0%
Total	201	25	226	88.94%	

Table 9. Intermediate group – summary of morphological forms (session 3, task 1)

Morphological forms	Correct	Incorrect	Total	% Correct	% Overall
indicative present	92	3	95	96.84%	54.44%
future	31	1	32	96.87%	18.34%
conditional present	22	7	29	75.86%	13.02%
futur antérieur	8	0	8	100%	4.73%
subjunctive present	7	6	13	53.84%	4.14%
imparfait	4	0	4	100%	2.36%
past infinitive	3	1	4	75%	1.77%
futur proche	2	2	4	50.0%	1.18%
subjunctive past	0	2	2	0%	0%
Total	169	22	191	88.48%	

Table 10. Advanced group – summary of morphological forms (session 3, task 1)

Morphological forms	Correct	Incorrect	Total	% Correct	% Overall
indicative present	60	0	60	100%	37.04%
future	48	1	49	97.96%	29.63%
conditional present	27	2	29	93.1%	16.67%
futur antérieur	7	0	7	100%	4.32%
past infinitive	7	0	7	100%	4.32%
futur proche	4	1	5	80%	2.47%
participle present	3	0	3	100%	1.85%
subjunctive present	3	0	3	100%	1.85%
imparfait	2	1	3	66.67%	1.23%
subjunctive past	0	1	1	0%	0%
conditional past	0	1	1	0%	0%
passé composé	1	0	1	100%	.61%
Total	162	7	169	95.86%	

The 'correct' column refers to the number of tokens used appropriately given the context (e.g. 54 tokens of future were used appropriately, that is, on target), while the 'incorrect' column refers to the number of tokens used inappropriately given the context (e.g. 2 tokens encoded with the future should have been another morphological form such as indicative present). The '% correct' refers to the percentage of tokens used appropriately, while the '% overall' gives the percentage for a given morphological form used correctly. Thus, for instance, the correct indicative present forms account for 53.73% of the morphological forms the Beginning group produced.

All three groups were very accurate in their production of most morphological forms particularly for the forms used the most such as the indicative present and the future, which may not be surprising because a free production task allows the learners to use the forms they feel most comfortable with, and to avoid the ones about which they may feel uncertain or hesitant. Note that they may be sure of the morphological form to use, but not of its inflection.

The three morphological forms used the most often – indicative present, future, conditional present – are the same across all groups who produced quite a few variety of forms, as many as 12 for the Advanced group, but with few tokens.

The use of the indicative present decreases as the proficiency level increases (from to 53.73% and 54.44% for the Beginning and Intermediate groups down to 37.04% for the Advanced group), but the other two morphological forms – future and conditional present – do not seem to pattern following proficiency level.

A one-way Anova did not reveal any significant effect for any of the morphological forms.

5.3   Production task: Session 4, task 1

For the last production task, the participants were asked to write about where they were from, where they grew up, whether they would like their children to grow up the same way, and what their best childhood memory was. This topic was intended to elicit mainly past tense forms.

Table 11 presents a summary of the word, verb tokens and types produced by group, as well as the number of morphological forms and errors. There are no

Table 11. Production task summary by groups (session 4, task 1)

		Beginning	Intermediate	Advanced
Total number of words	average	137.86	123.47	165.69
	range	77–265	66–167	95–236
Verb tokens	average	19.21	16	19.23
	range	10–33	11–24	9–31
Verb types	average	11.86	11.53	12.76
	range	8–16	8–16	8–21
Morphological forms	average	4.36	4.47	4.84
	range	1–7	2–6	2–7
Morphological errors	average	2.21	.8	1
	range	0–7	0–6	0–3

major differences between groups except for the fact that the Advanced group produced a greater average of words than the other two groups, but not of verb tokens and slightly more of verb types. The higher the level of proficiency, the fewer the morphological errors, and both the average and range remain low even for the Beginning group (2.21 and 0–7, respectively).

The next three tables – Tables 12, 13 and 14 – display the types of morphological forms participants used, as well as their (in)correct use based on context.

Table 12. Beginning group – summary of morphological forms (session 4, task 1)

Morphological forms	Correct	Incorrect	Total	% Correct	% Overall
indicative present	83	3	86	96.51%	35.93%
passé composé	70	9	79	88.61%	30.30%
imparfait	56	7	63	88.89%	24.24%
conditional present	9	2	11	81.82%	3.89%
subjunctive present	5	2	7	71.42%	2.16%
future	6	0	6	100%	2.59%
infinitive	n/a	5	5	n/a	n/a
passé composé passive	1	0	1	100%	.04%
futur antérieur	0	1	1	0	0%
past infinitive	1	0	1	100%	.04%
subjunctive imperfect	0	1	1	0	0%
past subjunctive	0	1	1	0	0%
Total	231	31	262	88.17%	

Table 13. Intermediate group – summary of morphological forms (session 4, task 1)

Morphological forms	Correct	Incorrect	Total	% Correct	% Overall
indicative present	93	3	96	96.87%	38.11%
imparfait	60	1	61	98.36%	24.59%
passé composé	56	7	63	88.89%	22.95%
conditional present	19	0	19	100%	7.78%
subjunctive present	8	1	9	88.89%	3.27%
future	6	0	6	100%	2.45%
participle present	2	2	4	50.0%	.08%
plus-que-parfait	0	1	1	0%	0%
Total	244	15	259	94.08%	

Table 14. Advanced group – summary of morphological forms (session 4, task 1)

Morphological forms	Correct	Incorrect	Total	% Correct	% Overall
indicative present	100	4	104	96.15%	41.49%
passé composé	52	3	55	94.54%	21.57%
imparfait	52	2	54	96.29%	21.57%
subjunctive present	15	0	15	100%	6.22%
conditional present	14	0	14	100%	5.81%
future	3	1	4	75%	1.24%
futur proche	2	1	3	67%	.08%
plus-que-parfait	1	2	3	33.3%	.04%
passé composé passive	2	0	2	100%	.08%
subjunctive past	0	2	2	0%	0%
conditional past	0	1	1	0%	0%
Total	241	16	257	93.77%	

Participants in all groups correctly encoded a very high percentage of the tokens they produced, even if we consider only the morphological forms which have a large amount of tokens as opposed to just a few. Thus, the Beginning group used mostly the indicative present, the *passé composé* and *imparfait* with accuracy rates of 96.51%, 88.61% and 88.89%, respectively. Similarly, the Intermediate group was accurate for 96.87%, 98.36% and 88.89% of the same morphological forms; the conditional present is also worth mentioning since with 19 tokens, it represents 7.78% of the total number of the tokens used, with a perfect accuracy rate of 100%. The five morphological forms that the Advanced group used the most often to encode verbal tokens – indicative present, *passé composé, imparfait*, subjunctive present, conditional present – also display nearly perfect to perfect accuracy rates (94.54% to 100%).

The one-way Anova run with all the morphological forms revealed a main effect only for *futur proche* (F (2,39) = 4.039, p =.025), that was only used by the Advanced group.

5.4   Summary

Four main trends appeared from the production tasks: (1) the tasks did not elicit a majority of targeted forms since, as shown in Figure 1, the participants mostly produced indicative present forms, but in decreasing frequency from Session 2 to Session 4; however, past tense forms only occurred in the appropriate task (Session 4) with the *passé composé* and *imparfait* accounting for the majority of forms across groups (54.54%, 47.54% and 43.14% for the Beginning, Intermediate and Advanced group, respectively); (2) all three groups used a wide variety of morphological forms; (3) they did so with very high or perfect accuracy levels across all three groups; (4) the most frequently used forms were the same across the three groups as displayed in Figures 2, 3, and 4.

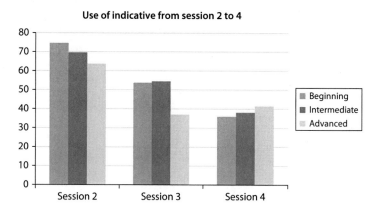

Figure 1. Use of indicative from session 2 to 4 (production tasks)

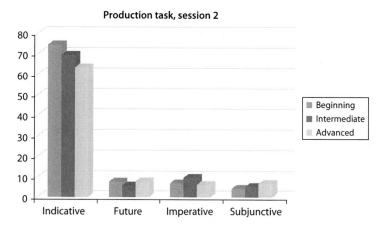

Figure 2. Morphological forms used in session 2 (production task)

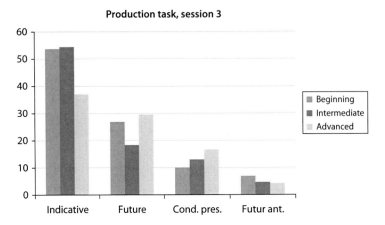

Figure 3. Morphological forms used in session 3 (production task)

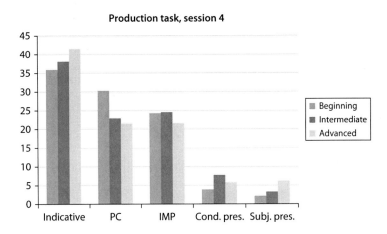

Figure 4. Morphological forms used in session 4 (production task)

CHAPTER 5.2

Findings

Cloze tests

Tous les moyens de l'esprit sont enfermés dans le langage; et qui n'a point réfléchi sur le langage, n'a point réfléchi du tout.

Alain

1. Cloze test: Session 2, task 2

The cloze test of session 2 targeted future temporality. The 20 tokens were distributed as follows: 2 *futur antérieur,* 7 indicative present, 11 future. Two sets of means are displayed in Table 15: CT/CF means 'correct tense/correct form', indicating that the appropriate verbal tense (i.e. morphological form) was used along with its appropriate form (i.e. inflectional ending) (e.g. *tu parleras* 'you will speak'), while CT/IF means 'correct tense/incorrect form', indicating that the appropriate verbal tense was used but with a nontarget inflectional ending (e.g. *tu parlera* instead of *tu parleras*).

The means show that the L2 learners' performance varied with the morphological form tested; it improved from the *futur antérieur* to the future and the present.[4]

The results of the two-way ANOVA in Table 16 indicate that there is indeed a significant tense effect (F (2,78) = 97.095, p < .001), a significant interaction between group and tense (F (4,78) = 3.183, p = .018), as well as a significant effect for group (F (2,39) = 927.295, p < .001). The means for 'correct tense/incorrect form' are relatively low (1.67% to 5.5%) except for the Advanced group on *futur antérieur* (7.69%). There was no significant difference between means for tense (F (2, 78) =.226, p = .798) and no interaction between group and tense (F (4, 78) = .950, p =.440) for CT/IF.

---

4. The data for the *futur antérieur* should be viewed cautiously as only two tokens could be encoded with this form.

Table 15. Means for correct tense/correct form and correct tense/incorrect form by group and tense (session 2, task 2)

	Group	Means CT/CF	SD	Means CT/IF	SD	overall	SD
future	Beginning	66.67%	21.68	4.17%	7.83	70.83%	22.34
	Intermediate	67.22%	17.94	5.00%	6.13	72.22%	19.33
	Advanced	85.25%	12.79	3.84%	4.32	89.10%	10.42
futur antérieur	Beginning	32.14%	20.63	3.57%	9.07	35.71%	23.44
	Intermediate	21.67%	18.58	1.67%	6.45	23.33%	19.97
	Advanced	59.61%	33.13	7.69%	12.01	67.31%	32.88
present	Beginning	82.85%	17.22	4.28%	8.51	87.14%	14.86
	Intermediate	88.00%	16.56	2.67%	7.03	90.67%	11.09
	Advanced	93.85%	12.60	3.08%	7.51	96.92%	15.39

Table 16. ANOVA for correct tense/correct form (session 2, task 2)

Within-subjects	Sum of squares	Df	Mean square	F	p
Tense	56022.333	2	28011.166	97.095	<.001
Tense by group	3672.981	4	918.248	3.183	.018
Error	22502.416	78	288.493		
Between-subjects	Sum of squares	Df	Mean square	F	p
Group	10655.782	2	5327.891	8.934	.001
Error	23259.297	39	596.392		

Table 17. ANOVA for correct tense/incorrect form (session 2, task 2)

Within-subjects	Sum of squares	Df	Mean square	F	p
Tense	28.857	2	13.429	.226	.798
Tense by group	225.676	4	56.419	.950	.440
Error	4634.333	78	59.419		
Between-subjects	Sum of squares	Df	Mean square	F	p
Group	64.944	2	34.472	.484	.620
Error	2615.060	39	67.053		

The means displayed in Table 18 reveal that even when they did not encode the predicates with the appropriate tense, the participants used correct inflectional endings, but with a significant effect for tense, group and an interaction between tense and group, as shown in Table 19.

Table 18. Incorrect tense/correct form by group and tense (session 2, task 2)

IT/CF	Group	Mean	SD
future	Beginning group	28.57%	22.57
	Intermediate group	27.22%	18.49
	Advanced group	10.89%	10.42
futur antérieur	Beginning group	64.28%	23.44
	Intermediate group	71.67%	18.58
	Advanced group	32.69%	32.88
present	Beginning group	12.85%	18.57
	Intermediate group	8.0%	12.69
	Advanced group	3.08%	11.09

Table 19. ANOVA on incorrect tense/correct form (session 2, task 2)

Within-subjects	Sum of squares	Df	Mean square	F	p
Tense	51412.464	2	30888.504	94.795	<.001
Tense by group	4243.880	4	1274.857	3.912	.010
Error	21151.887	78	325.846		
Between-subjects	Sum of squares	Df	Mean square	F	p
Group	10651.305	2	5325.653	8.40	.001
Error	24725.150	39	633.978		

Finally, the means for IT/IF are negligible. However, a group effect was found ($F(2, 39) = 3.874$, $p = .029$) (the means overall were 1.98% for the Beginning group, 2.29% for the Intermediate group and 0% for the Advanced group).

Tukey post hoc tests reveal that Beginning and Intermediate groups performed significantly differently from the Advanced group for CT/CF as well as CT/CF combined with CT/IF for the future and the present, but not for the *futur antérieur*.[5]

As also illustrated by Figure 1, the participants thus performed very differently on the three morphological forms tested in this first cloze test, and their performance improved with their level of proficiency. The Beginning group performed slightly better than the Intermediate group on *futur antérieur*, however the means are so low that this cannot have a significant implication.

---

5.   Future: Beginning and Advanced ($p = .004$), Intermediate and Advanced ($p = .003$); present: Beginning and Advanced ($p = .005$), Intermediate and Advanced ($p = .006$).

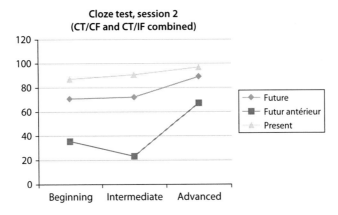

Figure 5. Cloze test, session 2 (means on CT/CF and CT/IF combined)

The predicates were also coded by lexical class – states, activities, telics – as described in Chapter 1. Table 20 displays the means for each group.

Table 20. Accuracy means by lexical class (cloze test, session 2)

	Beginning	SD	Intermediate	SD	Advanced	SD
States	74.28%	4.36	76.19%	4.36	89.0%	4.69
Activities	58.89%	5.22	63.33%	5.22	82.05%	5.61
Telics	62.5%	5.22	62.5%	5.22	88.46%	5.61

Table 21. ANOVA on lexical class by group (session 2, task 2)

Within-subjects	Sum of squares	Df	Mean square	F	p
Lexical class	3173.517	2	1586.759	8.329	<.001
Lexical class by group	755.255	4	188.814	.991	.417
Error	21151.887	78	325.846		
Between-subjects	Sum of squares	Df	Mean square	F	p
Group	11232.618	2	684784.590	944.685	<.001
Error	28995.244	40	724.881		

The accuracy means displayed in Table 20 and the ANOVA findings displayed in Table 21 clearly show that there is a significant lexical class effect ($F (2, 4) = 8.329$, $p < .001$) as well as a group effect ($F (2, 40) = 944.685$, $p < .001$), but no interaction between the two ($F (2, 78) = .991$, $p < .417$).

The Advanced group's performance is consistently above 80% accuracy across lexical class, while the performance of the Beginning and Intermediate groups varies much more from a low of 58.89% on activities for the Beginning group to a high of 76.19% for the Intermediate group, also on activities. Both groups score 62.5% accuracy on telic predicates. As also illustrated by Figure 6, not only does the Advanced group systematically outperforms the other two groups, but its performance is also more even across lexical classes.

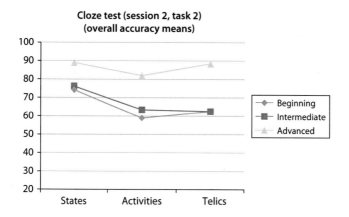

Figure 6. Accuracy means by lexical class and group (session 2, task 2)

Post hoc pairwise comparisons indicate that the Advanced group's performance is significantly different from the performance of the other groups ($p = .002$), but that there is no significant difference between the Beginning and the Intermediate groups ($p = .711$).

2. Cloze tests: Session 5, task 1

Both cloze tests administered in the last session (i.e. Session 5) targeted past temporality. Table 22 displays the means for the first one (task 1), combining the means for correct tense/correct form and correct tense/incorrect form under the 'overall' column. There were an equal number of tokens to be encoded with the *passé composé* and the *imparfait*, 7 each, and 5 tokens with the *plus-que-parfait*.

The means show a clear improvement from the lowest to the highest proficiency level for all three tense forms, confirmed by the statistical significance for tense ($F (2, 78) = 153.140 \ p = < .001$) and group ($F (2, 39) = 10.371, p = < .001$) displayed in Table 23. The learners' best performance is on the *passé composé*

Table 22. Means for correct tense/correct form and correct tense/incorrect form (session 5, task 1)

	Group	CT/CF		CT/IF		Overall
		Mean	SD	Mean	SD	Mean
passé composé	Beginning group	63.09%	16.294	16.67%	16.01	79.76%
	Intermediate group	81.11%	21.700	5.56%	8.13	86.67%
	Advanced group	93.59%	10.840	1.28%	4.62	94.87%
imparfait	Beginning group	47.95%	19.090	6.12%	9.23	54.07%
	Intermediate group	63.81%	25.249	3.81%	6.53	67.62%
	Advanced group	70.33%	25.058	4.39%	9.00	74.72%
plus-que-parfait	Beginning group	1.42%	5.345	0%	.00	1.42%
	Intermediate group	17.33%	27.115	1.33%	5.16	18.66%
	Advanced group	23.07%	21.363	1.54%	5.54	24.61%

Table 23. Two-way ANOVA for Correct Tense/Correct Form (session 5, task 1)

Within-subjects	Sum of squares	Df	Mean square	F	P
Tense	94835.683	2	47417.842	153.140	< .001
Tense by group	350.450	4	87.612	.283	.888
Error	24151.739	78	309.638		
Between-subjects	Sum of squares	Df	Mean square	F	P
Group	13095.912	2	6547.956	10.371	< .001
Error	24623.436	39	631.370		

(63.09%, 81.11%, 93.59%, respectively), followed by the *imparfait* (47.95%, 63.81%, 70.33%, respectively) and a poor performance on the *plus-que-parfait* (1.42%, 17.33%, 23.07%, respectively), clearly showing that this form is not yet part of the interlanguage of these instructed learners. The means for CT/IF make a notable difference only for the Beginning group's performance on the *passé composé* (16.01% bringing the overall mean to 79.76%), but the results of the two-way ANOVA displayed in Table 24 show a significant difference for both tense ($F(2, 78) = 7.669$, $p = .001$) and group ($F(2, 39) = 4.144$, $p = .023$), as well as an interaction between the two ($F(4, 78) = 4.535$, $p = .002$). The same effects are found for the two-way ANOVA run with the CT/CF and CT/IF means combined, as shown in Table 25.

Table 24. Two-way ANOVA for CT/IF (session 5, task 1)

Within-subjects	Sum of squares	Df	Mean square	F	P
Tense	993.940	2	496.970	7.669	.001
Tense by group	1175.609	4	293.902	4.535	.002
Error	5054.675	78	64.804		
Between-subjects	Sum of squares	Df	Mean square	F	P
Group	612.713	2	306.357	4.144	.023
Error	2883.382	39	73.933		

Table 25. Two-way ANOVA for Correct Tense/Correct Form and Correct Tense /Incorrect Form combined (session 5, task 1)

Within-subjects	Sum of squares	Df	Mean square	F	p
Tense	114931.835	2	57465.917	161.468	.001
Tense by group	433.736	4	108.434	.305	<.001
Error	27759.861	78	355.896		
Between-subjects	Sum of squares	Df	Mean square	F	p
Group	8083.796	2	4041.898	7.279	.002
Error	21655.859	39	555.278		

In other words, the learners do not appear to have much difficulties with the accuracy of morphological endings, whether they encode the predicate with the appropriate forms or not, since the means for IT/CF displayed in Table 25 indicate that when they provided the *passé composé* instead of the *imparfait*, for instance, they did use a correct inflectional ending (e.g. *ils sont partis* 'they left' or *nous marchions* 'we were walking').

Table 26. Means for incorrect tense/correct form (session 5, task 1)

	Group	CT/IF Mean	SD
passé composé	Beginning group	20.23%	17.515
	Intermediate group	13.33%	22.886
	Advanced group	5.13%	18.601
imparfait	Beginning group	44.9%	18.463
	Intermediate group	30.47%	25.819
	Advanced group	24.17%	20.524
plus-que-parfait	Beginning group	97.14%	7.262
	Intermediate group	81.33%	27.740
	Advanced group	75.38%	23.315

Again, a statistical significance is found for tense (F (2, 78) = 159.707, p = <.001), group (F (2, 39) = 7.015, p = <.001), and the interaction between the two (F (4, 78) = .247, p = <.001), as shown in Table 27.[6]

Table 27. Two-way ANOVA for Incorrect Tense/Correct Form (session 5, task 1)

Within-subjects	Sum of squares	Df	Mean square	F	p
Tense	114422.697	2	57211.349	159.707	< .001
Tense by group	354.121	4	88.530	.247	< .001
Error	27941.646	78	358.226		
Between-subjects	Sum of squares	Df	Mean square	F	p
Group	7736.663	2	3868.331	7.015	< .001
Error	21506.459	39	551.448		

The means by lexical class and group are shown in Table 28, while the results of the ANOVA are displayed in Table 29.

Table 28. Accuracy means by lexical class (session 5, task 1)

	Beginning	SD	Intermediate	SD	Advanced	SD
States	51.67%	7.61	63.33%	7.61	76.92%	8.17
Activities	43.33%	6.38	56.67%	6.38	61.54%	6.85
Telics	50.0%	3.53	60.0%	3.53	65.38%	3.79

Table 29. ANOVA on lexical class by group (session 5, task 1)

Within-subjects	Sum of squares	Df	Mean square	F	p
Lexical class	2201.220	2	1100.610	2.492	.089
Lexical class by group	480.620	4	120.155	.272	.895
Error	35333.333	80	441.667		
Between-subjects	Sum of squares	Df	Mean square	F	p
Group	8230.769	2	4115.385	5.250	.009
Error	28995.244	40	724.881		

---

6.   The means for IT/IF go from 0% for *passé composé* (all three groups) to 1.42% for *plus-que-parfait* (Beginning group) and no significant effect was found.

The accuracy means displayed in Table 28 and the ANOVA findings displayed in Table 29 indicate that there is a group effect ($F (2, 40) = 5.250, p = .009$), but no interaction between lexical class and groups. The Beginning group's performance is dismal with below chance means on all three lexical classes; the Intermediate group performed slightly better on states (63.3%) and telics (60.0%), but not on activities (56.67%), while the Advanced group's best performance is also on states (76.92%), and low on activities (61.54%) and telics (65.38%).

Figure 7 clearly illustrates both the lexical class and group effects.

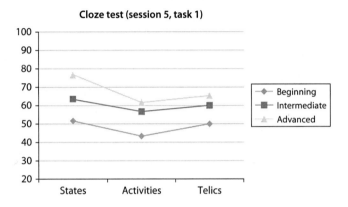

Figure 7. Accuracy means by lexical class and group (session 5, task 1)

Post hoc pairwise comparisons reveal a significant difference between the Beginning group and the Intermediate group ($p = .055$), as well as between the Beginning group and the Advanced group ($p = .003$), but not between the Intermediate and Advanced groups ($p = .202$).

3. Cloze tests: Session 5, task 2

The second cloze test targeting past temporality included 10 tokens to be encoded with the *passé composé*, 14 tokens with the *imparfait*, and 4 tokens with the *plus-que-parfait*.

The means for full accuracy (CT/CF) and for partial accuracy (CT/IF) are displayed in Table 30.

As in the first cloze test, the participants' performance on this second cloze test increases with their proficiency level and decreases from the *passé composé* to *imparfait* and *plus-que-parfait*. Regarding the *passé composé* – and only that form since they did well on the other two forms – the learners had more difficulties with the appropriate inflectional endings: the means for CT/IF are quite high for the Beginning group (57.86% CT/CF mean, 21.43% CF/IF mean) and the

Table 30. Means for correct tense/correct form (session 5, task 2)

	Group	CT/CF Mean	SD	CT/IF Mean	SD	Overall Mean	SD
passé composé	Beginning	57.86%	25.773	21.43%	13.50	79.29%	15.91
	Intermediate	68.67%	37.007	12.67%	23.74	81.33%	33.56
	Advanced	87.69%	10.127	3.08%	6.30	90.77%	6.40
imparfait	Beginning	55.61%	21.733	3.06%	3.66	58.67%	22.79
	Intermediate	65.24%	22.076	4.28%	7.54	69.52%	23.29
	Advanced	83.52%	13.796	1.65%	3.13	85.16%	13.50
plus-que-parfait	Beginning	5.36%	10.645	0%	.0	5.36%	10.64
	Intermediate	36.67%	38.806	3.33%	12.90	40.0%	39.86
	Advanced	50.00%	32.27	0%	.0	50.0%	32.27

Intermediate group (68.67% CT/CF mean, 12.67% CF/IF mean), but not for the Advanced group whose accuracy is quite high (87.69% CT/CF mean, 3.08% CF/IF mean). The Beginning group's performance is below chance for the *imparfait* (55.61%) and extremely poor for the *plus-que-parfait* (5.36%); the Intermediate group's performance is just above chance for the *imparfait* as well (65.24%) and equally poor for the *plus-que-parfait* (36.67%). The Advanced group performs well in encoding predicates with the *passé composé* (87.69%) and the *imparfait* (83.52%), but not the *plus-que-parfait* (50.0%); however, they do perform better than the other two groups, so it appears that the *plus-que-parfait* is a difficult and late-emerging morphological form among instructed learners.

The results of the two-way ANOVA displayed in Table 31 show that there is a significant difference for group, and the interaction of tense by group is close to significance (p =.054). Tense, group and the interaction between the two are significant for the CT/IF means, as shown in Table 32.

Table 31. Two-way ANOVA for Correct Tense/Correct Form (session 5, task 2)

Within-subjects	Sum of squares	Df	Mean square	F	p
Tense	42862.894	2	21431.447	41.725	.517
Tense by group	2302.056	4	575.514	1.120	.054
Error	40063.291	78	513.632		
Between-subjects	Sum of squares	Df	Mean square	F	p
Group	23571.724	2	11785.862	401.290	< .001
Error	39281.018	39	1007.206	11.702	< .001

When the participants did not supply the appropriate morphological form, they still provided an alternative form with correct inflectional endings, as indicated by the IT/CF means displayed in Table 33. In addition, a significant difference was found for tense, group, as well as an interaction between the two (see Table 34).[7]

Table 32. Two-way ANOVA for Correct Tense/Incorrect Form (session 5, task 2)

Within-subjects	Sum of squares	Df	Mean square	F	p
Tense	3055.647	2	1527.823	14.112	<.001
Tense by group	1457.374	4	364.343	3.365	.014
Error	8444.635	78	108.265		
Between-subjects	Sum of squares	Df	Mean square	F	p
Group	968.430	2	484.215	3.302	.047
Error	5718.968	39	146.640		

Table 33. Means for Incorrect Tense/Correct Form (session 5, task 2)

IT/CF	Group	mean	SD
passé composé	Beginning group	20.71%	15.91
	Intermediate group	18.67%	33.56
	Advanced group	9.23%	6.40
imparfait	Beginning group	40.82%	22.83
	Intermediate group	30.00%	23.41
	Advanced group	14.83%	13.50
plus-que-parfait	Beginning group	94.64%	10.64
	Intermediate group	60.0%	39.86
	Advanced group	50.0%	32.27

Table 34. Two-way ANOVA for Incorrect Tense/Correct Form (session 5, task 2)

Within-subjects	Sum of squares	Df	Mean square	F	p
Tense	61818.928	2	30909.464	58.683	.000
Tense by group	5332.506	4	1333.126	2.531	.047
Error	41083.813	78	526.716		
Between-subjects	Sum of squares	Df	Mean square	F	p
Group	15352.255	2	7878.127	9.552	< .001
Error	31339.748	39	803.583		

---

7.   The means for IT/IF are 0% for all groups on *passé composé* and *plus-que-parfait* and from 0% to 5.1% for the Beginning group on the *imparfait*.

The accuracy means by lexical class and group are displayed in Table 35, while the results of the ANOVA are shown in Table 36.

Table 35. Accuracy means by lexical class (session 5, task 2)

	Beginning	SD	Intermediate	SD	Advanced	SD
States	65.18%	5.02	73.33%	5.02	83.76%	5.39
Activities	42.67%	6.99	61.33%	6.99	73.84%	7.51
Telics	63.33%	4.40	70.0%	4.40	84.07%	4.73

Table 36. ANOVA on lexical class by group (session 5, task 2)

Within-subjects	Sum of squares	Df	Mean square	F	p
Lexical class	5647.958	2	2823.979	11.398	< .001
Lexical class by group	890.347	4	222.587	.898	.469
Error	19820.239	80	247.753		
Between-subjects	Sum of squares	Df	Mean square	F	p
Group	11535.874	2	5767.937	6.349	.241
Error	36340.645	40	908.516		

As also illustrated by Figure 8, the learners' performance improves with proficiency, the Advanced group scoring accuracy means from 73.84% on activities and above 80% on other two lexical classes (83.76% and 84.07% on states and telics respectively). All groups have more difficulties with activities where the Beginning group's performance is only 42.67%, their performance is about the same on states and telics. There is a significant effect for lexical class (F (2, 4) = 11.398, p < .001), but not for group (F (2, 40) = 6.349, p = .241), and no interaction between the two was found (F (2, 80) = .898, p = .469).

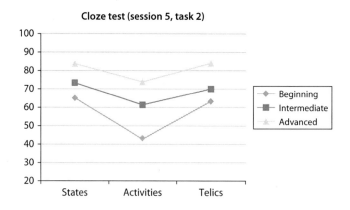

Figure 8. Accuracy means by lexical class and group (session 5, task 2)

4. Summary of the cloze tests

To sum up, let us now compare the findings for these two cloze tests targeting past temporality as illustrated by the graph in Figure 9.

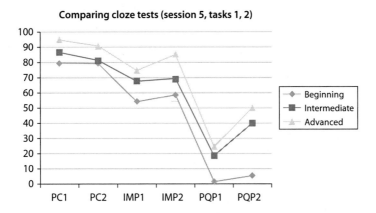

Figure 9. Comparing past temporality in cloze tests (Session 5)

The number 1 refers to the first cloze test (task 1) and the number 2 refers to the second cloze test (task 2) for each of the morphological forms (*passé composé, imparfait, plus-que*-parfait). There are clear differences between groups and morphological forms: the three groups are relatively comparable for the *passé composé* on both tasks; there is a distinct group effect for the *imparfait* – the higher the level of proficiency, the greater the performance and improvement from the first to the second cloze test; finally, none of the groups performed well on the *plus-que-parfait*, but both the Intermediate and Advanced groups performed better on the second than on the first cloze test; the Beginning group did not.

Finally, the data were also analyzed by lexical class – statives, activities and telics.

We saw that the learners' performance improved with their proficiency level, they all performed better with future temporality than with past temporality, and there was a lexical class effect (generally statives, telics and activities in decreasing order of accuracy).

The next three figures (Figure 10 to 12) illustrate the learners' performance across the three cloze tests by lexical class.

These figures indicate that there is a task effect as well since the learners' performance varied with the cloze test even when they had the same linguistic target, that is, past temporality for the last two cloze tests. It is not unusual to find task effects when more one type of elicitation task is administered (see e.g. Comajoan 2005). The worst performance for all groups was on the second cloze test (Session 5, task 2) and on activity predicates overall, confirming previous find-ings (Ayoun 2005b). These instructed learners thus display a tense-aspect system with semantic contrasts, but with varying degrees of mastery across the different lexical classes. It is encouraging to note that the participants' performance clearly improves with their proficiency level suggesting that they may eventually achieve a more even mastery across lexical classes and elicitation tasks.

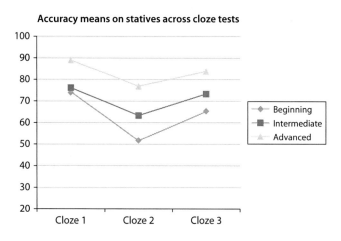

Figure 10.   Accuracy means on statives across cloze tests by groups

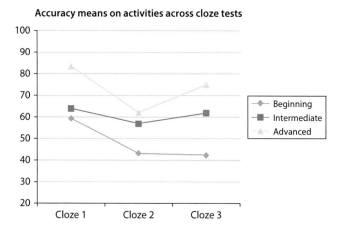

Figure 11.   Accuracy means on activities across cloze tests by groups

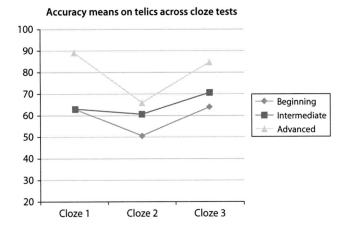

Figure 12. Accuracy means on telics across cloze tests by groups

CHAPTER 5.3

Findings

Sentence completion tasks

Tous les moyens de l'esprit sont enfermés dans le langage; et qui n'a point réfléchi sur le langage, n'a point réfléchi du tout.

Alain

1. Sentence completion: Session 3, task 2

Two controlled or guided production tasks in the form of sentence completion tasks were administered as the second task of session 3 targeting the subjunctive, and of session 4 targeting modals. The first sentence completion task targeted the present and past subjunctive. Participants were asked to complete 54 individual, complete sentences by providing the appropriate form of the verbs given in parentheses. All of the stimuli required the use of the present subjunctive (42 stimuli) or past subjunctive (12 stimuli) as opposed to the indicative. No distractors were included because the variety of semantic and syntactic triggers were deemed to be sufficient to act as distractors. A few stimuli are shown in (1):

(1) a. *Nous souhaitons tous que le mariage de Paul et Marie _____ (avoir lieu) en juin.*
'We would all like for Paul and Marie to get married in June'.

   b. *Marie est déçue qu'il _____ (pleuvoir) aujourd'hui.*
'Marie is disappointed that it's raining today'.

   c. *Mes parents ont interdit que nous _____ (sortir) seuls le soir.*
'My parents forbade us to go out alone at night'.

Again, CT/CF (correct tense/correct form) indicates complete accuracy (i.e. appropriate morphological form, here present or past subjunctive, with the appropriate inflectional ending), while CT/IF (correct tense/incorrect form) indicates partial accuracy (i.e. appropriate morphological form, but inappropriate inflectional ending).

Table 37 presents both sets of means by groups. First, although all the means are very low, we note an improvement in performance from the lowest to the highest proficiency levels, particularly for the present subjunctive (19.89%, 50.32% and

Table 37. Means for Correct Tense/Correct Form and Correct Tense/Incorrect Form (session 3, task 2)

	Group	CT/CF		CT/IF		Overall	
		Mean	SD	Mean	SD	Mean	SD
pres. subjunctive	Beginning	19.89%	19.46	0.34%	.864	20.24%	19.87
	Intermediate	50.32%	23.82	1.75%	2.28	52.06%	23.60
	Advanced	61.91%	18.28	2.20%	3.56	64.10%	16.70
past subjunctive	Beginning	4.17%	9.09	0.59%	2.22	4.76%	9.64
	Intermediate	25.0%	21.12	2.78%	4.06	27.78%	22.19
	Advanced	34.62%	30.20	6.41%	9.71	41.02%	32.17

61.91% for the Beginning, Intermediate and Advanced groups, respectively) that is statistically significant as shown in Table 38 (so is group, but not the interaction between tense and group), as also illustrated in Figure 13.

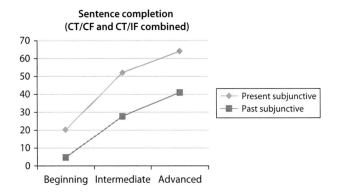

Figure 13. CT/CF and CT/IF combined on sentence completion task

Second, the performance of all groups is dismal on the past subjunctive (4.17%, 25% and 34.62% for the Beginning, Intermediate and Advanced groups, respectively). The CT/IF means make a small difference only for the Advanced group, bringing their mean from 34.62% to 41.02%, which indicates that the problem does not lie with inflectional morphology, but with the acquisition of the subjunctive/indicative contrast.[8]

---

8.   No significant differences were found for the CT/IF means.

Table 38. Two-way ANOVA for correct tense/correct form (session 3, task 2)

Within-subjects	Sum of squares	Df	Mean square	F	p
Tense	10859.773	1	10859.773	70.067	< .001
Tense by group	528.207	2	264.103	1.704	.195
Error	6044.652	39	154.991		
Between-subjects	Sum of squares	Df	Mean square	F	p
Group	18985.312	2	9492.656	12.713	< .001
Error	29120.049	39	746.668		

Table 39. Means for incorrect tense/correct form and incorrect tense/incorrect form (session 3, task 2)

		IT/CF		IT/IF		Overall
	Group	Mean	SD	Mean	SD	Means
present subjunctive	Beginning	75.85%	20.92	2.38%	1.86	78.23%
	Intermediate	39.36%	24.77	3.49%	5.15	42.85%
	Advanced	31.68%	19.08	0.55%	1.04	32.23%
past subjunctive	Beginning	82.74%	15.14	5.95%	7.61	88.69%
	Intermediate	47.78%	32.03	2.22%	4.94	50.0%
	Advanced	41.03%	26.01	3.21%	5.42	44.24%

The next table, Table 40, displays the means for IC/CF and IT/IF. Again, the IT/IF means are very low, even insignificant for the Advanced group (0.55%). Not surprisingly, given the participants' poor performance on CT/CF, the means for IT/CF are quite high particularly for the Beginning group (75.85% and 82.74% for the present and the past subjunctive, respectively), clearly indicating that the subjunctive mood is not yet part of their interlanguage. They chose the indicative instead.

Table 40. Two-way ANOVA for incorrect tense/incorrect form (session 3, task 2)

Within-subjects	Sum of squares	Df	Mean square	F	p
Tense	57.145	1	57.145	3.955	.054
Tense by group	96.184	2	48.092	3.328	.046
Error	563.521	39	14.449		
Between-subjects	Sum of squares	Df	Mean square	F	p
Group	71.488	2	35.744	1.059	.357
Error	1316.675	39	33.761		

Table 41. Two-way ANOVA for Incorrect Tense/Correct Form (session 3, task 2)

Within-subjects	Sum of squares	Df	Mean square	F	p
Tense	1411.937	1	1411.937	12.695	.001
Tense by group	20.849	2	10.424	.094	.911
Error	4337.431	39	111.216		
Between-subjects	Sum of squares	Df	Mean square	F	p
Group	29223.869	2	14611.935	14.323	<.001
Error	39785.771	39	1020.148		

As shown in Table 41, there is a significant effect for tense and group, but no interaction between tense and group; however, there is one for the IT/IF means which also shows a significant effect for tense as displayed in Table 40.

The data were also analyzed to see whether the learners did produce a subjunctive form, but not the appropriate one, and as shown in Table 42, it appears that they did for the past subjunctive (6.58%, 22.22% and 14.74% for the Beginning, Intermediate and Advanced group, respectively), but not for the present subjunctive. In other words, they produced indicative forms in present subjunctive contexts and present subjunctive forms in past subjunctive contexts.

Table 42. Means for incorrect subjunctive form (session 3, task 2)

IT/CF	Group	Mean	SD
pres subjunctive	Beginning group	1.53%	2.57
	Intermediate group	4.60%	6.51
	Advanced group	3.66%	4.82
past subjunctive	Beginning group	6.58%	5.82
	Intermediate group	22.22%	15.95
	Advanced group	14.74%	12.79

Table 43. Two-way ANOVA for incorrect subjunctive form (session 3, task 2)

Within-subjects	Sum of squares	Df	Mean square	F	p
Tense	2643.523	1	2643.523	30.301	<.001
Tense by group	575.935	2	287.967	3.301	.047
Error	3402.442	39	87.242		
Between-subjects	Sum of squares	Df	Mean square	F	p
Group	1274.304	2	637.152	7.040	.002
Error	3529.848	39	90.509		

Thus, although the means are low, it is still an encouraging finding for the L2 acquisition of the subjunctive mood. A significant effect was found for tense, group, as well as the interaction between tense and group (cf. Table 43).

As seen in Chapter 2, the subjunctive mood must be triggered by a semantic or syntactic element in the main clause. The stimuli exemplified 8 different triggering elements (with 6 to 8 stimuli per trigger) to investigate whether there is a trigger effect in the L2 acquisition of the subjunctive. The means for CT/CF are displayed in Table 44:

Table 44. Means by triggers on Correct Tense/Correct Form (session 3, task 2)

CT/CF	Beginning		Intermediate		Advanced	
Trigger	Means	SD	Means	SD	Means	SD
judgment	16.96%	6.24	38.33%	6.03	50.0%	6.47
emotion	21.42%	6.58	47.62%	6.36	51.65%	6.83
wish/regret	14.28%	6.41	50.0%	6.20	58.97%	6.65
order/interdiction	30.36%	7.59	56.67%	7.33	84.61%	7.88
conjunctions	19.64%	6.86	54.17%	6.62	73.08%	7.11
doubt/imposs.	18.57%	6.36	49.33%	6.15	62.31%	6.60
superlatives	1.19%	5.92	17.78%	5.72	23.08%	6.14
indf. antecedents	8.57%	8.84	42.67%	8.54	43.08%	9.18

Table 45. Two-way ANOVA by trigger and group on Correct Tense/Correct Form (session 3, task 2)

Within-subjects	Sum of squares	Df	Mean square	F	p
Trigger	48254.024	7	6893.432	21.312	<.001
Trigger by group	8178.549	14	584.182	1.806	.038
Error	88302.459	273	323.452		
Between-subjects	Sum of squares	Df	Mean square	F	p
Group	90527.255	2	45263.628	14.677	<.001
Error	120272.984	39	3083.923		

A quick examination of the CT/CF means show that the learners' performance improves with the proficiency level and that it varies greatly with the type of trigger, as confirmed by the results of the two-way ANOVA presented in Table 45 which indicate that there is a significant effect for trigger and group as well as a significant interaction between trigger and group. The Beginning group's performance is below chance for all the triggers; although the Intermediate group's performance improves greatly (e.g. from 14.28% to 50% for wish/regret triggers), it remains at or just above chance level (i.e. highest mean is 56.67%); the Advanced group's performance varies as well greatly depending on the trigger – from as low as 23.08% for superlatives to 84.61% for order/interdiction – but it is a significant improvement over the other two groups.

Did the learners have difficulties with inflectional endings? Not according to the CT/IF means displayed in Table 46 which are extremely low for all triggers and groups with a few exceptions for the Advanced group on wish/regret (6.41%) and doubt/ impossibility (5.38%).

Table 46. Means by triggers on correct tense/incorrect form (session 3, task 2)

CT/IF	Beginning		Intermediate		Advanced	
Trigger	Means	SD	Means	SD	Means	SD
judgment	0%	1.22	3.33%	1.18	2.88%	1.27
emotion	0%	1.58	2.86%	1.53	3.29%	1.64
wish/regret	1.19%	2.43	6.67%	2.34	6.41%	2.52
order/interdiction	0%	1.02	0%	.993	1.92%	1.06
conjunctions	0%	.729	.83%	.704	.96%	.756
doubt/imposs.	1.43%	1.34	.67%	1.29	5.38%	1.39
superlatives	0%	.685	0%	.662	1.28%	.711
indf. antecedents	0%	1.16	1.33%	1.12	1.53%	1.21

There is still a significant effect for trigger and group, and the trigger and group interaction is significant as well as shown in Table 47.

Table 47. Two-way ANOVA by trigger and group on correct tense/incorrect form (session 3, task 2)

Within-subjects	Sum of squares	Df	Mean square	F	p
Trigger	615.977	7	87.997	3.661	.001
Trigger by group	314.443	14	22.460	.934	.522
Error	6562.273	273	24.938		
Between-subjects	Sum of squares	Df	Mean square	F	p
Group	384.141	2	192.070	4.398	.019
Error	1703.103	39	43.669		

If the L2 learners did not produce subjunctive, they obviously produced indicative forms as indicated by the IT/CF means displayed in Table 48.

Table 48. Means by triggers on incorrect tense/correct form (session 3, task 2)

IT/CF	Beginning		Intermediate		Advanced	
Trigger	Means	SD	Means	SD	Means	SD
judgment	74.11%	7.38	36.67%	7.13	33.65%	7.66
emotion	70.41%	7.87	32.38%	7.60	28.57%	8.17
wish/regret	76.19%	6.16	30.00%	5.92	28.21%	6.39
order/interdiction	66.07%	7.20	31.67%	6.96	13.46%	7.47
conjunctions	77.68%	7.05	36.67%	6.81	21.15%	7.32
doubt/imposs.	73.57%	7.19	38.00%	6.95	25.38%	7.46
superlatives	94.05%	7.28	74.44%	7.03	74.36%	7.55
indf. antecedents	90.00%	9.25	56.00%	8.94	52.31%	9.60

Again, they show very high levels of accuracy for the inflectional endings. The usual effects for trigger, group and interaction of group with trigger are shown in Table 49.

Table 49. Two-way ANOVA by trigger and group on Incorrect Tense/Correct Form (session 3, task 2)

Within-subjects	Sum of squares	Df	Mean square	F	p
Trigger	61900.375	7	8842.911	24.816	<.001
Trigger by group	7560.316	14	540.023	1.515	.105
Error	97281.252	273	356.342		
Between-subjects	Sum of squares	Df	Mean square	F	p
Group	117676.936	2	58838.468	15.648	<.001
Error	146647.891	39	3760.202		

Conversely, the IT/IF means are negligible (cf. Table 50) and the only significant effect is for tense (cf. Table 51).

The CT/IF means – a subjunctive form was used, but not the appropriate one – displayed in Table 52 are also rather low with a few exceptions: judgment for all three groups, emotion for the Intermediate and Advanced groups, as well as wish/regret and order/interdiction, but only for the Intermediate group.

Table 50. Means by triggers on Incorrect Tense/Incorrect Form (session 3, task 2)

IT/IF	Beginning		Intermediate		Advanced	
Trigger	Means	SD	Means	SD	Means	SD
judgment	0%	1.88	3.33%	1.14	0%	1.23
emotion	4.08%	1.67	3.81%	1.61	2.19%	1.73
wish/regret	7.14%	1.99	3.33%	1.92	0%	2.07
order/interdiction	1.78%	1.46	1.67%	1.41	0%	1.51
conjunctions	2.68%	1.97	5.00%	1.90	1.92%	2.05
doubt/imposs.	3.57%	1.99	5.33%	1.92	3.07%	2.07
superlatives	4.62%	1.20	0%	1.16	0%	1.25
indf. antecedents	1.43%	.825	0%	.797	0%	.856

Table 51. Two-way ANOVA by trigger and group on Incorrect Tense/Incorrect Form (session 3, task 2)

Within-subjects	Sum of squares	Df	Mean square	F	p
Tense	535.747	7	78.535	2.604	.013
Tense by group	529.790	14	37.842	1.287	.214
Error	8024.594	273	29.394		
Between-subjects	Sum of squares	Df	Mean square	F	p
Group	321.468	2	160.734	2.035	.144
Error	3081.122	39	79.003		

Table 52. Means for incorrect subjunctive form (session 3, task 2)

CT/IF	Beginning		Intermediate		Advanced	
Trigger	Means	SD	Means	SD	Means	SD
judgment	8.93%	2.99	17.50%	2.89	13.46%	3.11
emotion	4.08%	2.98	13.33%	2.88	14.28%	3.09
wish/regret	1.19%	1.96	10.00%	1.90	6.41%	2.04
order/interdiction	1.78%	2.73	10.00%	2.64	0%	2.83
conjunctions	0%	1.38	2.50%	1.33	2.88%	1.43
doubt/imposs.	2.86%	1.89	6.00%	1.82	3.85%	1.96
superlatives	0%	2.09	7.78%	2.02	1.28%	2.17
indf. Antecedents	0%	1.11	0%	1.07	3.08%	1.15

As expected given these means, a significant effect was found for trigger and group as well as for the interaction between the two (cf. Table 5.53).

Table 53. Two-way ANOVA for incorrect subjunctive form (session 3, task 2)

Within-subjects	Sum of squares	Df	Mean square	F	p
Trigger	5464.72	7	780.675	13.959	<.001
Trigger by group	1419.384	14	101.385	1.813	.037
Error	15267.792	273	55.926		
Between-subjects	Sum of squares	Df	Mean square	F	p
Group	2111.153	2	1055.576	6.084	.005
Error	6766.526	39	173.501		

Table 54 combines the means for overall tense accuracy, that is for verbs encoded with a subjunctive form, showing that L2 learners were aware of the indicative/subjunctive alternation.

Table 54. Means for overall accuracy in tense (session 3, task 2)

Overall accuracy	Beginning		Intermediate		Advanced	
Trigger	Means	SD	Means	SD	Means	SD
judgment	16.96%	6.11	41.67%	5.91	52.88%	6.35
emotion	21.43%	6.43	50.48%	6.22	54.94%	6.68
wish/regret	15.47%	6.43	56.67%	6.21	65.38%	6.68
order/interdiction	30.36%	7.29	56.67%	7.05	86.54%	7.57
conjunctions	19.64%	6.93	55.00%	6.69	74.04%	7.19
doubt/imposs.	20.00%	6.55	50.00%	6.32	67.69%	6.79
superlatives	1.190%	6.01	17.78%	5.81	24.35%	6.24
indf. antecedents	8.57%	8.98	44.00%	8.67	44.61%	9.32

The means are still extremely low for the Beginning and Intermediate groups, while they are slightly better for the Advanced group (67.69% for doubt/impossibility, 74.04% for conjunctions, 86.54% for order/interdiction). There is a significant effect for tense, trigger and the interaction between the two (cf. Table 55).

To sum up the findings of this sentence completion task, it appears that L2 learners do not acquire the alternation between the indicative and the subjunctive until they are at an advanced level of proficiency and even then, their performance varies tremendously with the type of semantic and/or syntactic triggers, and they clearly do not master the indication-subjunctive alternation yet. These findings are

Table 55. Two-way ANOVA for overall accuracy in tense (session 3, task 2)

Within-subjects	Sum of squares	Df	Mean square	F	p
Trigger	50211.723	7	7173.103	21.806	<.001
Trigger by group	9053.916	14	646.708	1.966	.020
Error	89804.409	273	328.954		
Between-subjects	Sum of squares	Df	Mean square	F	p
Group	102638.429	2	51319.214	16.896	<.001
Error	118456.541	39	3037.347		

in line with those reported in Bartning (2005) and Howard (2008, 2012), reviewed in the preceding chapter.

Although participants in all three groups produced accurate subjunctive forms in the production task of sessions 2, 3, and 4, they accounted for a very small percentage of the overall accurate forms used. The means are reproduced below in Table 56.

Table 56. Subjunctive forms in production tasks by group

	Production task session 2	Production task session 3	Production task session 4
Beginning	4.23%	0%	2.16%
Intermediate	5.19%	4.14%	3.27%
Advanced	6.64%	1.85%	6.22%

And again, proficiency level makes a small difference.

2. Sentence completion task: Session 4, task 2

The second sentence completion task administered in session 4 targeted three modal verbs, *devoir, pouvoir* and *savoir*. *Il faut que* and *vouloir* were excluded because previous research showed that they were acquired early. The participants were presented with 60 stimuli composed of a context sentence followed by a sentence with a modal verb which they were instructed to conjugate at the appropriate form as in (2):

(2)   *Je ne pourrais pas vous accompagner parce que*
      -> je _____ (devoir) absolument terminer ce projet avant midi.
      'I won't be able to go with you because
      I really must finish this project before noon'

The reader may recall that French modal verbs behave like lexical verbs in that they can be encoded with all indicative, subjunctive and conditional forms.

The CT/CF means are displayed in Table 57 and show a performance improvement with proficiency level for each of the three modal verbs, from at or below chance level for the Beginning group to above chance level for the Intermediate group and a slight improvement for the Advanced group (60.71%, 70.71% and 76.92% for *devoir, pouvoir* and *savoir*, respectively). The two-way ANOVA results shown in Table 58 indicate that there is a significant effect for modal and for group, but no interaction between modal and group.

Table 57. Means for Correct Tense/Correct Form (session 4, task 2)

CT/CF	Devoir		Pouvoir		Savoir	
	Mean	SD	Mean	SD	Mean	SD
Beginning	43.88%	7.853	55.22%	13.460	54.76%	17.817
Intermediate	53.57%	12.734	64.36%	15.553	70.00%	15.685
Advanced	60.71%	12.542	70.71%	14.178	76.92%	14.495

Table 58. Two-way ANOVA for Correct Tense/Correct Form (session 4, task 2)

Within-subjects	Sum of squares	Df	Mean square	F	p
Modal	4737.679	2	2368.840	15.499	<.001
Modal by group	223.136	4	55.784	.365	.833
Error	11921.278	78	152.837		
Between-subjects	Sum of squares	Df	Mean square	F	p
Group	6868.374	2	3434.187	11.868	<.001
Error	11285.640	39			

The CT/IF means are negligible (cf. Table 59), but there is a significant effect for modal (cf. Table 60).

Table 59. Means for Correct Tense/Incorrect Form (session 4, task 2)

CT/IF	Devoir		Pouvoir		Savoir	
	Mean	SD	Mean	SD	Mean	SD
Beginning	1.27%	2.26	3.02%	4.32	1.19%	4.45
Intermediate	1.43%	2.95	3.07%	3.09	1.11%	4.30
Advanced	1.37%	3.10	3.25%	4.39	0%	.0

Table 60. Two-way ANOVA for Correct Tense/Incorrect Form (session 4, task 2)

Within-subjects	Sum of squares	Df	Mean square	F	p
Modal	125.127	2	62.564	5.522	.006
Modal by group	9.865	4	2.466	.218	.928
Error	883.693	78	11.329		
Between-subjects	Sum of squares	Df	Mean square	F	p
Group	2.608	2	1.304	23.930	.922
Error	625.359	39	16.035	.081	

A significant effect was found for modal and group, as well for the IT/CF means, as displayed in Tables 61 and 62, respectively.

Table 61. Means for Incorrect Tense/Correct Form (session 4, task 2)

IT/CF	Devoir		Pouvoir		Savoir	
	Mean	SD	Mean	SD	Mean	SD
Beginning	53.32%	6.78	41.75%	12.69	42.86%	19.29
Intermediate	44.29%	11.03	32.56%	13.23	28.89%	17.21
Advanced	37.91%	10.56	26.04%	14.05	23.08%	14.49

Table 62. Two-way ANOVA for Incorrect Tense/Correct Form (session 4, task 2)

Within-subjects	Sum of squares	Df	Mean square	F	p
Modal	4530.22	2	2265.211	15.474	<.001
Modal by group	131.572	4	32.893	.225	.924
Error	11418.055	78	146.385		
Between-subjects	Sum of squares	Df	Mean square	F	p
Group	6012.664	2	3006.332	11.004	<.001
Error	10655.115	39	273.208		

As confirmed by the means for IT/IF which are 0% for all modals and groups, except for the Beginning group (1.53% for *devoir*, and 1.19% for *savoir*), whatever morphological form is chosen, it carries the appropriate inflectional ending. Thus, combining the means for CT/CF with CT/IF to get an overall picture of appropriate morphological encoding for these three modals, we obtain the data in Table 63.

Table 63. Means for overall correct (session 4, task 2)

CT/CF and CT/IF	Devoir		Pouvoir		Savoir	
	Mean	SD	Mean	SD	Mean	SD
Beginning	45.15%	7.36	58.24%	12.69	55.95%	19.17
Intermediate	55.00%	11.59	67.43%	13.23	71.11%	17.21
Advanced	62.08%	10.56	73.96%	14.05	76.92%	14.49

Table 64. Two-way ANOVA for overall correct (session 4, task 2)

Within-subjects	Sum of squares	Df	Mean square	F	p
Modal	4899.454	2	2449.727	16.183	<.001
Modal by group	176.259	4	44.065	.291	.883
Error	11807.323	78	151.376		
Between-subjects	Sum of squares	Df	Mean square	F	p
Group	6687.763	2	3343.882	12.431	<.001
Error	10490.579	39	268.989		

Again, there is a steady improvement with proficiency level, showing that instructed L2 learners can probably eventual acquire modal expressions, but that it takes time. They are not yet a productive part of these learners' interlanguage. There is still a significant effect for modal and group, but no interaction.

Some of the stimuli allowed for more than one appropriate morphological form, so the data were also coded for up to three possible morphological forms, the first one being the most target-like or likely, and the second (and even third where possible) morphological form being also possible given the context. Two-way ANOVAs were run to determine how the participants performed for each possible morphological form (present, *imparfait*, future, present conditional, past conditional, *passé composé*, n/a).

Table 65 exhibits the means for overall correct (CT/CF and CT/IF) by group.

Table 65. Means for overall correct (CT/CF and CT/IF) for first possible tense

CT/CF-CT/IF	Beginning		Intermediate		Advanced	
	Means	SD	Means	SD	Means	SD
present	75.39%	10.12	85.18%	11.54	84.05%	8.99
imparfait	36.43%	17.36	44.67%	17.26	51.53%	19.93
future	57.14%	33.14	36.67%	29.68	50.0%	28.86
present conditional	45.92%	16.02	55.24%	17.79	69.23%	22.47
past conditional	18.25%	18.28	33.33%	25.19	61.53%	22.95
passé composé	22.86%	18.98	42.67%	24.91	40.0%	18.25

Table 66. Two-way ANOVA for overall correct on first possible tense

Within-subjects	Sum of squares	Df	Mean square	F	p
Tense	60602.953	5	12120.591	31.445	<.001
Tense by group	14032.333	10	1403.233	3.640	<.001
Error	75164.370	195	385.458		
Between-subjects	Sum of squares	Df	Mean square	F	p
Group	11383.768	2	5691.884	7.586	.002
Error	29261.927	39	750.306		

Not surprisingly, when the indicative present was an option, it was used by a majority of the participants in all groups, followed by the future and the present conditional. The two-way ANOVA results presented in Table 66 show that a significant effect was found for tense, group, and the interaction between the two.

The second most common second possible tense was future, followed by the present conditional and passé composé, as shown in Table 67. A significant effect was found for tense and for group but there was no interaction between the two (cf. Table 68).

Table 67. Means for overall correct (CT/CF and CT/IF) for second possible tense

CT/CF-CT/IF	Beginning		Intermediate		Advanced	
	Means	SD	Means	SD	Means	SD
present	67.14%	23.01	76.0%	22.92	78.46%	17.24
imparfait	25.0%	32.52	43.33%	31.99	30.77%	25.31
future	92.85%	26.72	100%	.0	92.03%	27.73
present conditional	68.68%	10.65	82.56%	7.94	87.57%	13.52
past conditional	33.93%	25.20	50.0%	18.89	55.77%	32.52
passé composé	78.57%	42.58	93.33%	25.81	92.31%	27.73
n/a	44.96%	7.51	52.55%	14.65	62.44%	12.82

Table 68. Two-way ANOVA for overall correct on second possible tense

Within-subjects	Sum of squares	Df	Mean square	F	p
Tense	133756.745	6	22292.791	43.837	<.001
Tense by group	3971.983	12	330.099	.651	.797
Error	118997.290	234	508.535		
Between-subjects	Sum of squares	Df	Mean square	F	p
Group	10211.938	2	5105.969	6.328	.004
Error	31466.253	39	806.827		

Finally, the *imparfait* was the morphological form used the most often as the third possible way to encode the modal verbs, as presented in Table 69. There is again a significant effect for tense, but not for group, and there was no interaction between tense and group (cf. Table 70).

Table 69. Means for overall correct (CT/CF and CT/IF) for third possible tense

CT/CF-CT/IF	Beginning		Intermediate		Advanced	
	Means	SD	Means	SD	Means	SD
present	35.71%	49.72	53.33%	51.63	23.07%	43.85
imparfait	78.57%	42.58	93.33%	25.81	92.31%	27.73
future	51.72%	6.89	61.61%	9.80	69.09%	10.61

Table 70. Two-way ANOVA for overall correct on third possible tense

Within-subjects	Sum of squares	Df	Mean square	F	p
Tense	53889.869	2	26944.934	23.956	<.001
Tense by group	6117.201	4	1529.300	1.360	.256
Error	87730.967	78	1124.756		
Between-subjects	Sum of squares	Df	Mean square	F	p
Group	4346.399	2	2173.199	1.686	.199
Error	50274.730	39	1289.096		

3.   Summary

The findings for the modal verbs are summarized with Figure 14 that shows two clear trends: a proficiency level effect and a modal verb effect.

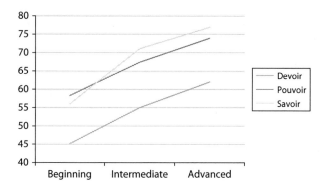

Figure 14. Means for Correct Tense/Correct Form by modals and groups

The higher the proficiency level, the better the performance from below chance for the Beginning group on *savoir* to above chance and more encouraging means for the Advanced group on *pouvoir* (73.96%) and *savoir* (76.92%). The findings for alternative morphological forms show that: (a) in the minimal context that a single stimulus provides, modal verbs can be encoded with several morphological forms adding to their subtlety and complexity; (b) learners are not necessarily selecting the first option, but their second and/or third options are target-like, just not the first option that a native speaker would select.

4. Discussion and conclusion

The main purpose of the present study was to gain a better and more complete perspective on the tense, aspect, mood/modality system that L2 learners build as they progress along the continuum from the L2 initial state to the L2 end state, that is, ideally, ultimate attainment. To this end, the participants, who were placed in one of three proficiency levels (beginning, intermediate or advanced) based on a GJT, were administered three different elicitation tasks (production, cloze test, sentence completion) over the course of five sessions. Four research questions were investigated following previous findings.

4.1 Research questions

4.1.1 *Does the L2 learners' interlanguage grammar display contrasts and systematicity? Do they acquire aspectual, modal and mood contrasts (e.g. indicative vs subjunctive)?*

Yes and no. Yes, the learners' interlanguage grammar displays contrasts between perfective and imperfective expressed by the *passé composé* and the *imparfait*, but no, because: (a) they do not perform systematically and consistently; they perform much better on free production tasks – tasks that allow them to use the forms with which they feel comfortable, and avoid the forms about which they are unsure – than on tasks such as a cloze test which require only one appropriate and obligatory response; (b) they perform better with aspectual contrast than with mood contrasts or modal verbs.

Let us review again the data on past temporality that was elicited with a production task and two cloze tests:

The accuracy means displayed in Table 71 shows that learners at all proficiency levels were very accurate in producing predicates encoded with the *passé composé* and *imparfait*; the Advanced group and the Intermediate remained at about the same accuracy levels on the cloze tests for the *passé composé*, while the

Table 71. Past temporality by tasks and groups

	Production task		Cloze test 1			Cloze test 2		
	PC	IMP	PC	IMP	PQP	PC	IMP	PQP
Beginning	88.6%	88.9%	79.8%	54%	1.42%	79.3%	58.7%	5.36%
Intermediate	88.9%	98.4%	86.7%	67.6%	18.7%	81.3%	69.5%	40%
Advanced	94.5%	96.3%	94.8%	74.7%	24.6%	90.8%	85.2%	50%

Beginning group's performance was worse particularly on the first cloze test. However, the performance of all groups declined noticeably for the *imparfait* on both cloze tests, and they clearly have not acquired the *plus-que-parfait* at this point.

The subjunctive was also elicited with two tasks, a production task and a sentence completion task.

Table 72. Subjunctive means by tasks and groups

	Production task			Sentence completion	
	Subj.Pres.		Subj.Past	Subj.Pres.	Subj.Past
	Produced	Accurate	Produced	Elicited	
Beginning	4.23%	83.3%	0	20.2%	4.76%
Intermediate	5.19%	85.7%	0	52.1%	27.8%
Advanced	6.64%	94.4%	0	64.1%	41.0%

The subjunctive made up a very small percentage of the L2 learners' overall production, although when they did use it, they did so with good to high accuracy levels. However, the sentence completion task findings indicate that overall, they are not yet sufficiently sensitive to the indicative-subjunctive alternation to perform well. The Beginning group's performance is extremely poor, the Intermediate group's performance is at chance level, and while better, the Advanced group's performance is still very low at 64.1% accuracy.

Moreover, there was a clear context effect as was displayed above and is reproduced here as Table 73. The data have been rearranged in a decreasing order of accuracy based on the means for the Advanced learners.[9]

---

9. The order is the same for the Intermediate with the exception of the indefinite antecedents and judgment. The Beginning group performed better on the emotion trigger than on three other triggers.

Table 73. Means by triggers on correct tense/correct form (session 3, task 2)

CT/CF	Beginning		Intermediate		Advanced	
Trigger	Means	SD	Means	SD	Means	SD
order/interdiction	30.36%	7.59	56.67%	7.33	84.61%	7.88
conjunctions	19.64%	6.86	54.17%	6.62	73.08%	7.11
doubt/imposs	18.57%	6.36	49.33%	6.15	62.31%	6.60
wish/regret	14.28%	6.41	50.0%	6.20	58.97%	6.65
emotion	21.42%	6.58	47.62%	6.36	51.65%	6.83
judgment	16.96%	6.24	38.33%	6.03	50.0%	6.47
indf. antecedents	8.57%	8.84	42.67%	8.54	43.08%	9.18
superlatives	1.19%	5.92	17.78%	5.72	23.08%	6.14

In the production task (session 2, task 1), the participants' use of the subjunctive was triggered by the following expression as displayed in Table 74.

Table 74. Subjunctive triggers in production task (session 2, task 1)

Beginning	Intermediate	Advanced
avant que	*bien que*	*avant que*
quoique	*je ne veux pas*	*à moins…que..*
je ne veux pas que	*je propose que*	*il vaut mieux*
il faut que	*il faut que*	*il faut que*
il est important que		*je (ne) veux (pas) que*
		je ne crois pas que
		pour que tu..

The triggers displayed in Table 74 mostly express an order/interdiction (*je (ne) veux (pas) que, il faut que*) or are conjonctions (*avant que, bien que, pour que, quoique, à moins que*), thus matching the accuracy means of the triggers in Table 73.

To sum up, findings are positive on the perfective/imperfective aspectual distinction, yet mixed because of the task effect, while they are mostly negative on the indicative-subjunctive mood alternation.

4.1.2 Does the L2 learners' performance improve with their proficiency level eventually leading to near-native performance levels?

Yes, there is a clear improvement in performance with proficiency level from the Beginning to the Intermediate, and finally the Advanced group. However, the most proficient group, the Advanced group, does not consistently perform at near-native levels as measured by accurate means.[10]

Figure 15 shows the L2 learners' performance on each of the forms and tasks.

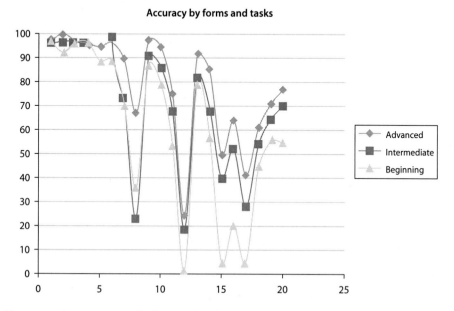

Figure 15. Accuracy means by forms and tasks

A cursory look at Figure 15 illustrates a definite trend: the lines representing the accuracy means for each group pattern remarkably well. They also indicate a proficiency level effect with the Advanced group consistently outperforming the other two groups, but the Intermediate group does not always outperform the Beginning group. Finally, all groups reach near perfect accuracy means, but also display extremely low ones.

The next three figures, Figures 16, 17, 18, show the same means for each group individually.

---

10. NS means are generally expected to be at 90% or above.

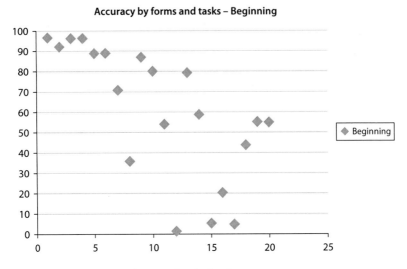

Figure 16. Accuracy means by forms and tasks for the Beginning group

Figure 3 reveals that out of 20 accuracy means, 6 are below chance level (i.e. 50%) and 9 are at or above 80% (i.e. a good score).

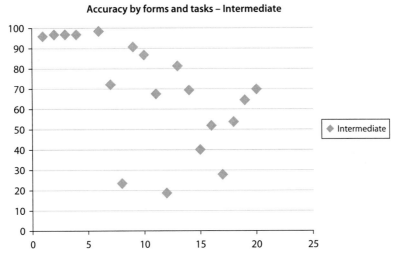

Figure 17. Accuracy means by forms and tasks for the Intermediate group

Figure 17 shows that 6 out of 20 accuracy means are at or below chance level, while 8 means are at or above 80%.

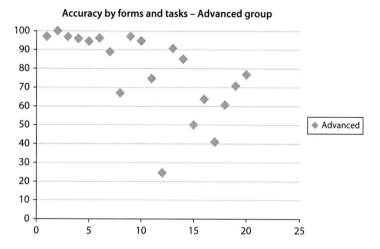

Figure 18. Accuracy means by forms and tasks for the Advanced group

Figure 18 shows that 3 out of 20 means are at or below chance level, while 11 means are above 80%, up to 98%.

All three groups are at or below 50% on the *plus-que-parfait* (cloze tests 2 and 3) and the past subjunctive (sentence completion task 1); the Beginning and Intermediate groups are at or below 50% on *futur antérieur* (cloze test 1), present subjunctive (sentence completion task 1) and *devoir*; in addition, the Beginning group is at or below 50% on the *imparfait* (cloze test 2), *pouvoir* and *savoir* (sentence completion task 2).

To sum up, although it is clear that even the Advanced group's performance is mixed, exhibiting task and morphological form effects, the L2 learners' performance does improve with proficiency.

4.1.3 *Do the L2 learners acquire targetlike use of inflectional morphology?*
Yes, they displayed very high accuracy means for all the forms they used in all three tasks whether they encoded the predicates with the appropriate morphological form or not, they did so with accuracy. In addition to the fully accurate means (CT/CF), this was indicated by the IT/CF (incorrect tense/correct form) means: even when they chose a nontarget morphological form, they produced it with targetlike inflection morphology.

We now turn to the three predictions that the study was designed to test.

4.1.4 *Will there be an elicitation task effect and will it vary with proficiency?*
The first part of the prediction was supported as the L2 learners' performance depended on elicitation task that was used. The participants performed better on

the production tasks than on the cloze test (although with a form effect) or the sentence completion tasks. For instance, regarding future temporality, Table 75 combines the participants' overall accuracy means on the cloze test and the production task for comparison purposes.

Table 75. Future temporality on cloze test and production task

	Cloze test			Production task			
	Future	Fut. Ant.	Present	Future	Fut. Ant.	Present	Cond. Pres
Beginning	70.83%	35.71%	87.14%	96.43%	100%	92.31%	86.95%
Intermediate	72.22%	23.33%	90.67%	96.87%	100%	96.84%	75.86%
Advanced	89.10%	67.31%	96.92%	97.96%	100%	100%	93.1%

The second part of the prediction was supported as well: the lower proficiency levels were more sensitive to the type of elicitation task, performing better on the production task than on the cloze test for instance as found previously (e.g. Ayoun 2000, 2005b; Geeslin 2006) and very early on (Tarone 1983). The participants' competence level may not have been sufficiently high to performance consistently on different elicitation tasks requiring different metalinguistic skills.

In a study designed to compare L2 Spanish learners' performance in selecting the appropriate mood (indicative vs subjunctive) across three elicitation tasks, Kornuc (2004) hypothesized that accuracy would decrease as the task difficulty increased. She used a written sentence-completion task, a written dialogue-completion task, and an oral interview. The hypothesis was confirmed with the subjunctive stimuli, but not the indicative, suggesting that the relationship between mood selection and task difficulty is unclear.

It is not unusual to find a task effect in TAM studies (e.g. Ayoun 2005b; Ayoun & Rothman 2013) as expected from the still developing interlanguage grammars of L2 learners at lower proficiency levels. Various task-related factors, from procedural factors (e.g. setting, instructions, order in which the tasks are administered) to stimulus factors (e.g. context, meaning, parsability) may impact the participants' judgments in various elicitation tasks with well-established caveats (e.g. Cowart 1997; Gass 1994; Hedgcock 1993; Schütze 1996; Sorace 1996).

All tasks require parsing, processing, decision-making and are more or less demanding. Thus, sentence completion tasks and cloze tests are certainly more difficult than free production tasks in the form of the personal narratives. They require that participants first read, process and understand the entire text without the benefit of tense-marked predicates as indications of the storyline. Then, they are forced to adopt the narrator's viewpoint. Last but not least, if they misinterpret the semantics or viewpoint of a few predicates early on in the storyline, they are likely to continue making erroneous assumptions throughout the task as the storyline should be coherent.

One would presume that increasing proficiency levels should eventually lead to a more consistent performance across various elicitation tasks, but the literature clearly shows that empirical findings are rarely consistent across measures and a remnant of "fuzziness" or "indeterminacy" (Sorace 1996; Sorace & Filiaci 2006) seems to characterize all grammars, non-native and native alike.

4.2   From a minimalist perspective

The reader may recall that the task of Anglophone, instructed learners of L2 French was to acquire: (a) The strong features of functional categories (e.g. Infl); (b) the relevant functional categories themselves: AgrP (Agreement Phrase) for agreement; TP (Tense Phrase) for tense, and MoodP (Mood Phrase) for modality that corresponds to traditional modality values (e.g. epistemic, irrealis, deontic); (c) a complex morpho-syntax (i.e. inflectional paradigms for the morphological forms); (d) for past temporality, the perfective-imperfective aspectual distinction; the appropriate mapping of the formal feature [+perfective] with *passé composé* morphology, and the feature [–perfective] with *imparfait* morphology; the three aspectual values conveyed by the *imparfait* (imperfective, durative, iterative); (e) *concordance des temps* or tense sequences (e.g. if clauses, when clauses with future temporality); (f) prospective aspect for future temporality; (g) the indicative-subjunctive alternation with a variety of syntactic and semantic triggers; (h) the complex and subtle semantic distinctions expressed by modal verbs.

Following others (e.g. Ayoun & Rothman 2013; Duffield et al. 2003; Montrul & Slabakova 2002), I assumed that L2 grammars are constrained by Universal Grammar, and that functional categories and features are in principle acquirable, *contra* the claims made by impairment hypotheses. The findings of this study support the claim that adult L2 learners can acquire functional categories which are not present in their L1, and that they can set feature values to the appropriate target language strength (i.e. strong in French). For instance, their productive and accurate use of perfective and non-perfective morphology indicates that they have acquired the appropriate feature strength of AspP.

Although the mapping of the functional categories onto the appropriate morphology in French is complicated by the large number of endings for each verb (e.g. Terrell 1986), to which are added phonological difficulties, because the *imparfait* endings for instance sound very similar to other forms (Harley 1986), participants produced a wide variety of morphological forms with great accuracy. Practically all lexical verbs, auxiliaries and past participles were properly inflected for tense, number and gender, with a few rare gender agreement errors. Moreover, bare forms were non-existent. If L2 grammars were permanently impaired, learners would not perform with such accuracy rates in obligatory contexts. However, findings are still mixed because the learners' performance varies with the elicitation task and some morphological forms.

The participants performed poorly on forms that exhibit low frequency in the input (i.e. *futur antérieur*, subjunctive), as will be discussed in Chapter 6. They also performed poorly on morphological forms situated at interfaces (e.g. syntax-semantics for the subjunctive), supporting the main claim that the Interface hypothesis makes (e.g. Sorace 2011): interface-conditioned properties are more complex than properties limited to a single domain, increasing the difficulty of acquisition and the possibility of residual optionality even at near-native proficiency.

CHAPTER 6

Pedagogical implications for foreign language learners and teachers

Tout refus du langage est une mort.
Roland Barthes

6.1 Introduction

The teaching of foreign languages started with Latin and Greek in the 17th century, initially leading to the grammar translation method; then, the 19th and 20th centuries saw new teaching approaches such as the direct method, the audiolingual method, the Total Physical Response (Asher 1977), the natural approach (Terrell 1986) or communicative language teaching, and yet, in spite of such a long tradition of teaching languages, it is generally believed that instructed language learners rarely reach native-like proficiency, even in French Canadian immersion settings where children benefit from a longer exposure both in language and content courses.

Although foreign language teaching can be classified as a branch of applied linguistics, there has been tension and misunderstanding between foreign language teachers and applied linguists, at times even with those who carry out classroom-based research, for their findings, however interesting they may be, rarely include concrete, practical pedagogical applications. If some researchers argue that one key aspect of second language acquisition (SLA) research is to inform foreign language pedagogy (e.g. Larsen-Freeman 1998; Pica 2005), others wonder whether SLA findings have benefitted second language teaching at all, if for no other reason than these two fields have different goals and concerns (e.g. Block 2000).

If caution about interpreting and suggesting applications of SLA findings to foreign classrooms was warranted over 40 years ago (e.g. Hatch 1978; Tarone, Swain & Fathman 1976) when some experimental studies may have been limited in various ways (e.g. scope, methodology), this is no longer the case as studies' methodologies have become increasingly rigorous as well as more fine-grained and focused on foreign language pedagogy. For instance, classroom-based research and immersion studies are directly motivated by foreign language pedagogy, and hence have immediate, practical applications for foreign language classrooms.[1] I would thus disagree with statements claiming that "much of the research is no longer directly concerned with pedagogic issues" (Ellis 2000: 45).

Moreover, doctoral programs at American universities such as the SLAT (second language acquisition and teaching) interdisciplinary program at the University of Arizona that boasts over 70 students shows that an increasing number of them are majoring or minoring in pedagogy (R. Ariew, personal communication, September 2012).[2] Another large program in Second Language Studies at Indiana University states in its online introduction that both their M.A. and Ph.D. programs are "designed to train the next generation of foreign and second language professionals as both researchers and teachers".[3] And about 50% of the doctoral students enrolled in the Second Language Acquisition program at the University of Wisconsin-Madison are interested in the foreign language education in the U.S., while others focus on ESL or multilingualism, "in particular, how global population flows observed in various regions of the world inpact on the diaspora population's language acquisition, maintenance, loss or sense of self" (J. Mori, personal communication, September 2012).

These young scholars and educators will in all likelihood contribute to bridging the ideological and practical gaps between SLA research and foreign language teachers who themselves appear eager to participate in doing so, if the findings of a survey reported in Nassaji (2012) are any indication.

Nassaji (2012) used a written questionnaire to collect qualitative and quantitative data among Canadian ESL teachers (n = 82) and Turkish EFL teachers (n = 119).[4] Although very few had published research articles (4%) or read articles often (48%) mostly for lack of time (80%), most "had taken courses in SLA (74%) or SLA research methods (63%)" and almost all indicated that they found such courses "useful or very useful (91% and 80%, respectively)" (*ibid*: 346). The most

---

1.   There is a plethora of classroom-based and/or purely experimental studies investigating very practical issues such as corrective feedback, input and interaction, students' learning styles based on their personality and motivation. See Nassaji and Fotos (2010), Norris and Ortega (2006), among others, for assessments of the relevance of SLA research and theory to foreign language classroom.

2.   In the 2012 academic year, 68% of the doctoral students were pedagogy majors and 18% were pedagogy minors. The full name of the specialization is L2 pedagogy and program administration; the other three areas of specialization are L2 use, L2 analysis and L2 processes and learning.

3.   http://www.indiana.edu/~dsls/

4.   ESL stands for English as a second language, while EFL stands for English as a foreign language.

interesting finding may be that "[t]he majority of the teachers (79%) […] agreed or strongly agreed that knowing about SLA research improves second language teaching. On the other hand, about two thirds (60%) disagreed with the statement that SLA research is not relevant to language teaching" (*ibid*: 349). And when asked about their expectations of SLA research, teachers provided a wide range of responses with by far the most common being "effective instructional strategies" *ibid*: 353). As Nassaji concludes, teachers should not be viewed "simply as readers of research findings, but as active contributors, question generators and initiators of insight" (*ibid:* 356).

The following statement was accurate in 2000 and continues to be even more relevant now, as it will be in the future:

> The influence of SLA research is now evident in textbooks and teacher training programs and in proposals for curriculum design (see e.g. Long & Crookes 1992). Some aspects of SLA research and theory have become so completely integrated into mainstream FL/SL pedagogy that they are referred to without reference to their sources. Notions such as *the silent period, focus on form,* or *developmental stages* are often taken for granted by teachers trained since the 1980s.
> (Lightbown 2000: 438)

As others have expressed (e.g. Lightbown 2000; Pica 2005), reciprocal collaborations between SLA researchers and teachers hold the promise of positive outcomes for all concerned – researchers, teachers and learners.[5]

6.2 Current pedagogical issues

A commonly heard complaint by instructors and students alike is that accounts of tense, aspect, mood/modality (TAM) systems in textbooks are at best inadequate, and at worst misleading, be it for *FLE*[6] learners in Europe (e.g. Barbazan 2010; Confais 1995; Judge 2002) or in North America for L2 instructed learners (e.g. Blyth 2005 for Romance languages; DeCarrico 1986 for English; Ayoun 2001; Lepetit 2001 for French; Rothman 2008 for Spanish).

---

5. As examples of successful collaboration between instructors and researchers, Lightbown (2000: 453) cites Kowal and Swain (1994, 1997), Doughty and Varela (1998), White and Goulet (1995).

6. *FLE* stands for Français langue étrangère, 'French as a foreign language'.

One significant issue is the use of terminology for various concepts: the distinction between tense, time and temporality is usually not established,[7] while the notions of aspect or mood/modality are rarely, if ever, mentioned, and instructed learners are thus not made aware of the difference between perfective and imperfective, or between perfective and progressive, for instance. Moreover, once the concept of temporality is established, the notion of atemporality could be introduced, so that learners do not automatically assume that a given tense represents a given temporality, since that is clearly not the case.

Another relatively simple and basic concept is the difference between transitive and intransitive verbs. Thus, most textbooks introduce the *passé composé* by stating that some verbs use *être* while others use *avoir* without a principled explanation. Instructed learners are misled down a garden path full of inaccuracies instead of being made aware of the fact that verbs used transitively require *avoir*, while verbs used intransitively and reflexively require *être* in compound tenses. It is just an example of a simple but accurate principle that would be tremendously helpful to classroom learners (see also Section 8 below).

Anecdotal evidence and some empirical evidence (e.g. Salaberry 1997) also indicate that classroom learners tend to associate past temporality with *passé composé* as a default past tense – possibly because it is introduced first and early on – leaving out the *imparfait* and the *plus-que-parfait* as the two most obvious relevant possibilities.[8]

Second, certain 'rules' are overgeneralized to the point of being misleading, such as stating that verbs indicating a 'frame of mind' (i.e. statives) (e.g. *penser* 'think', *savoir* 'know', *vouloir* 'want', *espérer* 'hope') are usually encoded with the *imparfait* (Rideout 2002). This is a linguistically accurate description, but it is incomplete, and thus potentially misleading because it only includes the prototypical use of statives as shown in (1) and (2):

(1) a. *Marc voulait étudier seul, alors je suis partie.*
          Marc want-IMP study alone, so I leave-PC
          'Mark wanted to study by himself so I left'

      b. *Marc n'a pas voulu m'aider.*
          Marc want-PC not me help
          'Mark refused to help me'

---

7. This is especially important for L2 French learners because French has only one word *'temps'* for both 'time' and 'tense'.

8. The *passé simple* may be introduced as a literary tense. It is less relevant here as its use is indeed limited to written, literary contexts.

(2)   a.   *Je savais   qu'il allait   pleuvoir.*
             I   know-IMP   that   it go-IMP   rain
             'I knew it was going to rain'

      b.   *Je l'ai su   tout de suite.*
             I   it know-PC   right   away
             'I knew right away'

Instructed learners need to be taught the difference between prototypical and non-prototypical uses as it is a crucial semantic distinction that cannot be ignored if they are to ever achieve advanced levels of proficiency. Of course, simplifications are necessary for ease of exposition (particularly for beginning learners), however they should not be confused with oversimplifications which should be avoided.

Third, different morphological forms, referred to as tenses in textbooks, are often presented in isolation, one after the other, rather than showing how they relate to each other. As seen in Chapter 1, languages exhibit systems of time relationships that should be presented as such. A good starting point could be the Reichenbach timeline (Speech, Event, Time) to allow learners to understand the relationship between *passé composé* and *plus-que-parfait*, or between future and *futur antérieur* for instance.[9] This would also help them understand the tense sequences in complex clauses as shown in the examples in (3):

(3)   a.   *Quand tu   auras fini,   nous dînerons.*
             when   you   finish-FutAnt, we   eat-Fut
             'When you're done, we'll eat'.

      b.   *Il n'aurait pas pu savoir   qu'il pleuvrait.*
             he   could   not   know-PastCond   that   it rain-Cond
             'He could not have known that it would rain'

      c.   *Je doute   que Marc soit parti   seul.*
             I   doubt-Pres   that   Marc   leave-PastSubj   alone
             'I doubt that Mark left alone'

The ESL (English as a second language) field appears to be facing similar issues. Thus, DeCarrico (1986: 668) explains that "[…] the basic problem seems to be that in ESL grammar texts, the systematic nature of the forms and of the semantics with respect to time relationships is either not explained adequately or is simply left vague. For instance, hypothetical past is normally introduced after lessons on simple past and present perfect".

DeCarrico (1986: 678) suggests a specific five-step sequence for teaching English modals that groups them semantically, takes into account the actual

---

9.   See Chapter 1.

time frames as well as the time relationships between the various modals and morphological forms.

A major difficulty is thus to present very complex and subtle syntactic, semantic and morphological concepts in a way that is accessible to beginning foreign language learners, and yet comprehensive and accurate. This is a task that should be undertaken collaboratively by foreign language teachers, theoretical linguists and SLA researchers, as suggested in the introduction.

6.3   A selected literature review of classroom-based studies in TAM

A small selection" of classroom-based studies focusing on tense, aspect or modality/mood will be reviewed here in order to illustrate the variety of learnability hypotheses that have been proposed so far. Additional studies will be mentioned under their respective proposed hypotheses in Section 6 below. We start with French immersion studies in Canada.[10]

6.3.1   French immersion studies in Canada

As Lyster (2008) notes in his review of immersion studies in Canada, Lambert and Tucker's (1972) seminal study was the first to use the term 'immersion' to characterize an experiment in bilingual education that took place in Montreal in 1965, prompted by Anglophone parents who were concerned that the second language pedagogical approaches at the time would not allow their children to become sufficiently proficient in French in an increasingly francophone Quebec. The positive results led to the creation of more immersion programs across Canada.

However, even total immersion (i.e. 100% of the curriculum is taught in French) lasts only two to three years, whereas in partial immersion (i.e. 50% of the curriculum is taught in French) lasts from one to several years, which may be one reason why although immersion students achieve much higher proficiency levels in French than instructed learners in non-immersion settings, they still are "clearly less proficient on most grammar variables, and especially on verbs in the oral grammar test" than French native speakers of the same age (Harley, Cummins,

---

10.   Immersion studies are also of course classroom-based studies as well but they are reviewed separated from other classroom-based studies because immersion students are instructed in different conditions than the students who are typically enrolled in foreign language classes in the United States or Europe (e.g. age at beginning of instruction, purely language courses versus content-based courses in French).

Swain & Allen 1990:16).[11] Specific difficulties with the verbal domain include the distinction between the perfective and imperfective, as well as conditionals (Harley 1986, 1989, 1992; Harley et al. 1990; Lyster 1994, 2008; Swain & Lapkin 1990).

Day and Shapson (1991) used a pre-test, 6-week, post-test design to address these persistent grammatical difficulties by testing the functional, communicative approach with the conditional in polite requests and hypothetical situations. Six grade 7 early French immersion classes received curriculum materials designed to encourage the students to use the conditional in natural communicative situations and with games and exercices, while another six grade 7 classes composed the control group (for a total of 315 students). Findings indicate that the experimental group performed significantly better than the control group on the cloze test and the composition, both in the immediate and follow-up tests (administered 11 weeks later), but not on the oral interview, suggesting that a well thought-out and carefully planned curricular intervention can lead to an improvement of immersion students overall, but that continued and sustained efforts over a longer time period are nonetheless necessary.

French immersion settings in Canada have also been a fertile ground to test the efficiency of various forms of feedback in form-focused instruction classrooms as we will see below.

6.3.2 Classroom-based studies in North America

Classroom-based studies in foreign language contexts (i.e. the L2 is not used outside of the classroom as opposed to the immersion context of Canada where French is not only used but an official language) have also been used as testing grounds for different instructional approaches, types of feedback and the usefulness of new computer- and web-based technologies as opposed to traditional, text-based approaches.

Thus, Ayoun (2001) investigated the effectiveness of three types of written feedback – implicit negative feedback in the form of recasts, pre-emptive positive evidence as modelling, explicit negative feedback as traditional grammar instruction – in the acquisition of the aspectual distinction between the *passé composé* and the *imparfait* with a pre-test, repeated exposure over 4 weeks, post-test design. Quantitative data analyses indicated that participants in the recast group

---

11. For a more complete description of immersion programs in Canada, see Burger and Chrétien (2001), Genesee (2004, 2006), Lyster (2008) among others. For evaluations of immersion programs see Genesee (1987, 1992, 1998), Lambert and Tucker (1972), Swain and Lapkin (1982), Turnbull, Lapkin and Hart (2001), Lyster (2004a), among others.

performed significantly better than the traditional grammar group, but not the modelling group, partially supporting the hypothesis that implicit negative feedback is the most effective form of feedback. It was also found that all participants improved in their use of the *passé* composé, but not the *imparfait*. The follow-up study, Ayoun (2004), used qualitative data in an effort to better understand these differential outcomes; unfortunately, the qualitative analyses muddied the waters, so to speak, because it became more difficult to differentiate the three different treatments: (a) participants in the traditional group outperformed the other two groups in accuracy and frequency of use of the *passé composé*; (b) all three groups decreased in their accuracy and frequency of use of the *imparfait,* but the traditional grammar group outperformed the other two; (c) overall, the traditional grammar group displayed a greater aspectual use of predicate frequency and type in the *imparfait*. It was concluded that the prediction of the Aspect Hypothesis, according to which lexical class of predicates influences the use of past tense morphology, was partially confirmed. It was also suggested that different forms of negative evidence may be more effective with different grammatical structures.

Fernández (2008) investigated whether online delivered explicit information in the context of processing instruction (VanPatten 1996, 2002, 2004; VanPatten & Oikkenon 1996) would be more effective in the L2 acquisition of the Spanish subjunctive than no explicit information.[12] Explicit information is defined as "the information that learners receive about the L2 and how it works" (*ibid*: 277). Explicit information could be effective because it is hypothesized to encourage learners to notice forms in the input (e.g. DeKeyser 2003). The study compared a processing input group (n = 42) with a structured input group (n = 42)[13] targeting the 3rd person singular in expressions of doubt with 20 stimuli (and 10 distractors). Participants were instructed to listen to the subordinate clause, and then indicate which of the two main clauses presented on the computer screen was the trigger clause. The processing input group read the instructions before reading the explicit input presented on seven frames that moved automatically; then, they listened to the structured input stimuli one at a time as two pictures appeared on the screen for them to select one. The structured input group went through the same procedure, but saw the structured input right after reading the instructions. Both groups received positive or negative feedback following each answer. It is concluded that two out of three hypotheses were supported: the processing

---

12.   OVS order was another linguistic target of this study which is a replication of Farley (2000).

13.   The goal of structured input or modified input is to encourage learners to adopt different, more effective, processing strategies.

instruction group performed better than the structured input group in processing the input correctly and responding faster (presumably making the connection between the form and its meaning), but the two experimental groups did not perform with the same accuracy after the first four correct stimuli (i.e. referred to as "reaching criterion" in the study). However, the claim that this study tested instructional approaches is questionable because the materials were delivered online, and participants did not benefit from classroom dynamics or any type of personal interaction;[14] moreover, there were two few targeted items (20 plus 10 distractors), and one may also argue that the order of presentation of the two clauses was counter-intuitive (i.e. subordinate first, then trigger).

Izquierdo (2008) also chose to investigate the potential effect of form-focused multimedia instruction (interactive written/aural narratives, video cartoons with visual enhancement, input processing instruction and feedback) on the aspectual distinction between *passé composé* and *imparfait*, focusing more specifically on the prototypical *vs.* nonprototypical uses. The Hispanophone participants' developmental readiness was measured by an aspectual pre-test with an equal number of prototypical and nonprototypical contexts (e.g. a stative predicate encoded with the *imparfait* is a prototypical use of that predicate) and they were placed in one of three groups: E1-RD (n = 12) and E2-RD (n = 17) were rated as being developmentally ready for non-prototypical marking, but participants in the former group were only exposed to prototypical stimuli below their competence, while the latter were only exposed to non-protypical stimuli at their competence level; E2-NR (n = 13) were rated as not being developmentally ready and were exposed to non-prototypical marking. All groups were exposed to perfective and imperfective forms. Four one-hour lessons were administered over a period of four weeks followed by an immediate post-test and a delayed post-test; past tense production and comprehension were measured with three different elicitation tasks (cloze task, situational task for written comprehension, listening preference task for listening comprehension) and reaction times were recorded. Findings show that participants greatly improved on the production task (particularly the lower level proficiency learners), but not on the listening task; they performed better with perfective than imperfective and it was concluded that they needed longer and more explicit exposure in the least prototypical contexts as also concluded elsewhere (e.g. Ayoun 2001, 2004).

These three studies illustrate both the great potential and difficulties of measuring and testing the efficacy of various instructional approaches. They will be further developed below.

---

14. It is one of the shortcomings of the study acknowledged by the researcher.

6.4   Input, saliency and frequency

To be at least relatively easily acquirable, forms must not only be present in the input, but also be salient and frequent. That is not the case for at least three different morphological forms in the TAM system as corroborated by the findings of the study reported in Chapter 5 indicating that the participants had difficulties with: (a) low frequency morphological forms (*futur antérieur*, present and past subjunctive) with complex tense sequences (futur and *futur antérieur*) as well as semantic and syntactic triggers (present and past subjunctive); (b) semantically complex and subtle morphological forms (modal verbs).

It appears that input frequency impacts even bilingual language acquisition among children as research shows that the delay that can be observed in bilingual children compared to monolingual children is directly attributed to such differences in each language (e.g. Marchman, Martínez-Sussman & Dale 2004; Paradis, Nicoladis & Crago 2007). For instance, Nicoladis, Song and Marentette (2012) compared the acquisition of English past tense marking by 5–12 year old French-English bilingual and Chinese-English bilingual children. Findings indicate that these bilingual children were acquiring English past tense marking like monolinguals, showing a small transfer effect from the first language, and with a slower rate. Similarly, Paradis, Nicoladis, Crago and Genesee (2011) compared the acquisition of past tense marking by French-English bilingual children with French monolingual children.[15] It was found that the bilingual children were "less accurate than their monolingual peers with regular and irregular verbs in English, and with irregular verbs in French. Differential exposure to each language at home, as measured by parental report, had an impact on how accurate children were with the past tense in each language, and on how their accuracy compared with that of monolinguals". In other words, findings indicate that "acquisition rates for bilinguals are sensitive to input variation, both in terms of quantity of input in each language and in terms of type/token frequency properties of morphological structures" (*ibid*: 572). But the developmental delay was short-lived which lead the authors to speculate "whether additional mechanisms might be operative in bilingual acquisition that could compensate for reduced input and, in so doing, enable children to catch up for some morphosyntactic structures relatively rapidly" (*ibid*: 573).

However, since it is unlikely that adult L2 learners benefit from the same compensatory acquisition mechanisms, variations in input, frequency and

---

15. It was hypothesized that regular past tense forms in both language would be acquired before irregular past tense forms because they display higher type frequencies; authors were thus predicting that there would be differences in acquisition rates.

saliency must be addressed in foreign language classrooms. As we will see below, frequency and perceptual saliency increase the likelihood of a form to be noticed (Schmidt 1990).

6.4.1 *Futur antérieur*

According to the frequency survey reported in Engel (2001), the *futur antérieur* is extremely rare, accounting for 0% to 1.7% of all the tense forms used in newspapers and magazines.[16] And only 32 tokens were found in another corpus of five written media from 1998 (most of them were in *Le Monde*).

Nor is the *futur antérieur* introduced along with the *futur proche* and the *futur* in foreign language classrooms. That is the case in for instance, *Français-Monde*, an introductory textbook used at major North American universities for the first year of instruction, although it does indicate that "[s]ome expressions in French are followed by the future, making them different from English": *après que* 'after', *aussitôt que* 'as soon as', *dès que* 'as soon as', *quand* 'when', *une fois que* 'once' (*Français-Monde*: 353). This textbook also states that "[i]n most conversational situations the French use the present or the immediate future to describe future situations. In more formal contexts and after certain expressions, they use the future tense" (*ibid*: 252). Aside from the fact that the future is not restricted to formal contexts, the textbook is missing an opportunity to introduce the *futur antérieur* as an another tense form that can, and in some instances, must, be used after these expressions with a temporal meaning as in (4):

(4) a. *Dès que tu auras fini,   tu pourras nous rejoindre.*
      as soon as you finish-FutAnt, you can-Fut join us
      'As soon as you're done, you will be able to join us'

   b. *Aussitôt que l'avion   aura décollé,   les passagers*
      as soon as the plane take off-FutAnt, the passengers
      pourront se déplacer.
      can-Fut move
      'As soon as the plane takes off, passengers will be able to move about the cabin'

   c. *Les tableaux seront vendus une fois qu'ils auront été catalogués.*
      paintings be-Fut sold once they catalogue-FutAnt
      'Paintings will be sold as soon as they are/have been catalogued'

---

16. Engel (2001) mentions that a slight increase in the use of the *futur antérieur* is reported in Gonzalez (1995).

In each instance, the predicate encoded with the *futur antérieur* expresses an event that must take place in the future and before the event expressed in the other clause. When the *futur antérieur* is finally introduced in the second year of instruction, classroom students are not encouraged to establish a temporal link between these three future forms.

Moreover, although it is infrequent in the input and thus lacking in saliency, the status of *futur antérieur* has long been debated (see e.g. Engel 2001; Gobert & Maisier 1995): is it temporal, aspectual or modal? It is viewed as mostly temporal with secondary modal effects (Wilmet 1976), mostly modal (Yvon 1953), both temporal and aspectual (e.g. Grevisse 1993; Vet 1993). As a modal, the *futur antérieur* can express a probability for an event situated in the past as in (5a), or a possibility for an event that may happen in the future as in (5b):

(5) a. *Paul n'est pas encore arrivé? Il se sera perdu.*
         Paul not yet arrive-PC. He get lost-FutAnt
         'Isn't Paul here yet? He may have gotten lost'

     b. *Quand elle aura trouvé un témoin, elle pourra écrire*
         when she find-FutAnt a witness, she can-Fut write
         son article
         her article
         'When she finds a witness, she will be able to write her article'

Using a 40 page written corpus drawn from 1989 to 1991 issues of the magazine *L'Express*, Gobert and Maisier (1995) list no less than eighteen modal uses of the *futur antérieur*, six of which are classified as 'conjectural', and twelve as 'affectif/ expressif'. In the latter, the *futur antérieur* is actually the equivalent of the *passé composé* because it expresses the perfective, as in one of their examples reproduced here in (6a); it is also paraphrased in (6b):

(6) a. *Jamais, depuis sa nomination, M. Rocard n'aura subi pareille*
         never, since his nomination, Mr. Rocard endure-FutAnt such
         disgrâce dans l'opinion.
         disgrace in the public opinion
         'Mr Rocard never had to endure such disgrace in public opinion since
         he was nominated'   (*L'Express*, n. d., Gobert & Maisier 1995:1007).

     b. *Il n'a jamais subi pareille disgrâce.*
         he never endure-PC such disgrace
         'He never had to endure such disgrace'

This use of the *futur antérieur* as a perfective form, the equivalent of a *passé composé*, has also been described as a present perfect (Steinmeyer 1987) and a past perfective (Vet 1992). As summarized in Engel (2001:216), "both temporal and aspectual functions are primary, although specific contexts will favor the *accompli* over the anterior interpretation, and vice-versa", or a "tense-aspect with additional modal functions" (*ibid*: 217).

The same way scholars rightly argue that it is absolutely necessary to "take into account tense, aspect, typology of situations and the use of tense in texts in any model for the interpretation of French past tenses" (*ibid*: 217, citing Salkie 2000), foreign language materials and instructors cannot present them in isolation, they need to be taught in context as well as in relation to temporality, aspect and mood.

6.4.2   The indicative-subjunctive alternation

Although both the present and past subjunctive are part of standard French and hence are included in foreign language materials and classrooms, they turn out to be low frequency forms in the input according to corpus studies. Thus, Blaikner-Hohenwart (2006) studied the use of the subjunctive in two types of corpora and found only 56 subjunctive occurrences in pages 1–24 of the newspaper *Le Monde* (9/1/1996), 50 subjunctive occurrences in 105 pages in the magazine *Elle* (7/7/1995), and could not find a single subjunctive occurrence in the magazine *Prima* (9/1995).[17] Finally, only 85 subjunctive occurrences were found in the novel *Les belles images* by Simone de Beauvoir (approximately 154 pages depending on the edition); it is interesting to note that 50% of these occurrences were triggered by *il faut/il faudrait que, j'aime/j'aimerais que, je veux que, pour que*, which correspond to the findings in the present study.

A different corpus study, Blanche-Benveniste (2005), uses spoken French from the University of Provence; 580 different verbs were extracted from 29 780 finite forms out of 700 000 words recorded from NS conversations.[18] The five more frequent verbs are the auxiliaries *être* 'be' (26 541 tokens), *avoir* 'have' (23 133 tokens), *faire* 'do' (6 413 tokens), *dire* 'say, tell' (5 150 tokens) and the modal verb *devoir* 'must' (3 726 tokens), and they are the only verbs to use a large number of the 45 possible morphological forms (35 forms for *avoir* and 31 forms for *être*).[19]

Another reason for the subjunctive to be lacking in saliency in the input is because of the fact that some forms are homophonous with the indicative. Thus,

---

17.   My sincere thanks to Attila Pohlmann for the German to English translation of this article.

18.   See also Blanche-Benveniste and Adam (1999) for more details about the corpus.

19.   These corpora using standard French spoken in France differ from the corpora using *Québécois* French in Poplack (1992, 2001) in which is appears that the indicative has replaced the subjunctive in a wide variety of contexts, and that the subjunctive survives only following *falloir* 'to be necessary', *vouloir* 'want' and *aimer* 'like'.

the present indicative forms of the regular verbs ending in -er – which form the largest group of verbs, approximately 4000 (Grevisse & Goose 1980)[20] – are all homophonous with the present subjunctive (e.g. *entre, entres, entre, entrent*), except for the first and second person plural; moreover, they are homophonous with another indicative form, the *imparfait* (e.g. *entrions, entriez*). The present subjunctive form is phonetically salient on verbs with irregular paradigms, as well as verbs ending in -ir (e.g. *finisse, finisses, finisse, finissions, finissiez, finissent*) and -re (e.g. *prenne, prennes, prenne*), except for the first and second person plural which are homophonous with the *imparfait* (e.g. *prenions, preniez*). Taking these unmarked subjunctive forms into account lowers the estimated overall frequency of the subjunctive based on written and oral corpora from 2% to 1% in the spoken language, and from 3% to 2% in the written language (Di Vito 1994).

Finally, foreign language learners in instructed settings are usually told that the indicative mood expresses certainty whereas the subjunctive mood conveys uncertainty and subjectivity, which is an accurate generalization; however, the indicative-subjunctive alternation is plagued with puzzling exceptions. For instance, an expression such as *le fait que* 'the fact that' clearly indicating a fact does trigger the indicative as one would expect, but it can also trigger the subjunctive. Loengarov (2005) uses a corpus of 137 822 104 words from 1831–1993 (Frantex corpus) to select 576 occurrences of *le fait que* introducing a subject relative clause (without an adjective such as *le seul fait que* or adverb such as *le fait aussi que* which may influence the mood selection). Overall, indicative forms account for about 50% of the corpus, while subjunctive forms account for 20–30%; during the 1960s, there was almost an equal number of subjunctive and indicative forms, then clearly more subjunctive than indicative forms from 1970 on. Thus, sentences as shown in (7a, b) are common:

(7) a. *Le fait que Paul ne soit pas venu est étonnant.*
the fact that Paul come-PastSubj not is surprising
'The fact that Paul did not come is surprising'

   b. *Il a protesté contre le fait que son frère reçoive plus*
he complained about the fact that his brother get-PresSubj

   d'argent de poche que lui.
more money that him
'He complained about the fact that his brother gets a bigger allowance than he does'

---

20. Verbs in -er are the highest in frequency type (Bybee 1995; Nicoladis, Palmer & Marentette 2007; Paradis & Crago 2001).

Moreover, the subjunctive is required after the expression *le seul fait que* 'the mere fact that' as in (8):

(8)   *Le   seul   fait   que   vous ayez hésité   est de mauvaise augure.*
       The mere fact that you   hesitate-PastSubj is a bad   sign
       'The mere fact that you hesitated is a bad sign'

When *fait* is modifying with an adjective, the subjunctive or indicative may be triggered depending on the adjective as in (9a, b) (examples from Loengarov 2005):

(9)   a.   *C'est un fait bizarre qu'il ne soit   pas encore rentré.*
          it is   a   fact bizarre that he come-PastSubj not yet   go in
          'It's bizarre that he is not home yet'

    b.   *C'est un fait connu   qu' ils   sont amis.*
          it is   a   fact know-Adj that they are friends
          'Everyone knows that they are friends'

'*Bizarre*' triggers the subjunctive in (8a), but '*connu*' triggers the indicative in (8b).

To sum up, the complexities and subtleties of indicative-subjunctive alternation (cf Chapter 2), are compounded by the lack of frequency and saliency of the subjunctive forms in the input. Pedagogical approaches need to take these facts into account to facilitate the acquisition of the indicative-subjunctive alternation. As the findings reported in Chapter 5 indicate, the subjunctive is definitely acquired late as even the participants in the Advanced group struggled with the sentence completion task. Finally, instructors should keep in mind that the participants' performance varied tremendously with the different types of triggers (they performed best with expressions of order/interdiction and very poorly with superlatives and indefinite antecedents).

6.4.3 Modal verbs

As full lexical verbs, French modal verbs have complete paradigms for all moods and tenses (e.g. *je dois, tu dois, il doit, nous devons, vous devez, ils doivent; je pourrais, tu pourrais, il pourrait, nous pourrions, vous pourriez, ils pourraient*). As they also happen to be common verbs – albeit with an irregular morphology – their high frequency makes them very salient in the input. The difficulty is that modal verbs in French, as in all languages, are characterized by their complex and subtle polysemy (cf Chapter 2). Morever, an important contrast between English and French from a learnability perspective is that the polysemous semantic values of the modals (i.e. dynamic, deontic and epistemic modalities) are expressed by different moods and tenses in French, whereas English uses different modal auxiliaries. Thus, the difficulties that L2 learners generally already experience with various moods and tenses are compounded with the modal verbs.

The concept of mood/modality is not introduced in the typical first year textbook for French. *Pouvoir, savoir, devoir* are introduced early on during that first year, but only to emphasize their irregular morphological paradigms. It is only stated that *pouvoir* is used to make polite requests in the conditional.

6.5   Back to basics

Assuming motivated and engaged classroom learners who are eager to learn, what would be an effective pedagogical approach to teach them the French TAM system?

After summarizing the main empirical findings related to aspectual distinctions in Ayoun and Salaberry (2005), Blyth (2005) proposes three main principles that teachers may want to keep in mind when teaching aspect: "(1) design pedagogical interventions to enhance the input in keeping with students' developmental readiness; (2) base grammatical explanations and activities as much as possible on the students' own visual perception of events; and (3) choose appropriate narrative texts and tasks that take into account cognitive and linguistic complexity, as well as native speaker norms" (*ibid*: 218). These three principles are an excellent starting point for teaching not only aspect, but also mood and modality, but let us go back to even more basic concepts and principles of second language learning and how teachers may use them in the classroom.

6.5.1   The classroom language learner

Language learners are aided in their task by: (a) an acquisition device that is composed of at least three modules – a conceptual module, a perceptual module, and a computational module; (b) general learning mechanisms. In addition, an adult language learner is characterized by his or her cognitive abilities, the language interactions in the L1 and L2, as well as by other general activities be they personal, professional or school-related. In other words, it is important to keep in mind that however motivated adult language learners may be and however greater their cognitive capacities may be, they cannot be entirely dedicated to learning an L2 the same way a child is entirely focused on acquiring his or her L1.

According to DeKeyser and Koeth (2011: 396), among the most important cognitive aptitudes for L2 learning are "analytical ability (closely related to verbal aptitude and even general intelligence), memory (including various aspects) and phonetic sensitivity". They also mention the importance of working memory, implicit learning, emotional intelligence (citing Goleman 1996), as well as cognitive styles such as field independence or tolerance of ambiguity (Kozhevnikov 2007;

Price 2004; for applications in SLA, see e.g. Ehrman 1996; Ehrman & Oxford 1995; Hokanson 2000; Johnson, Prior & Artuso 2000; Littlemore 2001) (*ibid*: 397). After an extensive literature review, they conclude that working memory is the most critical cognitive component in second language learning "over a wide range of learner ages, proficiency, language skills and learning environments" (*ibid*: 402).

Finally, a variety of individual learner-internal affective factors such as anxiety, motivation, attitude, and/or perceived competence may impact the learners' interlanguage development (see e.g. Bernaus, Moore & Azevedo Cordeiro 2007; Dewaele 2009; Dörnyei & Schmidt 2001; Gardner 1980, 1985, 2000; Masgoret & Gardner 2003; Schumann 1975; Zafar & Meenakshi 2012).[21]

An adult language learner may thus be represented as in Figure 6.1:

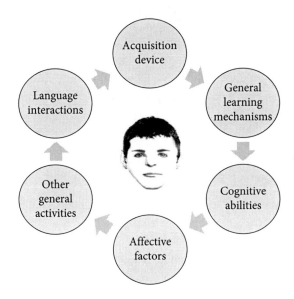

Figure 6.1. Adult language learner

Foreign language learning in instructed settings require the following basic elements as illustrated in Figure 6.2. Although they are discussed individually for ease of exposition, these elements clearly overlap; input and intake, or input and

---

21. See in particular Masgoret and Gardner (2003), a meta-analysis that investigates how the five attitudinal/motivation variables of the socio-educational model proposed by Gardner (1985, 2000) – attitudes toward the learning situation, motivation, integrative orientation, instrumental orientation – correlate with second language achievement.

output, for instance, are intrinsically related although they appear in two different modules in Figure 6.2.

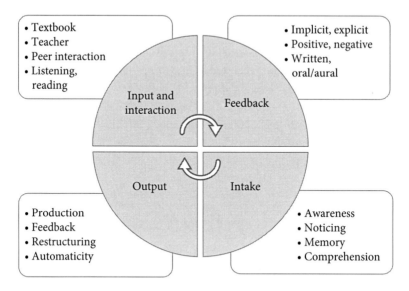

Figure 6.2. Four basic elements

6.5.2   Input and interaction

The language input is the exposure to the second language that the learner receives and as "perhaps the single most important concept of second language acquisition" (Gass 1997: 1), it has been the focus of much research from a generative perspective (e.g. Caroll 2001; Schwartz 1993), as well as from a non-generative perspective (see Mitchell & Myles 2004 for an overview). It can come from several sources: from reading the textbook in preparation for class; from the instructor during explanations and activities; interacting with peers during classroom activities and tasks; listening and reading with various media (e.g. computer-based media, movies, televised news).

However, as it is generally agreed that the foreign language classroom does not provide an adequate environment for successful language learning due to inherent limitations (e.g. time, materials, artificial interactions), two very productive lines of research have been investigating the best approach(es) to make the most of the input to which foreign language classroom learners are exposed: input processing instruction (e.g. VanPatten 1996, 2002, 2004; VanPatten & Oikkenon 1996), and focus-on-form instruction (e.g. Doughty & Williams 1998; Long 1988, 1991). Both approaches aim at better directing the learners' attention during input processing to compensate for the inadequacies of the input. They will be reviewed below.

6.5.3 Intake

Intake is distinct from input. Not all input becomes intake that is generally understoood as an intermediate process between input and actual language acquisition (e.g. Chaudron 1983, 1985; Sharwood Smith 1986; Slobin 1985; VanPatten 1985, 1990). For input to become intake – that is, incorporated into the learner's current grammar or interlanguage as stored data or final intake (Chaudron 1985) – it must be noticed and understood. Or as Leow (1993:334) puts it, intake is "that part of the input that has been attended to by second language learners while processing the input. Intake represents stored linguistic data that may be used for immediate recognition and does not necessarily imply language acquisition".

In their model of language acquisition that incorporates linguistic, sociolinguistic and psycholinguistic aspects, Gass and Selinker (1994) contend that intake occurs at the third level, preceded first by apperceived input, then comprehended input; it is then followed by integration and finally output. Frequency, affect (i.e. motivation, attitude), prior knowledge and attention are cited as essential factors for learners to successfully go through these stages, and in particular to notice and comprehend the input so that it may become intake.

Schmidt (1990, 1993, 1994, 1995, 2001; Schmidt & Frota 1986) convincingly argues that noticing is the *necessary* and sufficient condition for input to become intake.[22] I would stress that it is particularly necessary for instructed learners because little incidental learning (i.e. without consciously noticing; see Schmidt 1990) seems to occur in foreign language classrooms that typically place a very strong emphasis on explicit teaching and feedback.[23]

6.5.4 Output

Output refers to the learners' oral and written production of the foreign language they are learning. It is as important for learners to notice forms in the input as it is

---

22. For further discussion of the noticing hypothesis, see Robinson (1995, 2003) and Jin (2011) among others; for a critical review see Truscott (1998).

23. That is not to say that there is no implicit learning at all: the generative perspective adopted here assumes that adult SLA is UG-constrained, hence implicit learning does occur. If there is indeed a logical problem for SLA as suggested by empirical evidence (e.g. CITE), that is, learners show they possess knowledge of complex, abstract and subtle properties which they could not have derived from the input alone, and which are not explicitly taught. That knowledge is necessarily UG-constrained (e.g. White 2003). See O'Grady (2003:44) for a general nativism, also called cognitive nativism or emergentism, perspective that posits that "the entire grammar is the production of the interaction of the acquisition device with experience; no grammatical knowledge is inborn".

for them to notice that the gaps between their own output and the target language forms, so that they may restructure their interlanguage grammar as necessary, and continue moving along the continuum from the initial state to a successful end-state. Or, as initially stated by Swain (1985) and has become known as the output hypothesis, noticing a gap "pushes" the learner to modify his or her output as shown by some early empirical studies such as Nobuyoshi and Ellis (1993) that suggest that pushing learners to modify their output increases their control over forms they have already acquired.

Studies conducted in French immersion settings such as Swain and Lapkin (1995) led to a better understanding of the importance of output. Swain and Lapkin administered a writing task along with a think-aloud procedure to students in a grade 8 early French immersion class (n = 18), in order to categorize their decision-making processes (partially replicating Cumming 1990). They found that these teenage language learners did notice gaps in their linguistic knowledge even in the absence of negative feedback, and that they engaged in a thought process that may prove to be beneficial in their L2 learning in two ways: hypothesis testing and auto-maticity, as further developed in Swain (1993, 1995, 1998) that refined the original output hypothesis to add a metalinguistic function along with the functions of hypothesis testing and automaticity to the initial noticing function. Noticing (or consciousness-raising) was of course still another important function.[24]

Automatic processes are processes that have become so routinized that they require little thought or attention. They are the result of "consistent mappings of the same input to the same pattern of activation over many trials" (McLaughlin 1987: 134).[25] McLaughlin uses two concepts: the concept of automaticity (dichotomy between controlled and automatic processing) (Posner & Snyder 1975; Schneider & Shiffrin 1977; Shiffrin & Schneider 1977) and the concept of restructuring which consists in replacing existing structures with more efficient ones.

6.5.5   Feedback

There are so many different forms of feedback – implicit, explicit, negative, positive – that one may wonder what the best form of feedback may be and what may be the best way to provide it? It is a perennial question for all foreign language instructors when faced with the non-targetlike oral or written output of their

---

24. See Izumi (2003) (and reference cited therein) for a literature review of studies investigating the psycholinguistic processes relevant to the output hypothesis.

25. McLaughlin (1987) quotes empirical bilingual studies of semantic, lexical and syntactic encoding decoding and word retrieval. Differential effects of automaticity were found.

students. Based on current findings, it appears that the most appropriate answer is a frustrating one: it depends. However, language learners themselves express a strong preference for more and frequent corrective feedback rather than less (e.g. Brown 2009; Jean & Simard 2011; Lasagabaster & Sierra 2005).

As Ellis (2007:360) concluded at the end of a study that investigated the differential effects of corrective feedback on regular past tense -*ed* and comparative -*er*, "what is needed in future research is to determine how linguistic factors may determine when different types of feedback will work for acquisition".

In the longitudinal study investigating for three different types of feedback in the L2 acquisition of the aspectual distinction between the *passé composé* and the *imparfait* reviewed above, Ayoun (2001) found that implicit negative feedback in the form of written recasts appeared to be more effective than explicit negative feedback and traditional grammar instruction, although all groups improved from pre- to post-test. However, in Ayoun (2004), the follow-up study that investigated the differential outcomes between the *passé composé* and the *imparfait* with qualitative data, it became more difficult to differentiate the three different treatments. Unfortunately, these mixed findings are typical of laboratory and classroom studies investigating different forms of feedback.[26]

Let us just mention Yang and Lyster (2010) because it focuses on past tense forms (there are fewer feedback studies targeting TAM than other linguistic features), and two types of feedback in form-focused instruction. Chinese-speaking learners of L2 English (n = 72) were placed in one of two conditions: (a) corrective feedback (i.e. metalinguistic cue, repetition, clarification request, elicitation); (b) prompts or recasts (i.e. instructor's reformulation of an erroneous utterance with or without encouragement for the student to provide a correction). The results of pre-tests, immediate post-tests, and delayed post-tests in oral and written production tasks showed the prompt group improved significantly on all measures, the recast group improved on four, while the control group improved on three. Prompts led to greater accuracy in producing regular past tense forms, while prompts and recasts had comparable effects on the accuracy of irregular past tense forms.

Goo and Mackey (2013:32) review a large number of L2 empirical studies to conclude that no "study to date has provided clear-cut, convincing evidence that recasts are significantly less effective than metalinguistic feedback or prompts due to methodological limitations". They also make the important point that recasts and prompts make different and unique contributions to L2 development

---

26. For recent findings see Egi (2007a, 2007b), Ellis, Loewen and Erlam (2006), Leeman (2003), Lyster (2004b), Ranta and Lyster (2007), among many others.

(e.g. "modified output naturally follows the prompts, but not the recasts"; *ibid*). Finally, they suggest that "research time would be better spent exploring how the effectiveness of corrective feedback interacts with such mediating factors as noticing and attention (especially via recent eye-tracking techniques, see Smith 2013), individual cognitive differences in cognitive capacities (e.g. short-term memory, working memory, see Goo 2012), social factors (e.g. learning setting, social status of interlocutors, see Philip & Mackey 2010), and the type of target (e.g. whether recasts and prompts facilitate the acquisition of L2 pragmatics and phonology)" (*ibid*: 33).

In another review article, this one on oral corrective feedback in various settings as well as with different linguistic targets, Lyster, Saito and Sato (2013) stressed the importance of different types of feedback in different learning situations with learners of various ages and proficiency levels. Implicit and explicit corrective feedback are both needed even if empirical findings do not always show a clear advantage for one over the other as it was the case in a study on noun-adjective agreement errors (Erlam & Loewen 2010). In this case, it may have been because the treatment consisted of only one hour of interactive tasks. However, significant effects for oral interaction were found.

The best approach may thus be to use a repertoire of different types of feedback (particularly with metalinguistic information) as their effectiveness varies with the linguistic target and the learners' proficiency levels as well as their age (e.g. Lyster 2004b). As Ellis (2012: 263) noted, "it may be fundamentally mistaken to look for the most effective type of strategy".

6.5.6   Metalinguistic knowledge

It may be necessary for classroom learners to increase their metalinguistic knowledge in order to improve their hypothesis testing eventually leading to a better restructuring of their interlanguage grammar. Although explicit instruction facilitates student awareness of grammatical forms and meanings, they need the appropriate tools to better comprehend them.

Paradis (2006:1) stresses the importance of metalinguistic knowledge for it "allows learners to monitor the output of linguistic competence and thus increases their production of correct forms, the frequency of which may eventually (though indirectly) establish the implicit procedures that will sustain their automatic use. [...] With increase of proficiency, the use of metalinguistic knowledge is either speeded up or gradually replaced by the use of implicit linguistic competence [...]".

Alderson, Clapham and Steel (1997), who administered a battery of linguistic and metalinguistic tests to 509 college freshmen enrolled in French classes, only found a weak correlation between metalinguistic knowledge and proficiency in

French. However, Han and Ellis (1998) point out that metalinguistic knowledge is not as important for beginning learners as it is for intermediate and advanced learners. Moreover, Swain, Lapkin, Knouzi, Suzuki and Brooks (2009) show that "languaging" – for instance, talking out loud or to ourselves, attempting to explain something to someone – "is an important part of the language learning process as it transforms inner thoughts to external knowing (externalization) and, conversely, it transforms external knowing into internal cognitive activity (internalization) (*ibid*: 5). I would argue that language acquisition may be facilitated by metalinguistic knowledge.

6.6 Current instructional approaches and hypotheses

6.6.1 Processing instruction

The main objective of Processing instruction (VanPatten 2002, 2005) is to increase language learners' intake by encouraging them to make appropriate form-meaning connections. Two types of structured input activities are designed to facilitate input processing: affective activities (with more than one correct answer because learners express their personal feelings or beliefs) and referential activities (with only one correct answer between two dichotomous interpretations such as present *vs* past temporality).

An example of a referential activity and of an affective activity would be as follows (adapted from Farley 2000):

(10) Referential activity: your best friend
Instructions: you will hear the second part of a statement that someone made about your best friend. Circle the phrase that is correct for each statement.
Student hears: … *il sorte souvent* 'he go-SubjPres out often'
and selects from: (a) *je sais que…* 'I know that' and (b) *je ne pense pas que…* 'I don't think that

(11) Affective activity: *Le Monde*
Instructions: please read the following opinions about *Le Monde* and check off the ones you agree with.
Je ne pense pas que Le monde… 'I don't think that *Le Monde*'
a. *ait des articles intéressants* 'have-SubjPres interesting articles'
b. *dise souvent la vérité* 'say-SubjPres often the truth'
c. *soit lu par les jeunes* 'be-SubjPres read by young people'

Referential activities seem to be effective for learning morpho-syntax because they cannot be completed without providing accurate L2 target forms, that is, they are task-essential (Loschky & Bley-Vroman 1993); and learners receive negative feedback which allows them to figure out whether they are on track or not, and if so, to make appropriate adjustments.

Affective activities are designed to strengthen the form-meaning connections that are created during referential activities by helping language learners relate to the L2 forms in a more meaningful and personal way (Farley 2000, 2005; VanPatten 2005; Wong 2004). Both types of activities are most beneficial when presented jointly, particularly when referential activities are followed by affective activities because the former activities promote conscious attention to form while the latter activities serve as "implicit reinforcement" (Marsden 2006:524). Of course, one cannot guarantee that learners do focus on the relevant features, but complementary activities are always better than a single type of activity. Moreover, the relative effectiveness of tasks almost always varies with the linguistic target. Thus, Fernández (2008) found that participants' performance on referential activities improved on pre-verbal direct object pronouns, but not on the subjunctive.[27]

Processing instruction has been well researched targeting a variety of morphosyntactic forms, but not necessarily TAM forms (e.g. Sanz & Morgan-Short 2004; VanPatten & Cadierno 1993; VanPatten & Oikkenon 1996; VanPatten & Wong 2004; Wong 2004).[28] Several studies investigated the acquisition of the subjunctive in Spanish (e.g. Collentine 1998; Fernández 2008; Henshaw 2012), the future in Italian (Benati 2001), the English past tense (e.g. Benati 2005); however, only a few studies targeted TAM in French. One notable exception is Marsden (2004, 2006).[29]

Marsden (2004, 2006) is presented as a focus-on-form study with a pre-tests, post-tests and delayed post-tests design that compared a referential activity (with attention to forms and meaning) to Enriched input (grammar explanation but without attention to the forms or meanings). Two experiments conducted with two groups of instructed learners targeted verb inflections for number and person, as well as present and past tense. The Processing input condition included a short grammar and processing explanation followed by both referential and affective activities, while the Enriched input condition was composed of the same short grammar explanation followed by listening and reading activities. Findings show that Processing instruction led to greater gains than Enriched input, but I would

---

27.   See also Farley (2005) as well as Sanz and Morgan-Short (2004).

28.   For some concerns about Processing instruction see for instance Carroll (2004), Doughty (2004), DeKeyser, Salaberry, Robinson and Harrington (2002) or Harrington (2004).

29.   See also Mégharbi (2007) for a study comparing the effectiveness of processing instruction with output-based instruction in the acquisition of the aspectual distinction between the *passé composé* and the *imparfait*.

have to agree with Marsden (2004:551) that "further research is required to consider how interactions might occur among different input activity types, the developmental stage of the learner, outcome measurements, prior teaching, and the explicit grammar component of P[rocessing] I[nstruction]".

6.6.2 Focus on form(s) and focus on meaning

Focus-on-meaning instruction is concerned with classroom activities that emphasize primarily, if not exclusively, communication and negotiation of meaning to the detriment of forms and grammatical accuracy since this "actually had a negative effect on the second language classroom" (Hammond 1988:414) (see also Krashen 1982, 1993; Krashen & Terrell 1983), while focus-on-forms instruction is a structuralist approach to language that stresses forms rather than the meaning(s) they express, and classroom activities are characterized by an explicit presentation of grammatical structures and rules by the instructor (Burgess & Etherington 2002; Nassaji & Fotos 2004). "Form-focused instruction" is also defined as "any pedagogical effort which is used to draw the learners' attention to language form either implicitly or explicitly" (Spada 1997:73). Long's (1991) definition of focus-on-form is slightly different: the intended outcome is the allocation of attentional resources to a form, that it, noticing (Long & Robinson 1998). Focus-on-form instruction recognizes the importance of grammatical instruction, but insists it must be embedded in meaning-oriented classrooms.

The effectiveness of one approach over another may also depend on the learners' proficiency level. Beginning learners benefit equally from both as they still have so much to learn, while intermediate and advanced learners appear to benefit more from explicit teaching. I would agree with others (e.g. Ellis & Laporte 1997; Herdina & Jessner 2000; Long & Robinson 1998; Poole 2005) that these two approaches complement, rather than exclude each other: the ideal classroom promotes communicative activities while attending to language forms and using various ways of providing implicit and explicit negative feedback as necessary. Empirical research indeed shows that explicit attention to form in communicative contexts is more effective (Spada 1997; Norris & Ortega 2000).

More recently, Spada and Lightbown (2008) make a distinction between two types of form-focused instruction depending on whether the activities are isolated or integrated, and note that both types can be beneficial depending on the usual factors: the targeted linguistic factor, the learning conditions, and learner factors such as proficiency and developmental readiness. Thus, they suggest that isolated form-focused instruction may be helpful in learning "features that are relatively simple to explain or illustrate, but are not particularly salient in oral language. Drawing attention to them in isolation may help learners see/hear language features they have not been noticing in the input, the first step on the path to acquisition" (*ibid*: 195). However, they are in no way suggesting that these isolated grammar lessons become the mainstay of language instruction; they are only suggested as a 'starting point or a follow-up for communicative or content-based activities" (*ibid*: 201).

A comparative analysis of five empirical studies targeting various forms – two focus on *passé composé vs imparfait* and the conditional mood – in Lyster (2004a: 321) arrives at similar conclusions with learners in French immersion settings: " a balanced distribution of opportunities for noticing, language awareness and controlled practice with feedback" are the hallmarks of an effective form-focused instruction.[30]

6.6.3   Counterbalance hypothesis

Learners in immersion settings take content courses in the target language, that is French, which is of course a positive and important part of their education, but which also means that as language learners, they face the double challenge of having to focus on the content of the course and the target language forms at the same time.

Lyster's (2008: 126) Counterbalance hypothesis – or instructional counter-balance (Lyster 2007; Lyster & Mori 2006, 2008) – that aims at "integrating form-focused and content-based instruction through counterbalanced instruction" rests on Skehan's (1998) suggestion to encourage form-oriented learners to become more meaning-oriented and conversely, to push meaning-oriented learners to become more form-oriented, thereby striking a balance. In other words (cited in Lyster 2008):

> In the case of analytic learners, the intention is to build a greater concern for fluency and the capacity to express meanings in real time without becoming excessively concerned with a focus on form... In the case of memory-oriented learners, the intention is to set limits to the natural tendency to prioritize communicative outcome above all else.   (Skehan 1998: 171–172)

Lyster and Mori (2008) push Skehan's argument further to include "learners whose learning style and expectations have been shaped to a large extent by the overall

---

30. See also McCormick (2008) for a study testing the acquisition of the English present perfect by adult ESL learners in two different types of form-focused instruction (contextualized, explicit FFI with or without contrastive analysis with L1). Findings show that participants in the first condition outperformed the other experimental condition and the control group.

communicative orientation of their classroom setting" (*ibid*: 126) to the detriment of attention on forms. They thus argue that pedagogical intervention is necessary to draw learners to a different direction. In other words, it is hoped that a counterbalanced approach would result in a more balanced competence for these immersion students.

Lyster (2008) cites several of the form-focused studies reviewed above as providing empirical evidence for his hypothesis, and concludes that meaning-oriented interactions that prevail in content-based classroom are not likely to result in long-term, significant improvements, whereas controlled production activities along with tasks designed to elicit awareness and noticing are more likely to trigger significant restructuring of the learners' interlanguage.

The Counterbalance hypothesis also contends that different forms of negative feedback may be appropriate depending on the linguistic target, but suggests that although recasts are quite useful, various prompts (e.g. clarification requests, metalinguistic clues) may be more effective in helping learners correct their output (e.g. Lyster 2004b). Instructors are also encouraged to use a wide range of practices from form-focused to content-based interventions as well as to see these two approaches as interacting with one another as opposed to being separate, discrete units.

To sum up, the Counterbalance hypothesis sounds like a good, empirically- and common sense-based approach that is very likely to benefit not only immersion students, but also language learners in all instructed settings as they move from exclusively foreign language courses to content courses taught in that foreign language.

6.6.4   Teachability hypothesis and Processability theory

Pienemann's (1984, 1987, 1989) Teachability hypothesis was initially proposed and tested with a small study conducted with Italian-speaking elementary school children (n = 10) who were learning German in mostly a naturalistic context. The study was designed with the intent to "beat the order of acquisition through formal instruction" (Pienemann 1989:58). It was found that learners had to be developmentally ready to acquire a new structure (based on canonical word orders), and that stages "cannot be skipped" (Long 1988) because each stage represents a different processing stage. Instruction is helpful "only if the interlanguage is close to the point when the structure to be taught is acquired in the natural setting" (*ibid*: 60). Pienemann (1989:54) further specified that "the constraints imposed by language processing play a decisive part in determining the specific order in which given sets of L2 items are acquired by different individuals".

Thus, instruction, and particularly a focus-on-form approach, can be beneficial; instructors just need to take the learners' developmental readiness into account.[31] However, it is also important to stress that the goal of the Teachability hypothesis is not to propose specific instructional methods to teachers, but rather to bring out the psycholinguistic processes that underlie language learning and that should inform pedagogical approaches.

It is this emphasis on processing that led to the wider theoretical framework of the Processability theory of which the Teachability hypothesis is now understood as a subset (Pienemann 1998, 2005). Following Kaplan and Bresnan (1982), Pienemann (2005: 2) views the language processor as "the computational routines that operate on (but are separate from) the native speaker's linguistic knowledge. Processability theory primarily deals with the nature of those computational routines and the sequence in which they become available to the learner". It is assumed that L2 learners have to create language-specific processing routines following the general structure of the language processor.

In a pre-, immediate- and post-test design study, Tracy-Ventura (2008) set out to test both Pienemann's (1998) Teachability hypothesis and form-focused *vs* meaning-focused instruction in the acquisition of past tense morphology with L2 Spanish learners. Pre-tests were used to group participants (n = 56) in one of five stages of preterit and imperfect acquisition; they were also placed in one of three conditions (form-focused developmentally ready, form-focused advanced, meaning-focused comparison). The effectiveness of the conditions depended on the acquisition stage: form-focused developmentally ready instruction was more effective at the emergence stage of development, while explicit instruction was effective for the accuracy of the imperfect on the cloze test even at the advanced stage. When it came to the oral interview and written narration tasks, there was no difference in effectiveness between explicit instruction and meaning-focused instruction, both were equally effective for improving the accuracy of both past tense forms.

6.6.5 Competing systems hypothesis

Rothman (2008) contends that the pedagogical rules that are taught to classroom learners compete with Universal Grammar in such a way that learners are plagued by performance problems even at highly advanced proficiency levels. As established by previous L2 Spanish and Portuguese studies (e.g. Goodin-Mayeda & Rothman 2007; Rothman & Iverson 2007), L2 learners do show that they can acquire syntactic and semantic knowledge of aspectual distinctions, but Rothman hypothesizes that the inaccurate, simplified pedagogical rules to which they are

---

31. Others (e.g. Doughty & Williams 1998; Lightbown 1985; Weinart 1994) have suggested however that a pedagogical focus on more advanced forms for which learners are not yet ready could be beneficial even if the effects are not immediately noticeable. They can be retrieved later when the learners are ready to do so.

exposed in instructed settings "can override linguistic competence (generative system) of the L2 learner at the level of performance" (*ibid*: 85). It is further argued that "even when interlanguage reaches a steady-state in advanced learners that is representationally native-like in particular domains, the learned knowledge system can intercede, especially in highly monitored output, resulting in systematic errors. The prediction, therefore, is that once grammatical properties have been acquired at the mental representation level, this system can interfere with production, but not comprehension" (*ibid*: 85–86).

To test the Competing Systems hypothesis, Rothman set out to compare Anglophone instructed learners (n = 20) (who were also Spanish instructors) with naturalistic learners (n = 11) and native speakers of Spanish (n = 20) in their acquisition of the perfective/imperfective distinction instantiated by the preterit and the imperfect. All three groups performed a cloze paragraph multiple-choice test and a guided production task (fill-in-the-blank). Findings indicate that the naturalistic learners performed like the native speakers, while the instructed learners' performance significantly differed from these two groups on both elicitation tasks. The non-target-like verbal productions of the instructed learners in the cloze test can be traced to verbs which are taught as English translation equivalents, or to copula verbs (i.e. *ser* 'be', *haber* 'have'), which are taught as being almost always encoded with the imperfect (e.g. *sabía* vs *supe* 'knew'); a third context concerns the adverbials (i.e. *siempre* 'always', *cuando* 'when') which are taught as triggering either the preterit or the imperfect as default forms. The guided production task was designed to test preterit and imperfect uses that are not taught explicitly.

The findings thus confirm that instructed learners are misled by oversimplified, narrowly focused pedagogical rules that are limited to prototypical uses, ignoring nonprototypical uses. Since naturalistic L2 learners perform like native speakers, it seems reasonable to conclude that, as contended by the Competing Systems hypothesis, the linguistic system that instructed learners build interfers with their performance that would otherwise be more target-like. Of course, pedagogical rules could be modified to be more inclusive and accurate, as will be suggested below. As also concluded by Rothman (2008: 101), "[t]o test the verifiability of the Competing Systems Hypothesis as well as to isolate other areas of grammar in which native-like performance may be affected by a separate system of learned pedagogical rules, additional studies are warranted", but it is an interesting and promising area of research.[32]

---

32. See Gass and Mackey (2012) for a state-of-the-art edited volume on many of the issues covered here including the role of feedback, processability theory, noticing/attention/ awareness, aptitude and input process. See also Hinkel (2011), a two volume handbook on second language acquisition.

6.7 Computer-based technologies

The phrase ""traditional text-based technologies" refers to traditional classroom instruction in combination with the two most common tools students use to write and submit their papers and essays: paper and pencil or word processing software" (Castañeda 2011:695). Text-based technologies are still used in foreign language classrooms, however, they have been increasingly combined with computer-based technologies which started being a part of academic life in general since the early 1970s, and have only gained in prominence.

Warschauer (2004:22; cited in Chun 2011), distinguishes three stages to research in computer-assisted language learning (CALL), indicating the view of language to which each stage corresponds, as well as the primary use of technology as reproduced (and partially adapted) in Table 6.1:[33]

Table 6.1. The three stages of CALL

Stage	1970–1980s: structural CALL	1980s–1990s: communicative CALL	Twenty-first century: integrative CALL
technology	mainframe	computers	multimedia and Internet
teaching paradigm	grammar translation and audiolingual	communicative language teaching	content based
view of language	structural	cognitive	socio-cognitive
main use of computers	drill and practice	communicative exercices	authentic discourse
main objective	accuracy	fluency	agency

Chun (2011:663) makes the point that "[j]ust as there is no one universally accepted theory of SLA or one universally proven methodology of language teaching, so too are there no CALL tools that are effective universally for all learners". As all language teachers are well aware of, there is no such thing as one size-fits-all when it comes to providing instruction in general. The same way instructors used a whole repertoire of teaching tools in traditional classrooms, they know they must continue to do so in virtual and/or hybrid classrooms. However, it is helpful to their language learning and literacy in general that the current generation of students are indeed "digital natives" (Warschauer 2001) in that they grew up surrounded by technology.

---

33. See also the introduction in Fotos and Browne (2004) and the chapters therein.

Chun (2011) reproduces another table (Ducate & Arnold 2006; Hubbard 2009) that summarizes the CALL tools available for linguistic skills along with relevant research that should prove very useful for instructors in deciding which computer-based technologies to incorporate into their teaching repertoire (cf Table 6.2).

Table 6.2. CALL for individual language skills

Skill	CALL tools	Research results
pronunciation (vowels and consonants)	visualizations of articulation, automatic speech recognition	Levis (2008); O'Brien (2006)
prosody, intonation	visualizations of speech curves	Chun (2002); Hardison (2004, 2005)
vocabulary	tutorials, multimedia glosses, CMC	Chun (2006); Horst, Cobb & Nicolae (2005); Taylor (2006)
grammar and syntax	tutorials, iCALL, CMC	Heift & Schulze (2007); Kern (1995); Nagata (1999)
pragmatics	CMC 1.0 & 2.0	Belz & Kinginger (2003); Sykes (2005)
speaking	CMC 1.0 & 2.0, audio and videoconferencing	C. Blake (2009); R. Blake (2005); Payne & Ross (2005)
listening	multimedia glosses, audio and videoconferencing	Jones (2006); Jones & Plass (2002)
reading	multimedia annotations, electronic dictionaries	Abraham (2008); Chun (2006)
writing	CMC 1.0 & 2.0	Ducate & Lomicka (2008); Murray & Hourigan (2006)
culture, intercultural communicative competence	videos, films, CMC 1.0 & 2.0	Abrams (2006); Dubreil (2006); Lomicka (2006); O'Dowd & Ritter (2006)
multiliteracies	viewing and creating Web pages	Gonglewski & DuBravac (2006); Kern (2000)
assessment	Web-based tools	Carr (2006); Douglas & Hegelheimer (2008)

CALL studies have also focused on psycholinguistic research with cognitive factors such as noticing. Of particular interest to this chapter is the study by Yanguas (2009) that found that when learners frequently requested or accessed multimedia glosses, they appeared to notice this input more, leading to a significantly better performance on vocabulary tests than learners who did not use or access the glosses as frequently.

In an earlier, exploratory study, Salaberry (2000b) asked 4 English-speaking learners of L2 Spanish to complete three different tasks (a cloze test, and two interaction tasks: an informal oral interview and an informal computed-mediated written exchange with the software Aspect as a type of synchronous communication) in order to investigate how the expression of past temporality (preterit *vs.* imperfect) may be affected in different environments. The learners performed with high accuracy on the cloze test, while they produced fewer tense marked verb tokens in the oral tasks as a consequence of topic-shifting likely to occur in conversations, but not in a guided task such as a cloze test.

Castañeda (2011) is another of the few studies that investigated the L2 acquisition of TAM systems using new technologies.[34] This longitudinal study (13 weeks) aimed at exploring the instructional effects of video/photo blogs and wikis in comparison with traditional text-based technologies in the aspectual distinction between perfective and imperfective by beginning English-speaking learners of Spanish.[35] One experimental group was assigned to the video/photo blog and the other to the video/photo wiki. Both the experimental groups and the control group received instruction on the Spanish preterite and imperfect followed by a writing assignment for a total of three weeks before taking a delayed post-test two weeks after the last instruction and writing assignment. Findings show that the participants in the experimental groups outperformed the control group, and the video/photo blog group outperformed the video/photo wiki group. However, it was also found that only the recognition scores benefitted from the video/photo blog experimental condition, the production scores did not. Overall, the experimental conditions facilitated the acquisition of the linguistic target, but Castañeda (2011: 706) stresses that "the combination of traditional instruction, CMC text-based technologies, YouTube videos, and Google images (visual input) were of crucial importance in this study".

There is no doubt that for teachers willing to embrace CALL as a continuing evolving technology with its own challenges and rewards, the possibilities and potential gains are worthwhile. As Chapelle and Hegelheimer (2004: 313) conclude, "[the] opportunities afforded the language teacher by technology at the start of the 21st century require a better-than-ever understanding of the principles of language teaching and a broader-than-ever set of skills and teaching practices".

---

34.   There are of course many studies looking at the use of new technologies with a variety of linguistic targets, but as the literature review has established, the outcomes depend on the linguistic target.

35.   "Blogs and wikis are a form of computer-mediated communication that allows interaction, beyond the traditional face-to-face classroom, among participants that are distributed across time and distance" (Godwin-Jones 2003).

6.8   A few practical suggestions

The purpose of this section is to present a few practical suggestions for language teachers to introduce the main concepts related to tense, aspect, mood and modality developed in this monograph, particularly those which are difficult for L2 learners.

Figure 6.3 displays the general guiding principles that should inform instructional approaches to TAM. The second column provides empirical support. The principles advocate using the learners' existing knowledge about universal concepts such as time, temporality, discourse, necessity, possibility, desire, etc, which correspond to the human experience as well as needs and desires to communicate feelings, thoughts, ideas and so on.

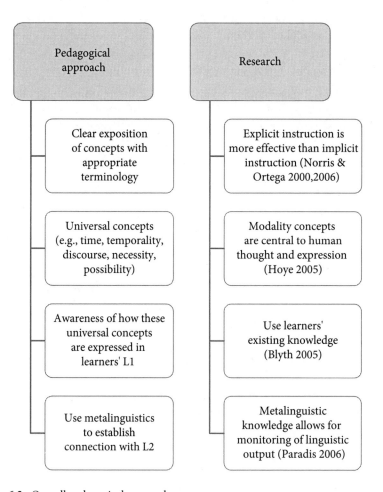

Figure 6.3. Overall pedagogical approach

It is important to not shy away from using the appropriate terminology: as noted elsewhere (Blyth 2005; Swain 1994), a delicate balance must be found between linguistic jargon that may overwhelm and confuse language learners and traditional, layman's terminology that may be unreliable and incomplete. I would like to suggest that one way to avoid this pitfall is to first explain the relevant concept in simple, layman's terms, and then to use the corresponding linguistic terminology. It is crucial to avoid misleading overgeneralizations for the sake of simplicity. Then, learners should be made aware of how basic TAM universal concepts are expressed in their L1, not so much to follow a strict contrastive exposition/analysis approach as to use a consciousness/awareness approach since it appears that the most effective classroom instruction is explicit while focusing on meaning.

Thus an effective roadmap may be as follows: awareness/consciousness (how basic universal concepts are expressed in their L1) => clear, thorough explanations of how they are expressed in the L2 => connect to existing L2 knowledge => stress that strict one-to-one correspondences between L1 and L2 are rare => mapping the concept to the morphology => working out the inflectional morphology => working out the syntactic component (e.g. past participle agreement) => working out the semantic component (e.g. polysemy of moods, modals) => working out the exceptions (see Appendix D for a concrete example).

Instructors must be sure to compensate for infrequent items in the input (e.g. distributional bias for prototypical use *vs* non-prototypical use of predicates – *elle a eu 20 ans* that research established is difficult for L2 learners (e.g. Salaberry 1998, 1999, 2005).

It is very important to choose simply stated, but wide-reaching principles over piecemeal instruction. For instance, L2 learners are aware that compound verbs are composed of an auxiliary and a past participle, but are generally confused about which auxiliary to use. Figure 6.4 displays a simple, yet accurate way to select auxiliaries in most cases, but not all, because as we will see below, a strict dichotomy of either transitive/ intransitive verbs or transitive/intransitive use cannot be maintained.

However, stating that verbs are either used transitively or intransitively as opposed to stating that verbs are either transitive or intransitive is not only more accurate than stating that verbs of movement are used with *être* for instance; moreoever, it eliminates the need to present some verbs as exceptions, as traditionally done in textbooks and grammars while preparing learners to adopt a broader and more flexible approach to verb uses that corresponds to the actual input they receive, as well as to the current growing trend of transitive verbs used without a direct object.

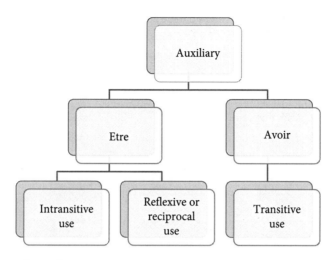

Figure 6.4. Auxiliary selection in compound tenses

Thus, generally, verbs used transitively require a direct object as in (12a), verbs used intransitively take an indirect object as in (12b), or no object at all as in (12c), while verbs used reflexively may take either as in (12d):

(12)   a.   *Attila a pris de belles photos.*
          'Attila took beautiful photos'.

        b.   *Paul est sorti avec ses amis.*
          'Paul went out with his friends'.

        c.   *Paul est sorti.*
          'Paul went out'.

        d.   *Les filles se sont promenées (avec leurs amis).*
          'The girls went out for a walk (with their friends)'.

This simple rule allows learners to understand the following examples in (13) more readily:

(13)   a.   *Paul est sorti avec ses amis.*
          'Paul went out with his friends'.

        b.   *Paul a sorti la poubelle.*
          'Paul took out the trash'.

There is no need to present (13b) as an exception (as traditionally done in textbooks) if the principle associating verbs used transitively with *avoir* and verbs used intransitively with *être* is explained to beginning learners: (13a) requires *être* since *sortir* is used with an indirect object, whereas (13b) requires *avoir* because *sortir* is now followed by a direct object.

However, aside from verbs used reflexively consistently require the auxiliary *être*, the strict traditional semantic dichotomy between transitive and intransitive is no longer tenable as a number of verbs used transitively do not always require a direct object as in (14):[36]

(14) a. *Gisèle a chanté (un opéra italien).*
          'Gisèle sang (an Italian opera).'

      b. *Morgan a écrit (des poèmes) sur une plage mexicaine.*
          'Morgan wrote (poems) on a Mexican beach.'

      c. *Nous avons payé (l'addition) et nous sommes partis.*
          'We paid (the bill) and left.'

Other verbs such as *dormir* 'sleep' never take a direct object (15a) unless it is a time adverbial (15b), but still require *avoir* presumably by analogy with *endormir* 'to put to sleep' (15c):

(15) a. *J'ai bien dormi.*
          'I slept well.'

      b. *j'ai dormi tout l'après-midi.*
          'I slept all afternoon.'

      c. *La pluie a endormi les enfants.*
          'The rain put the children to sleep.'

Moreover, the current trend alluded to above sees an increasing number of transitive verbs used without a direct object, as indicated by a corpus of newspapers, magazines and novels (Larjavaara 1999). Thus, it appears that *connaître* 'know', *dédicacer* 'dedicate', *admirer* 'admirer', *embaucher* 'hire', classified as symmetric verbs, that is, "two-place transitive verbs which can be used intransitively" in constructions where "the object becomes the subject" as in (16) are quite common (*ibid*: 108):

(16) a. *Jean culpabilise Marie.*
          'John makes Mary feel guilty.'

      b. *Marie culpabilise.*
          'Mary feels guilty.'

Larjavaara also suggests that the objects of these verbs are latent rather than missing, which explaining why they still require *avoir*, that is, they are still used transitively

---

36. Numerous attempts to classifiy French verbs along a strict transitive/intransitive dichomoty have failed as summarized for instance in Florea (1988).

although the direct object is not expressed, as shown by the ungrammaticality of the examples in (17):

(17)   a.   *Les visiteurs ont admiré les peintures en silence.*
       b.   *Les visiteurs ont admiré en silence.*
       c.   **Les visiteurs sont admiré les peintures en silence.*
            'The visitors admired the paintings silently.'

These examples indicate that whether the direct object is expressed as in (17a) or latent as in (17b), the auxiliary *avoir* is required; *être* yields an ungrammatical sentence.[37]

Instruction on auxiliary selection must be followed by instruction on past participle agreement rules: when a direct object precedes a verb used transitively, it agrees in number and gender with its past participle; that rule also applies to all verbs used transitively; when a verb is used intransitively or reflexively in an idiomatic expression, the subject agrees with the past participle in number and gender.

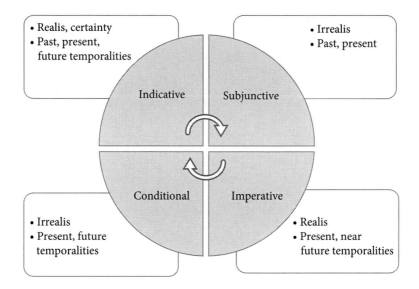

Figure 6.5. Mood selection

---

37.   The sentence *les visiteurs sont admirés en silence* is grammatical with a different meaning ('the visitors (not the paintings) are admired').

Finally, language learners in instructed settings must absolutely be made aware of the concepts of mood and modality. Figure 6.5 shows a basic way of selecting moods.

Language learners can draw on existing knowledge to understand the concepts of realis/certainty versus irrealis/incertainty; the former leading them to select an indicative tense based on the contextual temporality, the latter directing them to select the present/ past subjunctive or present/past conditional.

CHAPTER 7

Directions for future research

Sans la justesse de l'expression, pas de poésie.
Théodore de Banville

7.1 Introduction

The goal of this monograph was threefold: (a) to contribute to the already impressive body of research in the L2 acquisition of tense, aspect and mood/modality from a generative perspective, and in so doing, to present a more complete picture of the processes of L2 acquisition in general; (b) to bridge the gap between linguistic theory and L2 acquisition by showing how the latest theoretical minimalist assumptions apply to SLA research, so that they may inform each other; (c) to make empirical findings more accessible to language instructors by proposing concrete pedagogical applications.

7.2 Overview

The first chapter illustrated the complexity and subtleties of the TAM systems in French and English by highlighting similarities and differences between these two languages regarding the central concepts of time and temporality, lexical and grammatical aspect as well as morphological forms. Both languages use a variety of lexical, morphological, pragmatic and syntactic means to express past, present and future temporality, but differ in several respects. Thus, while the perfective *vs.* imperfective is the main aspectual opposition in French, it is between the perfective *vs.* progressive in English. The progressive is not grammaticalized in French, it is expressed by the lexical expression *être en train de*. Generally speaking, there are no one-to-one correspondences between morphological forms, or tense concordancing which displays a partial overlap for 'if' clauses for instance. Finally, what may be particularly difficult for anglophone learners of French is that a past tense form does not necessarily imply a past reference, a present tense form does not necessarily imply a present reference, while the *futur antérieur* can be the equivalent of a *passé composé*.

The second chapter's overview was another illustration that the lexical, semantic, and grammatical means of expression of mood and modality are as complex, subtle and sophisticated as the speakers' thoughts they are designed to convey. The universal concepts of possibility, certainty, probability and necessity are expressed by nouns, adjectives, adverbials, auxiliaries and verbs. English is characterized by morphologically and syntactically defective modal auxiliaries, French exemplifies morphologically and syntactically fully-fledged modal verbs. Moreover, mood/modality is not limited to modal auxiliaries and verbs, it also impacts temporality, blurring the lines between tense and modality. Although French is traditionally described as a mood language, it really is a mix between modality and mood.

Chapter 3 showed that from the feature matrix of the early days of generative syntax to a feature-based syntax in the current minimalist program, basic theoretical assumptions have been remarkably consistent. Traditional grammatical categories are now bundles of morpho-phonological, semantic and syntactic or formal features in a feature-based syntax. Following others, a word of caution was issued about using the latest theoretical assumptions to make learnability predictions for L2 learners. The Critical Period hypothesis was reviewed in light of the most recent empirical data to conclude that it is not sustainable. However, proponents of UG-constrained L2 grammars must still account for the inconsistent performance of L2 learners.

The generative literature review presented in Chapter 4 revealed an embarrassment of riches, but more studies focus on tense and aspect than on mood/modality. Most studies found evidence for successful L2 acquisition, with a progressive improvement in performance with proficiency, leading up to near-native performance, five reported mixed findings, while the only study (Hawkins & Liszka 2003) that claims to have found evidence in favor of impairment hypotheses is weakened by very small sample sizes (n = 2 to 5) as well as by a plausible alternative account (i.e. L1 prosodic transfer suggested by Campos 2009). It thus appears that L2 learners eventually acquire a TAM system with well established contrasts and systematicity, particularly for tense and aspect; no reliable conclusion can be reached for mood/modality for lack of empirical data. A permanent impairment preventing adult L2 learners to acquire new or different features would yield a much more erratic performance across various elicitation tasks without the high accuracy rates in required contexts reported in most of the studies reviewed. However, studies conducted with Russian and Spanish heritage speakers clearly indicate that TAM systems can undergo attrition and are vulnerable to incomplete acquisition.

Chapter 5 presented the empirical study conducted with L2 French learners at three proficiency levels who were administered production tasks, cloze tests and sentence completion tasks following a proficiency test. The findings were characterized by three main effects: proficiency, task and morphological forms effects, as the participants' performance improved with proficiency, the elicitation task (production tasks were easier than sentence completion or cloze tasks), and some morphological forms and lexical classes were better mastered than others. However, all groups produced a wide range of morphological forms with very high accuracy levels, notably on the production tasks. Overall, these instructed learners display a tense-aspect system with semantic contrasts, but with varying degrees of mastery across the different lexical classes. The participants performed poorly on forms that exhibit low frequency in the input as well as on morphological forms situated at interfaces, supporting the main claim of the Interface hypothesis. The findings support the minimalist claim that adult L2 learners can acquire functional categories even when they are not present in their L1, and that they can set feature values to the appropriate target language strength.

Finally, Chapter 6 aimed at bridging the gap between empirical findings and pedagogical applications stressing that foreign language teachers, theoretical linguists and SLA researchers can fruitfully collaborate to arrive at classroom tasks for instance. An overview of current instructional approaches and hypotheses was presented along with supporting evidence from relevant classroom studies. L2 learners' characteristics as well as basic elements of L2 acquisition – input and interaction, intake, feedback, output – were briefly reviewed as were computer-based technologies and how they evolved since the early 1970s along with pedagogical approaches from the grammar translation and audiolingual method to communicative language teaching and finally a content-based approach. Chun's (2011:663) best point may be that "[j]ust as there is no one universally accepted theory of SLA or one universally proven methodology of language teaching, so too are there no CALL tools that are effective universally for all learners".

7.3   Future research

As the literature review regarding the L2 acquisition of TAM in French presented in Chapter 4 showed, we still need to investigate: (a) the expression of present temporality (to the best of my knowledge, it has not yet been investigated in L2 French); (b) the expression of future temporality; (c) the acquisition of mood and modality; (c) the acquisition of modals and modal expressions. Then suggestions will also be made for methodology in teacher-centered research to test pedagogical hypotheses and approaches.

7.3.1 Present temporality

As reviewed in Chapter 1, with seven different functions from a punctual event to a future certainty or an immediate past, for instance, the indicative present in French is far from simple. Moreoever, and contrary to English, the present progressive is not grammaticalized (French uses lexical expressions instead, see Table 6), and the present indicative is required after certain adverbials (e.g. *depuis, il y a, voilà... que/cela fait...que*), as well as in tense concordancing in complex clauses (i.e. *si.., quand..*). The present indicative is the only tense to express present temporality, whereas English also uses the present progressive as already mentioned, an emphatic present with 'do', as well as the present perfect.

It would thus be interesting to investigate whether anglophone learners of L2 French do acquire the semantic distinctions expressed by the indicative present in simple clauses, the tense concordancing in complex clauses, and after adverbials. Do they attempt to use the *passé composé* in contexts where English requires the present perfect because of its similarity in form (auxiliary + past participle)?

7.3.2 Future temporality

Very few studies have investigated the expression of future temporality by L2 French learners aside from the studies reviewed above, so more data are needed from different elicitation tasks on not only *futur simple*, but also *praesens pro futuro* (present tense morphology) + time adverbial, *futur proche* (periphrastic future), and *futur antérieur* that appears to be difficult to acquire due to its lack of frequency and saliency as seen above. The stimuli of elicitation tasks should also include complex clauses as French requires the future in subordinate clauses when the predicate of the main clause is encoded with the future after *quand* 'when' or *dès que* 'as soon as', whereas English requires the indicative present.

7.3.3 Mood and modality

We need a lot more research in the development and acquisition of: (a) the complex and subtle indicative-subjunctive alternation; (b) the present and past conditional.

Current findings strongly suggest that the subjunctive is a late-acquired form, so highly advanced or near-native learners are needed to determine whether or not they eventually acquire it. The indicative is the default option while the subjunctive is a marked form that must be triggered by a semantic or syntactic expression. The accuracy means displayed above in Table 55 (Chapter 5) clearly showed a strong trigger effect even for the Advanced group which indicates that the variety of the triggers is an added difficulty in the acquisition of the indicative-subjunctive alternation. Future research may confirm the present trends (trigger effect and order of difficulty) with the same elicitation tasks and a larger number of stimuli, as well as different elicitation tasks to obtain converging evidence. One may choose to investigate a few triggers at a time rather than all of them in order to get more reliable results for each trigger since there are so many of them (8). It would also be interesting to compare English-speaking and Spanish-speaking (or another language instantiating a frequent use of subjunctive) learners of L2 French to determine whether or not L1 knowledge of the subjunctive facilitates its acquisition in L2 French.

The reader may recall that the indicative-subjunctive is not the only mood alternation in French (Chapter 2). There are three other atemporal moods – imperative, conditional, infinitive – which have barely been investigated from an L2 learning perspective, or at all. The most recent study investigating the use of the conditional with L2 French learners, Howard (2012), found that although it was used the most productively in required contexts (compared to the future and the subjunctive), it didn't go over 74% accuracy (see Chapter 4).

The conditional expresses irrealis (i.e. hypothetical aspect), it indicates that the event is construed as an alternative to reality, and its atemporality – it refers to the events that cannot be reliably placed in the past, present or future, although they suggest it – adds to its complexity for L2 learners. Are they able to identify the contexts in which the conditional is required (see Chapter 2)? Can they draw inferences from the other lexical and morphosyntactic elements of a complex clause (i.e. counterfactual *si* clauses with *imparfait*)?

Finally, the imperative and the infinitive appear to be acquired relatively early on based on anecdotal evidence, however, to the best of my knowledge, there is no empirical study targeting these two moods.[1]

7.3.4 Modals and modal expressions

We have only started to scratch the surface with the L2 acquisition of French modal verbs and expressions. Data are limited to those of the present study and to those obtained with immersion learners (e.g. Harley, Swain and colleagues, see Chapter 4). There are many other modal verbs and expressions to investigate (see Chapter 2) in order to understand how adult L2 learners acquire deontic, epistemic and dynamic modalities.

---

1. The infinitive is often mentioned in the production of beginning L2 learners before they fully distinguish between finite and non-finite forms though.

7.3.5   Methodology

The ideal empirical study would include: (a) a pre-test, multiple tasks, an immediate post-test and a delayed post-test;[2] (b) several different elicitation tasks as each one presents its own advantages, but also its drawbacks, and is only a partial window into the competence of the learners. However, together, they are much more likely to provide reliable, converging evidence; (c) large groups of L2 learners at different proficiency levels, all the way to near-native to test for ultimate attainment, with backgrounds as homogeneous as possible; (d) both quantitative and qualitative data.

Elicitation tasks need to be carefully chosen and designed based on the research questions. The literature review presented in Chapter 4 showed that current findings were obtained with an already impressive number of different tasks (e.g. narratives, cloze tests, compositions, oral interviews, story-telling, grammaticality judgment tasks, preference tasks, written translation, etc.), as well as with a variety of written and oral corpora. Future research needs to continue making use of a wide range of well-targeted and designed elicitations tasks (e.g. interpretation, production, comprehension, judgment tasks) to obtain reliable and converging data because various tasks complement each other. Native speaker and L2 learners alike are subject to performance constraints, but performance effects can be controlled or reduced with appropriately designed tasks.

Both cross-sectional and longitudinal studies make interesting and important contributions to our understanding of the acquisition of TAM systems, one is not better than the other, but we are in need of more longitudinal studies as they appear to be more rare than cross-sectional studies. Longitudinal research conducted in a study abroad context would be particularly interesting as it would introduce new elements such as an improved discourse-pragmatics interface that is important for the acquisition of mood and modality in particular. Both types of research should actively involve foreign language teachers who are such an important part in the ultimate attainment of instructed learners, particularly for the longitudinal research conducted in a study abroad context during which the teacher-learner interactions are much more frequent and thus potentially influential.

Last but not least, we should be careful to not lose sight of the two well-known, distinct, but equally important types of competence: competence as analytical knowledge from a generative perspective, and competence as both knowledge and ability from a sociolinguistic perspective as proposed by Hymes

---

2. Repeated testing and delayed post-tests are mostly limited to longitudinal studies as opposed to cross-sectional studies.

(1972), that is, the concept of communicative competence.[3] Although Hymes
(1972) initially proposed his concept of communicative competence in opposition
to the concept of grammatical competence, the two are not mutually exclusive, but
rather complementary and both are necessary. In practical terms, this means that
language instructors need to keep in mind that to be fully proficient, L2 learners
must acquire not only rules of usage, but also rules of use. In more general terms,
this illustrates the important point that different theoretical perspectives provide
a different piece of the puzzle, with each one contributing to our understanding
of L2 acquisition in general, and the development of TAM systems in particular.

---

3. Knowledge and ability was restated as knowledge and control (Bialystok & Sharwood
Smith 1985). See Widdowson (1989) for discussion.

Appendices

Appendix A – Summary of L2 French non-generative studies

Study	L1	Participants	Target	Elicitation task	Findings
Kaplan (1987)	English	college students (n = 16)	distinction between *PC* and *imparfait*	semi-structured oral interview	greater use and accuracy of PC than IMP
Harley (1989)	English	children in immersion classes (n = 270)	distinction between *PC* and *imparfait*	composition, cloze test, oral interview; 8 week treatment w/ functional approach	significant improvement in treatment condition but gains not maintained in posttest 3 months later
Swain & Lapkin (1990)	English	immersion students (grade 10) (n = 37)	conditional	written note taking task (among several others)	early immersion group produces significantly more tokens of conditional
Day & Shapson (1991)	English	early (grade 7) immersion students (n = 317)	conditional	cloze test, written composition, oral interview	significantly better performance of experimental groups on cloze and composition; all groups improved but unevenly so for control group
Harley (1992)	English	children in immersion classes (n = 36)	distinction between *PC* and *imparfait*	oral interviews, past tense narrations, future predictions	earlier development of *PC* than *IMP* and conditional, partial mastery of inflectional verbal system
Bergström (1995, 1997)	English	college students (n = 75)	distinction between *PC* and *imparfait*	written narrative, cloze test	task effect, *PC* acquired earlier than *IMP,* lexical class effect (dynamic verbs first then states in a gradual spread)

(Continued)

Study	L1	Participants	Target	Elicitation task	Findings
Schlyter (1990)	Swedish, German	adults (n = 2) children (n = 3)	tense-aspect development	corpus data	same order of morpheme acquisition for children and adults; temporal acquisition lags behind other areas
Schlyter (1996)	Swedish	3–7 year old children (n = 4)	distinction between *PC* and *imparfait*, foregrounding, backgrounding	recorded spontaneous story-telling	aspectual distinctions with temporal connectors made by time children are about 4 years old
Salaberry (1997)	English	college students	distinction between *PC* and *imparfait*	cloze test	learners differed from NSs for aspectually marked forms but not for unmarked forms with semantic lexical aspect
Salaberry (1998)	English	college students (n = 39)	distinction between *PC* and *imparfait*	written narrative, cloze test	L2 learners' performance differed from NSs' only for aspectually marked forms
Kihlstedt (1998)	Swedish	college students	distinction between *PC* and *imparfait*	oral data (conversations)	productive but limited use of both tenses; IMP limited to states with few semantic values
Ayoun (2001)	English	college students (n = 145)	distinction between *PC* and *imparfait*	written translation, GJT, preference task, production task	recasting most effective form of feedback compared to modeling and traditional grammar instruction; performance improved on PC but not on *imparfait*
Howard (2002)	English	college students (n = 18)	Aspect hypothesis, PC and IMP	oral interviews	*PC* used the most with telics then activities and statives last; order is reversed for the *imparfait*.

Study	L1	Participants	Target	Elicitation task	Findings
Moses (2002)	English	college students (n = 24)	future temporality	oral and written data	three developmental stages (pragmatic, lexical, morphological); first present, then periphrastic future and finally simple future
Nadasdi et al. (2003)	English	immersion students (n = 41)	future temporality	oral data	clear preference for periphrastic future, then simple future and present; L1 effect
Ayoun (2003)	English	college students (n = 34)	future temporality	cloze test, narrative	task (better on narrative than cloze) and proficiency effects; variety of morphological means
Ayoun (2004)	English	college students (n = 145)	distinction between *PC* and *imparfait*	written translation, GJT, preference task, production task	follow-up qualitative findings partially support Aspect hypothesis, tentative support for the *imparfait* spreading hypothesis
Bartning & Schlyter (2004)	Swedish	Adults	finite vs nonfinite forms, subject-verb plural agreement, TAM	two oral corpora (InterFra, Lund)	developmental stages are proposed; caveats: few data for some participants over a short period
Bartning (2005)	Swedish	adults (n = 8)	subjunctive	oral corpus (InterFra)	slow emergence of subjunctive increases from 23% accuracy among beginning learners to 86% among very advanced learners
Howard (2005)	English	college students (n = 18)	emergence and use of PQP	oral interviews	limited use even in appropriate contexts, *PC* used instead

(Continued)

Study	L1	Participants	Target	Elicitation task	Findings
Housen (2006)	Dutch	highschool students (n = 31)	TAM, (non) finite forms	oral production (story retell)	mixed findings, performance varies with aspect
Labeau (2007)	English	college students (n-63), bilinguals (n = 8)	*passé simple*	oral and written narratives based on fairy tale	very limited spontaneous use, slightly greater in guided task
Howard (2008)	English	college students (n = 18)	subjunctive	oral interviews	very limited subjunctive use but slight increase with proficiency
Izquierdo (2008)	Spanish	college students (n = 54)	PC, *imparfait*;	oral production and comprehension tasks, cloze	mixed findings, task effect
Howard (2012)	English	college students (n = 18)	futur, conditional, subjunctive	oral interviews	strong group and form effects, most productive use for conditional

Appendix B – Participants' background information

	Beginning (n = 14)	Intermediate (n = 15)	Advanced (n = 13)
gender	10 F, 4 M	9 F, 6 M	5 F, 8 M
age	22.5 (19–47)	22.4 (18–41)	24.46 (19–37)
status	sophomores (n = 3) juniors (n = 10) graduate (n = 1)	freshmen (n = 2) sophomores (n = 5) juniors (n = 2) seniors (n = 4) graduates (n = 2)	sophomores (n = 2) seniors (n = 3) graduates (n = 8)
major	French (n = 4) other (n = 10)	French (n = 9) other (n = 6)	French (n = 7) other (n = 5)
L1	English (n = 13) Spanish (n = 1)	English (n = 12) Spanish (n = 1) Vietnamese (n = 1) Arabic (n = 1)	English (n = 12) Spanish (n = 1)
L2	French (n = 13) Portuguese (n = 1)	French (n = 12) English (n = 3)	French (n = 11) English (n = 1) Spanish (n = 1)

	Beginning (n = 14)	Intermediate (n = 15)	Advanced (n = 13)
age L2	less than 5 (n = 1) 9–10 (n = 1) 13–14 (n = 6) 15–17 (n = 5) 18–20 (n = 1)	13–14 (n = 7) 15–17 (n = 4) 18–20 (n = 1) over 21 (n = 2)	6–8 (n = 1) 11–12 (n = 1) 13–14 (n = 4) 15–17 (n = 2) 18–20 (n = 4) over 21 (n = 1)
L2 setting	school (n = 14)	school (n = 13) both (n = 1) home (n = 1)	school (n = 11) both (n = 2)
L2 stay	yes (n = 6) no (n = 8)	yes (n = 11) no (n = 4)	yes (n = 12) no (n = 1)
L2 stay type	study (n = 4) vacation (n = 2)	study (n = 10) vacation (n = 1)	study (n = 8) residence (n = 3) vacation (n = 1)
L2 stay length	2 to 6 weeks	2 weeks to 5 months	3 weeks to 2 years
still learning	somewhat (n = 1) definitely (n = 13) not really (n = 1)	somewhat (n = 2) definitely (n = 12)	somewhat (n = 3) definitely (n = 8) not really (n = 2)
motivation	extremely (n = 4) very (n = 8) moderately (n = 2)	extremely (n = 4) very (n = 9) moderately (n = 1) not very (n = 1)	extremely (n = 7) very (n = 5) moderately (n = 1)

Appendix C – Production task summary (session 3, task 1)

Beginning group (n = 14)	words	Tokens	types	morphological forms	errors
BEG1	71	8	5	3	0
ratio	token/type .62			token/form .37	.0
BEG2	103	17	12	2	0
	ratio	.705		.117	.0
BEG3	146	19	12	4	2
	ratio	.63		.21	.105
BEG4	88	12	10	3	2
	ratio	.833		.25	.167
BEG5	107	10	8	3	0
	ratio	.80		.30	.0

(*Continued*)

Beginning group (n = 14)	words	Tokens	types	morphological forms		errors
BEG6	159	20	9	5		4
	ratio	.45		.25		.20
BEG7	158	20	12	5		9
	ratio	.60		.25		.45
BEG8	112	16	11	5		4
	ratio	.68		.31		.25
BEG9	61	10	8	3		1
	ratio	.80		.30		.01
BEG10	193	30	14	4		3
	ratio	.47		.13		.10
BEG11	95	13	10	4		1
	ratio	.769		.307		.076
BEG12	107	18	10	5		1
	ratio	.555		.277		.056
BEG13	147	17	15	3		3
	ratio	.882		.176		.176
BEG14	87	10	7	4		1
	ratio	.70		.40		.01
average	116.71	15.71		10.21	3.78	1.42
range	61–159	8–30		5–15	2–5	0–9

Intermediate group (n = 15)	words	tokens	types	morphological forms	errors
INT1	99	14	11	5	0
ratio		.78		.35	.0
INT11	125	17	10	4	4
ratio		.59		.23	.23
INT9	133	18	8	3	2
ratio		.444		.166	.11
INT10	131	19	15	7	4
ratio		.789		.368	.21
INT8	85	5	5	4	1
ratio		1.0		.80	.20

Intermediate group (n = 15)	words	tokens	types	morphological forms	errors
INT5	138	18	10	4	0
ratio		.555		.222	.0
INT7	88	8	7	4	1
ratio		.875		.50	.125
INT3	165	21	12	6	1
ratio		.57		.285	.047
INT6	63	11	9	5	2
ratio		.818		.454	.181
INT14	129	12	11	3	0
ratio		.916		.25	.0
INT15	80	12	10	5	0
ratio		.833		.416	.0
INT13	128	21	14	6	0
ratio		.67		.286	.0
INT4	110	16	10	5	3
ratio		.625		.31	.187
INT2	112	17	7	1	0
ratio		.41		.05	.0
INT12	105	14	10	4	0
ratio		.71		.28	.0
average	112.73	14.87	9.33	4.4	1.33
range	63–165	5–21	5–15	1–7	0–4

Group 3

Advanced group (n = 13)	words	tokens	types	morphological forms	errors
ADV1	182	23	19	5	1
ratio	type/token.83			token/form.22	token/error.04
ADV2	83	9	8	3	0
ratio	type/token.89			token/form.33	token/error.0
ADV3	60	9	4	2	1
ratio	type/token.44			token/form.22	token/error.11

(*Continued*)

Advanced group (n = 13)	words	tokens	types	morphological forms	errors
ADV4	119	18	7	4	0
ratio	type/token.388			token/form.22	token/error.0
ADV5	161	16	14	6	0
ratio	type/token.875			token/form.375	token/error.0
ADV6	165	16	9	4	1
ratio	type/token.56			token/form.25	token/error.06
ADV7	155	16	14	5	1
ratio	type/token.875			token/form.312	token/error.062
ADV8	173	16	11	6	1
ratio	type/token.687			token/form.375	token/error.062
ADV9	117	12	9	5	1
ratio	type/token.75			token/form.42	token/error.08
ADV10	133	20	17	4	1
ratio	type/token.85			token/form.20	token/error.05
ADV11	79	12	9	6	0
ratio	type/token.833			token/form.50	token/error.0
ADV12	131	17	11	5	0
ratio	type/token.647			token/form.294	token/error.0
ADV13	136	19	14	3	0
ratio	type/token.74			token/form.157	token/error.0
average	130.31	15.62	11.23	4.46	0.54
range	60–173	9–23	4–19	2–6	0–1

Apppendix C – Production task summary (session 4, task 1)

Group 1

Beginning group (n = 14)	words	tokens	types	morphological forms	errors
BEG1	104	11	8	4	2
ratio	token/type.727			token/form.36	token/error.18
BEG2	166	27	16	4	3
ratio	type/token.59			token/form.14	token/error.11
BEG3	104	17	10	4	1
ratio	type/token.588			token/form.23	token/error.05

Beginning group (n = 14)	words	tokens	types	morphological forms	errors
BEG4	97	15	12	3	4
ratio	type/token.666			token/form.20	token/error.27
BEG5	77	10	8	3	2
ratio	type/token.80			token/form.30	token/error.2
BEG6	101	13	8	5	1
ratio	type/token.615			token/form.384	token/error.07
BEG7	265	33	16	5	7
ratio	type/token.48			token/form.14	token/error.21
BEG8	156	22	10	6	2
ratio	type/token.45			token/form.27	token/error.09
BEG9	132	21	14	4	0
ratio	type/token.666			token/form.19	token/error.0
BEG10	228	31	15	5	0
ratio	type/token.483			token/form.161	token/error.0
BEG11	119	16	13	1	1
ratio	type/token.81			token/form.25	token/error.06
BEG12	130	19	12	6	1
ratio	type/token.63			token/form.315	token/error.052
BEG13	136	21	16	7	5
ratio	type/token.76			token/form.33	token/error.238
BEG14	115	13	8	4	2
ratio	type/token.615			token/form.307	token/error.153
average	137.86	19.21	11.86	4.36	2.21
range	77–265	10–33	8–16	1–7	0–7

Group 2

INT group (n = 15)	words	tokens	types	morphological forms	errors
INT1	126	17	13	3	0
ratio	token/type.764			token/form.176	token/error.0
INT2	97	11	8	2	0
ratio	token/type.727			token/form.181	token/error.0
INT3	163	23	12	5	0
ratio	token/type.521			token/form.217	token/error.0

(*Continued*)

INT group (n = 15)	words	tokens	types	morphological forms	errors
INT4	84	14	10	4	1
ratio	token/type.714			token/form.285	token/error.071
INT5	159	24	15	4	2
ratio	token/type.625			token/form.166	token/error.083
INT6	85	12	11	5	1
ratio	token/type.916			token/form.416	token/error.083
INT7	85	12	8	6	0
ratio	token/type.666			token/form.50	token/error.0
INT8	149	15	10	4	0
ratio	token/type.666			token/form.266	token/error.0
INT9	124	20	12	5	6
ratio	token/type.60			token/form.25	token/error.30
INT10	135	24	16	5	0
ratio	token/type.666			token/form.208	token/error.0
INT11	145	24	9	5	1
ratio	token/type.375			token/form.208	token/error.041
INT12	132	18	14	4	0
ratio	token/type.777			token/form.222	token/error.0
INT13	167	17	10	4	0
ratio	token/type.588			token/form.235	token/error.0
INT14	135	22	16	5	0
ratio	token/type.727			token/form.227	token/error.0
INT15	66	11	9	6	1
ratio	token/type.818			token/form.545	token/error.09
average	123.47	16	11.53	4.47	.8
range	66–167	11–24	8–16	2–6	0–6

ADV group (n = 13)	words	tokens	types	morphological forms	errors
ADV1	164	23	13	5	0
		.565		.217	0
ADV2	98	11	8	3	1
		.727		.272	.09
ADV3	95	9	8	5	2
		.89		.56	.22
ADV4	180	26	15	6	2
		.576		.23	.077
ADV5	195	30	19	6	3
		.633		.2	.10
ADV6	249	31	21	7	1
		.677		.225	.03
ADV7	152	15	10	4	0
		.666		.266	0
ADV8	236	29	16	6	2
		.551		.206	.06
ADV9	141	20	16	4	0
		.8		.2	0
ADV10	157	20	10	6	1
		.5		.3	.05
ADV11	130	12	10	2	1
		.833		.166	.08
ADV12	126	12	9	4	0
		.75		.33	0
ADV13	231	24	11	5	0
		.458		.208	0
average	165.69	19.23	12.76	4.84	1
range	95–236	9–31	8–21	2–7	0–3

Appendix D

A concrete example of an effective roadmap for the instruction of the aspectual distinction between the perfective and imperfective would be as follows. It is not intended to be exhaustive, it is a simple and basic illustration of how beginning learners may be exposed to difficult concepts.

a. Awareness/consciousness (how basic universal concepts are expressed in their L1): in English, the actions expressed by verbs are viewed as either completed or in progress. For instance: Mark played tennis yesterday vs Mark was playing tennis when I saw him.

b. Clear, thorough explanations of how they are expressed in the L2: French differs from English in that the actions expressed by verbs are viewed as either completed or not. If they were completed within their specific time frame (e.g. yesterday, all summer), they are said to be perfective and are expressed with the *passé composé*. If they were not completed within their specific time frame, they are said to be imperfective and are expressed with the *imparfait*. Thus, in *Marc a joué au tennis hier*, Mark started and finished playing tennis yesterday; whereas in *Marc jouait au tennis quand je l'ai vu*, the time frame is quite small (when I saw him) and during all that time he did not stop playing. The concept of time frame is very important. Consider the following examples: *Une belle femme est entrée, elle était blonde* 'a beautiful woman walked in, she was blonde'. The action of walking is expressed with the perfective because it was completed (the person did not get stuck at the door), but being blonde is a fact that did not change while the person was walking, it is imperfective, so it is expressed with the *imparfait*.

c. Connect to existing L2 knowledge: explain that the present (to which classroom learners are exposed first) is imperfective just like the imperfective, but that the present refers to an event/state that is still relevant whereas the *imparfait* refers to an event/state/description that is no longer relevant in the present.

d. Stress that strict one-to-one correspondences between L1 and L2 are rare: most of the time the English preterite will correspond to the *passé composé*, and the English progressive will correspond to the *imparfait*, but not always. Provide examples in context.

e. Mapping the concept to the morphology and working out the inflectional morphology: auxiliary selection for the *passé composé* (cf Chapter 6, Section 8), past participle forms, inflectional endings for *imparfait*

f. Working out the syntactic component: past participle agreement as stated in Chapter 6, Section 8.

g. Working out the semantic component: the *passé composé* is essentially perfective whereas the *imparfait* is imperfective, durative and iterative (with examples).

h. Working out the exceptions: introduce the distinction between prototypical and nonprototypical uses; *elle avait vingt ans vs elle a eu vingt ans*.

References

Abouda, L. 2002. Négation, interrogation et alternance indicatif-subjonctif. *French Language Studies* 12: 1–22.

Abraham, L. 2008. Computer-mediated glosses in second language reading comprehension and vocabulary learning: A meta-analysis. *Computer Assisted Language Learning* 21: 199–226.

Abrahamsson, N. 2012. Age of onset and nativelike L2 ultimate attainment of morphosyntactic and phonetic intuition. *Studies in Second Language Acquisition* 34: 187–214.

Abrams, Z.I. 2006. From theory to practice: Intracultural CMC in the L2 classroom. In Ducate & Arnold (eds), 181–209.

Abutalebi, J., Cappa, S.F. & Perani, D. 2001. The bilingual brain as revealed by functional neuro-imaging. *Bilingualism: Language and Cognition* 4: 179–190.

Achard, M. 1998. *Representation of Cognitive Structures. Syntax and Semantics of French Sentential Complements*. Berlin: Mouton de Gruyter.

Achard, M. 2002. The meaning and distribution of French moods and inflections. In *Grounding. The Epistemic Footing of Deixis and Reference*, F. Brisard (ed.), 197–249. Berlin: Mouton de Gruyter.

Adger, D. 2003. *Core Syntax*. Oxford: OUP.

Adger, D. 2006. Remarks on minimalist theory and move. *Journal of Linguistics* 42: 663–673.

Adger, D. & Ramchand, G. 2005. Merge and Move: Wh-depencies revisited. *Linguistic Inquiry* 36: 161–193.

Adger, D. & Smith, J. 2005. Variation and the minimalist program. In *Syntax and Variation. Reconciling the Biological and the Social* [Current Issues in Linguistic Theory 265], L. Cornips & K.P. Corrigan (eds), 149–178. Amsterdam: John Benjamins.

Aitchison, J. 1989. *The Articulate Mammal: An Introduction to Psycholinguistics*. London: Unwin Hyman.

Aikhenvald, A. 2004. *Evidentiality*. Oxford: OUP.

Alderson, J., Clapham, C. & Steel, D. 1997. Metalinguistic knowledge, language aptitude and language proficiency. *Language Teaching Research* 1: 93–121.

Allen, J.P.B., Cummins, J., Mougeon, R. & Swain, M. 1983. *The Development of Bilingual Proficiency: Second Year Report*. Toronto: Ontario Institute for Studies in Education.

Andersen, R. 1986. El desarrollo de la morfología verbal en el español como segundo idioma. In *Adquisición del lenguaje – Acquisição da linguagem*, J. Meisel (ed.), 115–138. Frankfurt: Klaus-Dieter Vervuert.

Andersen, R. 1991. Developmental sequences: the emergence of aspect marking in second language acquisition. In *Crosscurrents in Second Language Acquisition and Linguistic Theories* [Language Acquisition and Language Disorders 2], T. Huebner & C.A. Ferguson (eds), 305–324. Amsterdam: John Benjamins.

Andrews, B. 1992. Aspect in past tenses in English and French. *International Review of Applied Linguistics* 30: 281–297.

Asher, J. 1977. *Learning Another Language Through Actions: The Complete Teacher's Guidebook*. Los Gatos, CA: Sky Oaks Productions.

Au, T., Knightly, L, Jun, S. & Oh, J. 2002. Overhearing a language during childhood. *Psychological Science* 13: 238–243.

Au, T., Knightly, L, Jun, S., Oh, J. & Romo, L. 2008. Salvaging a childhood language. *Journal of Memory and Language* 58: 998–1011.

Authier-Revuz, J. 2004. La représentation du discours autre: Un champ multiplement hétérogène. In *Le discours rapporté dans tous ses états*, J. M. Lopez-Muñoz, S. Marnette & L. Rosier (eds), 35–53. Paris: L'Harmattan.

Ayoun, D. 1999. Verb movement in French L2 acquisition. *Bilingualism: Language and Cognition* 2: 103–125.

Ayoun, D. 2000. Web-based elicitation tasks in SLA research. *Language Learning and Technology* 3: 78–98.

Ayoun, D. 2001. The role of negative and positive feedback in the second language acquisition of *passé composé* and *imparfait*. *The Modern Language Journal* 85: 226–243.

Ayoun, D. 2003. *Parameter-Setting Theory and Language Acquisition*. London: Continuum.

Ayoun, D. 2004. The effectiveness of written recasts in the second language acquisition of aspectual distinctions in French: A follow-up study. *Modern Language Journal* 88: 31–55.

Ayoun, D. 2005a. Verb movement in the L2 acquisition of English by adult native speakers of French. *EUROSLA Yearbook* 5: 35–75.

Ayoun, D. 2005b. The acquisition of tense and aspect in L2 French from a Universal Grammar perspective. In Ayoun & Salaberry (eds), 79–127.

Ayoun, D. 2005c. The development of the future in L2 French. Talk given at the Second Language Research Forum, Teachers College, Columbia University.

Ayoun, D. 2007. The second language acquisition of grammatical gender and agreement. In *French Applied Linguistics* [Language Learning & Language Teaching 16], D. Ayoun (ed.), 130–170. Amsterdam: John Benjamins.

Ayoun, D. & Rothman, J. 2013. Generative approaches to the L2 acquisition of temporal-aspectual-mood (TAM) systems. In *Research Design and Methodology in Studies in L2 Tense and Aspect*, R. Salaberry & L. Comajoan (eds), 119–156. Berlin: Mouton de Gruyter.

Ayoun, D. & Salaberry, R. (eds). 2005. *Tense and Aspect in Romance Languages: Theoretical and Applied Perspectives* [Studies in Bilingualism 29]. Amsterdam: John Benjamins.

Ayoun, D. & Salaberry, R. 2008. The expression of temporality in English as a foreign language by French native speakers. *Language Learning* 58: 555–595.

Bach, E. 1965. On some recurrent types of transformations. In *Report of the Sixteenth Annual Round Table Meeting on Linguistics and Language Studies*, C. Kreidler (ed.), 3–18. Washington DC: Georgetown University Press.

Barbazan, M. 2010. Modèles explicatifs, modèles descriptifs: pour une interaction effective entre linguistique et cognition. *Cahiers Chronos* 21: 25–43.

Bardovi-Harlig, K. 2000. *Tense and Aspect in Second Language Acquisition: Form, meaning, and use*. Oxford: Blackwell.

Bardovi-Harlig, K. 2002. A new starting point? Investigating formulaic use and input in future expression. *Studies in Second Language Acquisition* 24: 189–198.

Bardovi-Harlig, K. 2004a. Monopolizing the future. How the go-future breaks into will's territory and what it tells us about SLA. *EUROSLA Yearbook* 4: 177–201.

Bardovi-Harlig, K. 2004b. The emergence of grammaticalized future. Expression in longitudinal production data. In *Form-Meaning Connections in Second Language Acquisition*, B. VanPatten (ed.), 115–137. Mahwah, NJ: Lawrence Erlbaum Associates.

Bardovi-Harlig, K. 2005. Tracking the illusive imperfect in adult second language acquisition: Refining the hunt. In *Aspectual Inquiries*, P. Kempchinsky & R. Slabakova (eds), 397–419. Dordrecht: Kluwer.

Bardovi-Harlig, K. & Bergström, A. 1996. Acquisition of tense and aspect in second language and foreign language learning: Learner narratives in ESL and FFL. *Canadian Modern Language Review* 52: 308–330.

Bartning, I. 1997. L'apprenant dit avancé et son acquisition d'une langue étrangère: Tour d'horizon et esquisse d'une caractérisation de la variété avancée. *Acquisition et Interaction en Langue Etrangère* 9: 9–50.

Bartning, I. 2005. Je ne pense pas que ce soit vrai – le subjonctif un trait tardif dans l'acquisition du français L2. In *Hommage à Jane Nystedt*, M. Metzeltin (ed.), 31–49. Wien: Drei Eidechsen.

Bartning, I. 2012. Synthèses rétrospectives et nouvelles perspectives développementales. Les recherches acquisitionnelles en français L2 à l'université de Stockholm. *Language, Interaction and Acquisition* 3: 7–28.

Bartning, I. & Schlyter, S. 2004. Itinéraires acquisitionnels et stades de développement en français L2. *French Language Studies* 14: 281–299.

Battye, A. & Roberts, I. 1995. Introduction. In *Clause Structure and Language Change*, A. Battye & I. Roberts (eds), 3–28. New York, NY: OUP.

Beard, R. 1987. Morpheme order in a lexeme/morpheme-based morphology. *Lingua* 72: 1–44.

Beck, M.L. 1998. L2 acquisition and obligatory head movement: English-speaking learners of German and the local impairment hypothesis. *Studies in Second Language Acquisition* 20: 311–348.

Belletti, A. 2004 (ed.). *Structures and Beyond. The Cartography of Syntactic Structures*, Vol. 3. New York, NY: OUP.

Belz, J.A. & Kinginger, C. 2003. Discourse options and the development of pragmatic competence by classroom learners of German: The case of address forms. *Language Learning* 53: 591–647.

Benmamoun, E. 2000. *The Feature Structure of Functional Categories*. New York, NY: OUP.

Benati, A. 2001. A comparative study of the effects of processing instruction and output-based instruction on the acquisition of the Italian future tense. *Language Teaching Research* 5: 95–127.

Benati, A. 2005. The effects of Processing Instruction, traditional instruction, and meaningful based output instruction on the acquisition of the English past tense. *Language Teaching Research* 9: 67–93.

Benveniste, E. 1974. *Problèmes de linguistique générale*. Paris: Gallimard.

Bergström, A. 1995. *The Expression of Past Temporal Reference by English-speaking Learners of French*. Ph.D. dissertation, Pennsylvania State University, State College.

Bergström, A. 1997. L'influence des distinctions aspectuelles sur l'acquisition du temps en français langue étrangère. *Acquisition et Interaction en Langue Etrangère* 9: 51–82.

Bernaus, M., Moore, E. & Azevedo Cordeiro, A. 2007. Affective factors influencing plurilingual students' acquisition of Catalan in a Catalan-Spanish bilingual context. *The Modern Language Journal* 91: 235–246.

Bever, T. 1981. Normal acquisition process explain the critical period for language learning. In *Individual Differences and Universals in Language Learning Aptitude*, K. Diller (ed.), 176–198. Rowley, MA: Newbury House.

Bhatt, R. 2007. *Interface Explorations. Covert Modality in Non-finite Contexts*. Berlin: Walter de Gruyter.

Bialystok, E. & Hakuta, K. 1994. *In Other Words: The Science and Psychology of Second Language Acquisition*. New York: Basic Books.

Bialystok, E. & Hakuta, K. 1999. Confounded age: Linguistic and cognitive factors in age differences for second language acquisition. In Birdsong (ed.), 161–181.

Bialystok, E. & Sharwood-Smith, M. 1985. Interlanguage is not a state of mind: An evaluation of the construct for second-language acquisition. *Applied Linguistics* 6: 101–117.

Biber, D., Finegan, E., Atkinson, D., Beck, A., Burges, D. & Burges, J. 1999. *The Longman Grammar of Spoken and Written English*. London: Longman.

Binnick, R. 1991. *Time and the Verb*. Oxford: Blackwell.

Birdsong, D. 1992. Ultimate attainment in second language acquisition. *Language* 68: 706–755.

Birdsong, D. 1999. Introduction: Whys and why nots of the Critical Period Hypothesis for second language acquisition. In Birdsong (ed.), 1–22.

Birdsong, D. 1999. *Second Language Acquisition and the Critical Period Hypothesis*. Mahwah, NJ: Lawrence Erlbaum Associates.

Birdsong, D. 2004. Second language acquisition and ultimate attainment. In *The Handbook of Applied Linguistics*, A. Davies & C. Elder (eds), 82–105. Oxford: Blackwell.

Birdsong, D. & Molis, M. 1998. Age and maturation in L2A: A replication of Johnson and Newport. Ms, University of Texas at Austin.

Bittner, M. 2005. Future discourse in a tenseless language. *Journal of Semantics* 22: 339–387.

Bittner, M. 2008. Aspectual universals of temporal anaphora. In *Theoretical and Cross-linguistic Approaches to the Semantics of Aspect* [Linguistik Aktuell/Linguistics Today 110], S. Rothstein (ed.), 349–385. Amsterdam: John Benjamins.

Blaikner-Hohenwart, G. 2006. Der subjonctif als 'gefrorene Morphosyntax'? *Zeitschrift für romanische Philologie* 122: 613–623.

Blake, C. 2009. Potential of text-based Internet chats for improving oral fluency in a second language. *The Modern Language Journal* 93: 227–240.

Blake, R. 2005. Bimodal CMC: The glue of language learning at a distance. *CALICO Journal* 22: 497–511.

Blanche-Benveniste, C. 2005. Structure et exploitation de la conjugaison des verbes en français contemporain. *Le Français aujourd'hui* 148: 75–87.

Blanche-Benveniste, C. & Adam, J.-P. 1999. La conjugaison des verbes: Virtuelle, attestée, défective. *Recherches sur le français parlé* 15: 87–112.

Bley-Vroman, R. 1989. What is the logical problem of language acquisition? In *Linguistic Perspectives on Second Language Acquisition*, S. Gass & J. Schachter (eds), 41–64. Cambridge: CUP.

Bley-Vroman, R. 1990. The logical problem of foreign language learning. *Linguistic Analysis* 20: 3–49.

Bley-Vroman, R. 2009. The evolving context of the fundamental difference hypothesis. *Studies in Second Language Acquisition* 31: 175–198.

Bley-Vroman, R., Felix, S. & Ioup, G. 1988. The accessibility of Universal Grammar in adult language learning. *Second Language Research* 4: 1–32.

Block, D. 2000. Revisiting the gap between SLA researchers and language teachers. *Links & Letters* 7: 129–143.

Blyth, C. 2005. From empirical findings to the teaching of aspectual distinctions. In Ayoun & Salaberry (eds), 212–252.

Bobaljik, J. 1995. Merge, move and the extension requirement. *MIT Working Papers in Minimalist Syntax* 27: 41–64.

Bohnemeyer, J. 2002. *The Grammar of Time Reference in Yukatek Maya*. Munich: Lincom.

Bonami, A. 2002. A syntax-semantics interface for tense and aspect in French. In *Proceedings of the 8th International HPSG Conference*, F. van Eynde, L. Hellan & D. Beerman (eds), 31–50. Stanford, CA: CSLI.

Bongaerts, T. 1999. Ultimate attainment in L2 pronunciation: the case of very advanced late L2 learners. In Birdsong (ed.), 133–159.

Bongaerts, T. 2003. Effets de l'âge sur l'acquisition de la prononciation d'une seconde langue. *Acquisition et Interaction en Langue Etrangère* 18: 79–98.

Bongaerts, T. 2005. Introduction: Ultimate attainment and the critical period hypothesis for second language acquisition. *IRAL* 43: 259–267.

Bongaerts, T., Planken, B. & Schils, E. 1997. Age and ultimate attainment in the pronunciation of a foreign language. *Studies in Second Language Acquisition* 19: 447–465.

Bongaerts, T., Planken, B., van Summeren, C. & Schils, E. 1995. Can late starters attain a native accent in a foreign language? A test of the Critical Period Hypothesis. In *The Age Factor in Second Language Acquisition*, D. Singleton & Z. Lengyel (eds), 30–50. Clevedon: Multilingual Matters.

Borer, H. 1984. *Parametric Syntax. Case studies in Semitic and Romance languages*. Dordrecht: Foris.

Borer, H. 1993. The projection of arguments. *Functional Projections, University of Massachusetts Occasional Papers* 17: 19–47.

Borer, H. 2005. *The Normal Course of Events. Structuring Tense*, Vol. 2. Oxford: OUP.

Borgovono, C. & Prévost, P. 2003. Knowledge of polarity subjunctive in L2 Spanish. *Proceedings of the 27th Boston University Conference on Language Development*, B. Beachley, A. Brown & F. Conlin (eds), 150–161. Somerville, MA: Cascadilla Press.

van Boxtel, S.J. 2005. *Can the Late Bird Catch the Worm? Ultimate Attainment in L2 Syntax*. Utrecht: LOT.

Bres, J. & Mellet, S. (eds). 2009. *Dialogisme et marqueurs grammaticaux*. Paris: Armand Colin.

Brown, A. 2009. Students' and teachers' perceptions of effective foreign language teaching: A comparison of ideals. *The Modern Language Journal* 93: 46–60.

Brown, C. 2000. The interrelation between speech perception and phonological acquisition from infant to adult. In *Second Language Acquisition and Linguistic Theory*, J. Archibald (ed.), 4–63. Malden, MA: Blackwell.

Burger, S. & Chrétien, S. 2001. The development of oral production in content-based second language courses at the University of Ottawa. *The Canadian Modern Language Review* 58: 84–102.

Burgess, J. & Etherington, S. 2002. Focus on grammatical form: Explicit or implicit. *System* 30: 433–458.

Bybee, J. 1985. *Morphology: A Study of the Relation between Meaning and Form* [Typological Studies in Language 9]. Amsterdam: John Benjamins.

Bybee, J., Perkins, R. & Pagliuca, W. 1994. *The Evolution of Grammar: Tense, Aspect and Modality in the Languages of the World*. Chicago, IL: University of Chicago Press.

Bybee, J. 1995. Regular morphology and the lexicon. *Language and Cognitive Processes* 10: 425–455.

Callan, D., Jones, J., Callan, A. & Akahane-Yamada, R. 2004. Phonetic perceptual identification by native- and second-language speakers differentially activates brain regions involved with acoustic phonetic processing and those involved with articulatory-auditory/orosensory internal models. *Neuroimage* 22: 1182–1194.

Campos, G. 2009. L2 production of English past morphology in Advanced Spanish natives: syntactic deficits of phonotactic transfer? In *Proceedings of the 10th Generative Approaches to Second Language Acquisition Conference*, M. Bowles, T. Ionin, S. Montrul & A. Tremblay (eds), 210–219. Somerville, MA: Cascadilla Proceedings Project.

Carnie, A. 2010. *Constituent Structure*, 2nd edn. Oxford: OUP.

Carr, N.T. 2006. Computer-based testing: prospects for innovative assessment. In Ducate & Arnold (eds), 289–312.

Carreira, M. 2004. Seeking explanatory adequacy: A dual approach to understanding the term heritage language learner. *Heritage Learner Journal* 2: 1–25.

Carroll, S.E. 2001. *Input and Evidence: The Raw Material of Second Language Acquisition*. Amsterdam: John Benjamins.

Carroll, S. 2004. Some comments on input processing and processing instruction. In VanPatten (ed.), 293–310.

Castañeda, D. 2011. The effects of instruction enhanced by video/photo blogs and wikis on learning the distinctions of the Spanish preterite and imperfect. *Foreign Language Annals* 44: 692–711.

Caudal, P. & Roussarie, L. 2005. Aspectual viewpoints, speech act functions and discourse structure. In *Aspectual Inquiries*, P. Kempchinsky & R. Slabakova (eds), 265–290. Dordrecht: Springer.

Caudal, P. & Vetters, C. 2005. Un traitement conjoint du conditionnel, du futur et de l'imparfait: Les temps comme fonction du langage. *Cahiers Chronos* 12: 109–124.

Celce-Murcia, M. & Larsen-Freeman, D. 1999. *The Grammar Book. An ESL/EFL Teacher's Course*, 2nd edn. Boston, MA: Heinle & Heinle.

Cenoz, J. & Jessner, U. (eds). 2000. *English in Europe. The Acquisition of a Third Language*. Clevedon: Multilingual Matters.

Cervoni, J. 1987. Les modalités. In *L'énonciation*, J. Cervoni (ed.), 65–103. Paris: Presses Universitaires de France.

Chapelle, C. & Hegelheimer, V. 2004. The language teacher in the 21st century. In *New Perspectives on CALL for Second Language Classrooms*, S. Fotos & C. Browne (eds), 299–316. Mahwah, NJ: Lawrence Erlbaum Associates.

Chaudron, C. 1983. Foreigner talk in the classroom – An aid to learning? In *Classroom Oriented Research in Second Language Acquisition*, H. Seliger & M. Long (eds), 127–145. Rowley, MA: Newbury House.

Chaudron, C. 1985. Intake: On models and methods for discovering learners' processing of input. *Studies in Second Language Acquisition* 7: 1–14.

Chiswick, B. & Miller, P. 2008. A test of the Critical Period hypothesis for language learning. *Journal of Multilingual and Multicultural Development* 29: 16–29.

Chomsky, N. 1959. A review of B.F. Skinner's Verbal Behavior. *Language* 35: 26–58.

Chomsky, N. 1965. *Aspects of the Theory of Syntax*. Cambridge, MA: The MIT Press.

Chomsky, N. 1981. *Lectures on Government and Binding. The Pisa Lectures*. Dordrecht: Foris.

Chomsky, N. 1989. Some notes on economy of derivation and representation. *MIT Working Papers* 10: 43–74.

Chomsky, N. 1991. Some notes on economy of derivation and representation. In *Principles and Parameters of Comparative Grammar*, R. Freidin (ed.), 417–454. Cambridge, MA: The MIT Press.

Chomsky, N. 1992. A minimalist program for linguistic theory. *MIT Occasional Papers in Linguistics* 1.

Chomsky, N. 1993. A Minimalist Program for linguistic theory. In *The View from Building 20: Essays in Linguistics in Honor of Sylvain Bromberger*, K. Hale & S.J. Keyser (eds), 1–52. Cambridge, MA: The MIT Press.

Chomsky, N. 1994. Bare Phrase Structure. *MIT Occasional Papers in Linguistics* 5.

Chomsky, N. 1995. *The Minimalist Program*. Cambridge, MA: The MIT Press.

Chomsky, N. 1999a. On the nature, use, and acquisition of language. In *Handbook of Child Language Acquisition*, T. Bhatia & W. Ritchie (eds), 33–54. San Diego, CA: Academic Press.

Chomsky, N. 1999b. Derivation by phase. *MIT Occasional Papers in Linguistics* 18: 1–43.

Chomsky, N. 2000. Minimalist inquiries: the framework. In *Step by Step: Essays on Minimalist Syntax in Honor of Howard Lasnik*, R. Martin, D. Michaels & J. Uriagereka (eds), 89–155. Cambridge, MA: MIT Press.

Chomsky, N. 2001. Derivation by phase. In *Ken Hale: A Life in Language*, M. Kenstowicz (ed.), 1–52. Cambridge, MA: The MIT Press.

Chomsky, N. 2002/2004. Beyond explanatory adequacy. *MIT Occasional Papers in Linguistics* 20. Reprint in *Structures and Beyond. The Cartography of Syntactic Structure*, Vol. 3, A. Belletti (ed.), 104–131. New York, NY: OUP.

Chomsky, N. 2005. Three factors in language design. *Linguistic Inquiry* 36: 1–22.

Chomsky, N. 2006. *Language and Mind*, 3rd edn. Cambridge: CUP.

Chun, D.M. 2002. *Discourse Intonation in L2: From Theory and Research to Practice* [Language Learning & Language Teaching 1]. Amsterdam: John Benjamins.

Chun, D.M. 2006. CALL technologies for L2 reading. In Ducate & Arnold (eds), 69–98.

Chun, D.M. 2011. Computer-assisted language learning. In *Handbook of Research in Second Language Teaching and Learning*, E. Hinkel (ed.), 663–680. London: Routledge.

Chung, S. & Timberlake, A. 1985. Tense, aspect, and mood. In *Language Typology and Syntactic Description*, Vol. III, T. Shopen (ed.), 202–258. Cambridge: Cambridge University Press.

Cinque, G. 1999. *Adverbs and Functional Heads*. Oxford: OUP.

Cinque, G. 2002 (Ed.). *Functional Structure in DP and IP. The Cartography of Syntactic Structures*, Vol. 1. Oxford: OUP.

Cinque, G. 2006. *Restructuring and Functional Heads: The Cartography of Syntactic Structures*. Oxford: OUP.

Clahsen, H. & Muysken, P. 1986. The availability of Universal Grammar to adult and child learners: a study of the acquisition of German word order. *Second Language Research* 5: 93–119.

Coates, J. 1983. *The Semantics of the Modal Auxiliaries*. London: Croon Helm.

Collentine, J. 1998. Processing Instruction and the subjunctive. *Hispania* 81: 576–587.

Comajoan, L. 2005. The acquisition of perfective and imperfective morphology and the marking of grounding marking in Catalan. In Ayoun & Salaberry (eds), 35–77.

Comrie, B. 1976. *Aspect*. Cambridge: CUP.

Comrie, B. 1985. *Tense*. Cambridge: CUP.

Confais, J.-P. 1995. *Temps modes aspects. Les approches des morphèmes verbaux et leurs problèmes à l'exemple du français et de l'allemand*. Toulouse: Presses Universitaires du Mirail.

Cook, V. 1992. Evidence for multi-competence. *Language Learning* 42: 557–591.

Copley, B. 2009. *The Semantics of the Future*. New York, NY: Psychology Press.

Cowart, W. 1997. *Experimental Syntax. Applying Objective Methods to Sentence Judgments*. Thousand Oaks: Sage Publications.

Cumming, A. 1990. Metalinguistic and ideational thinking in second language composing. *Written Communication* 7: 482–511.

Dahl, Ö. 1985. *Tense and Aspect Systems*. Oxford: Basil Blackwell.

Day, E. & Shapson, S. 1991. Integrating formal and functional approaches to language teaching in French immersion: An experimental study. *Language Learning* 41: 25–58.

DeCarrico, J. 1986. Tense, aspect and time in the English modality system. *TESOL Quarterly* 20: 665–682.

Declerck, R. 2006. The relation between temporal and modal uses of indicative verb forms. *Cahiers Chronos* 13: 215–227.

DeKeyser, R. 2003. Implicit and explicit learning. In *The Handbook of Second Language Acquisition*, C. Doughty & M. Long (eds), 313–348. Oxford: Blackwell.

DeKeyser, R. & Koeth, J. 2011. Cognitive aptitudes for second language learning. In *Handbook of Research in Second Language Teaching and Learning*, E. Hinkel (ed.), 395–406. London: Routledge.

DeKeyser, R., Salaberry, M., Robinson, P. & Harrington, M. 2002. What gets processed in processing instruction: A commentary on Bill VanPatten's Processing Instruction: Update. *Language Learning* 52: 805–823.

Dendale, P. 1994. Devoir épistémique, marqueur modal ou évidentiel? *Langue française* 102: 24–40.

Dendale, P. & Van Bogaert, J. 2007. A semantic description of French lexical evidential markers and the classification of evidentials. *Rivista di Linguistica* 19: 65–89.

Dendale, P. & Van Der Auwera, J. (eds). 2001. *Cahiers Chronos* 8. Amsterdam: Rodopi.

den Dikken, M. 2000. The syntax of features. *Journal of Psycholinguistic Research* 29: 5–23.

Dewaele, J.-M. 2009. Individual differences in second language acquisition. In *The New Handbook of Second Language Acquisition*, T. Bhatia & W. Ritchie (eds), 623–646. Bingley: Emerald.

Díaz, L., Bel, A. & Bekiou, K. 2007. Interpretable and uninterpretable features in the acquisition of Spanish past tenses. In *The Role of Formal Features in Second Language Acquisition*, J. Liceras, H. Zobl & H. Goodluck (eds), 485–512. London: Routledge.

Di Scullio, A.M. & Boeckx, C. 2011. (Eds). *The Biolinguistic Enterprise*. New York, NY: OUP.

Di Vito, N. 1994. French native speaker use of the subjunctive in speech and writing. In *Georgetown University Round Table on Languages and Linguistics*, J. Alatis (ed.), 253–263. Washington, DC: Georgetown University Press.

Do-Hurinville, T.D. 2000. L'emploi des temps verbaux dans la presse française contemporaine. Unpublished doctoral dissertation, Sorbonne Nouvelle, Paris 3.

Dominik, A.D. 2002. Les structures des énoncés à force illocutoire impérative en français moderne; un traitement minimaliste. Ph.D. dissertation, Université de Sherbrooke.

Dörnyei, Z. & Schmidt, R. 2001. *Motivation and Second Language Acquisition*. Honolulu, HI: University of Hawai'i Press.

Doughty, C. 2004. Commentary: When PI is focus on form it is very, very good, but when it is focus on forms. In *Processing Instruction: Theory, Research, and Commentary*, B. VanPatten (ed.), 257–272. Mahwah, NJ: Lawrence Erlbaum Associates.

Dowty, D. 1986. The effects of aspectual class on the temporal structure of discourse: Semantics or pragmatics? *Linguistics and Philosophy* 9: 37–61.

Doughty, C. & Varela, E. 1998. Communicating focus on form. In *Focus on Form in Classroom Second Language Acquisition*, C. Doughty & J. Williams (eds), 114–138. Cambridge: CUP.

Doughty, C. & Williams, J. 1998. (Eds). *Focus on Form in Classroom Second Language Acquisition*. Cambridge: CUP.

Douglas, D. & Hegelheimer, V. 2008. Assessing language using computer technology. *Annual Review of Applied Linguistics* 27: 115–132.

Dubreil, S. 2006. Gaining perspective on culture through CALL. In Ducate & Arnold (eds), 237–268.

Ducate, L. & Arnold, N. 2006 (Eds). *Calling on CALL: From Theory and Research to New Directions in Foreign Language Teaching*. San Marcos, TX: CALICO.

Ducate, L.C. & Lomicka, L. 2008. Adventures in the blogosphere: From blog readers to blog writers. *Computer Assisted Language Learning* 21: 9–28.

Ducrot, O. 1975. Je trouve que. *Semantikos* 1: 63–88.

Duffield, N., White, L., Bruhn de Garavito, J., Montrul, S. & Prévost, P. 2003. Clitic placement in L2 French: Evidence from sentence matching. *Journal of Linguistics* 38: 487–525.

Dunkel, H. & Pillet, R. 1957. A second year of French in the elementary school. *Elementary School Journal* 58: 142–151.

Egi, T. 2007a. Interpreting recasts as linguistic evidence: The roles of linguistic target, length, and degree of change. *Studies in Second Language Acquisition* 29: 511–537.

Egi, T. 2007b. Recasts, learners' interpretations, and L2 development. In *Conversational Interaction in Second Language Acquisition: A Collection of Empirical Studies*, A. Mackey (ed.), 249–267. Oxford: OUP.

Ehrman, M.E. 1996. *Understanding Second Language Learning Difficulties*. Thousand Oaks, CA: Sage.

Ehrman, M.E. & Oxford, R.L. 1995. Cognition plus: Correlates of language learning success. *The Modern Language Journal* 79: 67–89.

Elbert, T., Pantev, C., Wienbruch, C., Rockstroh, B. & Taub, E. 1995. Increased cortical representation of the fingers of the left hand in string players. *Science* 270: 305–306.

Ellis, N.C. 1996. Sequencing in SLA: Phonological memory, chunking, and points of order. *Studies in Second Language Acquisition* 18: 91–216.

Ellis, R. 2000. Second language acquisition: Research and language pedagogy. In *English Language Teaching in its Social Context*, C. Candlin & N. Mercer (eds), 44–74. London: Routledge.

Ellis, R. 2007. The differential effects of corrective feedback on two grammatical structures. In *Conversational Interaction in Second Language Acquisition: A Collection of Empirical Studies*, A. Mackey (ed.), 339–360. Oxford: OUP.

Ellis, R. 2012. *Language Teaching Research and Language Pedagogy*. Oxford: Blackwell.

Ellis, N.C. & Laporte, N. 1997. Contexts of acquisition: effects of formal instruction and naturalistic exposure on second language acquisition. In de Groot & Kroll (eds), 53–83.

Ellis, R., Loewen, S. & Erlam, R. 2006. Implicit and explicit corrective feedback and the acquisition of L2 grammar. *Studies in Second Language Acquisition* 28: 339–368.

Engel, D. 2001. Absolutely perfect? What is the status of *futur antérieur*? *Journal of French Language Studies* 11: 201–220.

Epstein, S., Flynn, S. & Martohardjono, G. 1996. Second language acquisition: Theoretical and experimental issues in contemporary research. *Behavioral and Brain Sciences* 19: 677–714.

Erlam, R. & Loewen, S. 2010. Implicit and explicit recasts in L2 oral French interaction. *The Canadian Modern Language Review* 67: 877–905.

Eubank, L. 1993/94. On the transfer of parametric values in L2 development. *Language Acquisition* 3: 183–208.

Eubank, L. 1996. Negation in early German-English interlanguage: More valueless features in the L2 initial state. *Second Language Research* 12: 73–106.

Eubank, L. & Gregg, K. 1999. Critical periods and (second) language acquisition: Divide et empera. In *Second Language Acquisition and the Critical Period Hypothesis*, D. Birdsong (ed.), 65–99. Mahwah, NJ: Lawrence Erlbaum Associates.

Fahtman, A. 1975. The relationship between age and second language productive ability. *Language Learning* 25: 245–253.

Farley, A. 2000. The Relative Effects of Processing Instruction and Meaning-based Output Instruction on the L2 Acquisition of the Spanish Subjunctive. Ph.D. dissertation, University of Illinois at Urbana-Champaign.

Farley, A. 2005. *Structured Input: Grammar Instruction for the Acquisition-oriented Classroom*. New York, NY: McGraw Hill.

Fernández, C. 2008. Reexamining the role of explicit information in processing instruction. *Studies in Second Language Acquisition* 30: 277–305.

Fitch, W.T., Hauser, M.D. & Chomsky, N. 2005. The evolution of the language faculty: Clarifications and complications. *Cognition* 97: 179–210.

Fleischman, S. 1982. *The Future in Thought and Language*. Cambridge: CUP.

Florea, L.S. 1988. Transitif vs. intransitif: Une division dichotomique en français? *Studia Universitatis Babe-Bolyai, Philologia* 33: 26–36.

Flynn, S. & Martohardjono, G. 1995. Toward theory-driven language pedagogy. In *Second Language Acquisition Theory and Pedagogy*, F. Eckman, D. Highland, P.W. Lee, J. Mileham & R. Rutkowski Weber (eds), 45–59. Mahwah, NJ: Lawrence Erlbaum Associates.

Fotos, S. & Browne, C. (eds). 2004. *New Perspectives on CALL for Second Language Classrooms*. Mahwah, NJ: Lawrence Erlbaum Associates.

Fotos, S. & Browne, C. 2004. The development of CALL and current options. In Fotos & C. Browne (eds), 3–14.

Foullioux, C. 2003. Le mode verbal et l'atténuation: À propos de *devoir*. *Thélème, Revista Complutense de Estudios Franceses*, Special issue: 109–120.

Franceschina, F. 2005. *Fossilized Second Language Grammars: The Acquisition of Grammatical Gender* [Language Acquisition and Language Disorders 38]. Amsterdam: John Benjamins.

Fukui, N. 1986. A Theory of Category Projection and its Applications. Ph.D. dissertation, MIT.

Fukui, N. 1988. Deriving the differences between English and Japanese: A case study in parametric syntax. *English Linguistics* 5: 249–270.

Gabriele, A. 2005. The Acquisition of Aspect in a Second Language: A Bidirectional Study of Learners of English and Japanese. Ph.D. dissertation, The City University of New York.

Gabriele, A. 2009. Transfer and transition in the SLA of aspect. *Studies in Second Language Acquisition* 31: 371–402.

Gabriele, A. & Maekawa, J. 2008. Interpreting tense in a second language. *Eurosla Yearbook* 8: 79–106.

Gabriele, A., Martohardjono, G. & McClure, W. 2005. Evaluating the role of attrition in the L2 acquisition of aspect: a study of Japanese learners of English. In *Proceedings of the 4th International Symposium on Bilingualism*, J. Cohen, K.T. McAlister, K. Rolstad & J. MacSwan (eds), 808–826. Somerville, MA: Cascadilla Press.

Gardner, R.C. 1980. On the validity of affective variables in second language acquisition: Conceptual, contextual, and statistical considerations. *Language Learning* 30: 255–270.

Gardner, R.C. 1985. *Social Psychology and Second Language Learning: The Role of Attitudes and Motivation*. London: Edward Arnold.

Gardner, R.C. 2000. Correlation, causation, motivation, and second language acquisition. *Canadian Psychology* 41: 10–24.

Gass, S. 1997. *Input, Interaction and the Second Language Learner*. Mahwah, NJ: Lawrence Erlbaum Associates.

Gass, S. & Selinker, L. 1994. *Second Language Acquisition. An Introductory Course*. Hillsdale, NJ: Lawrence Erlbaum Associates.

Gass, S. & Mackey, A. 2012. *The Routledge Handbook of Second Language Acquisition*. London: Routledge.

Gavis, W. 1997. What factors influence the use of stative verbs in the progressive form? Paper presented at the American Association of Applied Linguistics conference, Orlando, FL.

Gazdar, G., Klein, E., Pullum, G. & Sag, I. 1985. *Generalized Phrase Structure Grammar*. Cambridge, MA: Harvard University Press.

Geeslin, K. 2006. Linguistic contextual features and variation in L2 data elicitation. In *Selected Proceedings from the 7th CLASP*, C. Klee & T. Face (eds), 74–85. Somerville, MA: Cascadilla Press.

Genesee, F. 1987. *Learning Through Two Languages: Studies of Immersion and Bilingual Children*. Cambridge, MA: Newbury House.

Genesee, F. 1992. Second/foreign language immersion and at-risk English-speaking children. *Foreign Language Annals* 25: 199–213.

Genesee, F. 1998. A case study of multilingual education in Canada. In *Beyond Bilingualism: Multilingualism and Multilingual Education*, J. Cenoz & F. Genesee (eds), 243–258. Clevedon: Multilingual Matters.

Genesee, F. 2004. What do we know about bilingual education for majority language students? In *Handbook of Bilingualism and Multiculturalism*, T.K. Bhatia & W. Ritchie (eds), 547–576. Malden, MA: Blackwell.

Genesee, F. 2006. *The Suitability of French Immersion for Students Who Are at Risk: A Review of Research Evidence*. Ottawa, ON: Canadian Parents for French.

Gess, R. & Herschensohn, J. 2001. Shifting the DP parameter: A study of anglophone French L2ers. In *Romance Syntax, Semantics and their L2 Acquisition* [Current Issues in Linguistic Theory 216], C.R. Wiltshire & J. Camps (eds), 105–119. Amsterdam: John Benjamins.

Giorgi, A. & Pianesi, F. 1997. *Tense and Aspect: From Semantics to Morphosyntax*. Oxford: OUP.

Goad, H. & White, L. 2006. Ultimate attainment in interlanguage grammars: A prosodic approach. *Second Language Research* 22: 243–268.

Goad, H. & White, L. 2008. Prosodic structure and representation of L2 functional morphology: A nativist approach. *Lingua* 118: 577–594.

Goad, H., White, L. & Steele, J. 2003. Missing inflection in L2 acquisition: Defective syntax or L1-constrained prosodic representations? *Canadian Journal of Linguistics* 48: 243–263.

Gobert, D.L. & Maisier, V. 1995. Valeurs modales du futur et du conditionnel et leurs emplois en français contemporain. *The French Review* 68: 1003–1014.

Godwin-Jones, R. 2003. Blogs and wikis: environments for on-line collaboration. *Language Learning & Technology* 7: 12–16.

Goleman, D. 1996. *Emotional Intelligence: Why it can Matter more than IQ*. New York, NY: Random.

Goo, J. 2012. Corrective feedback and working memory capacity in interaction-driven L2 learning. *Studies in Second Language Acquisition* 34: 445–474.

Goo, J. & Mackey A. 2013. The case against the case against recasts. *Studies in Second Language Acquisition* 35: 1–39.

Goodin-Mayeda, C.E. & Rothman, J. 2007. The acquisition of aspect in L2 Portuguese and Spanish: Exploring native/non-native performance differences. In *Romance Languages and Linguistic Theory* [Current Issues in Linguistic Theory 291], S. Baauw, F. Drijkoningen & M. Pinto (eds), 131–148. Amsterdam: John Benjamins.

Gonglewski, M. & DuBravac, S. 2006. Multiliteracy: second language literacy in the multimedia environment. In Ducate & Arnold (eds), 43–68.

Gonzalez, E. 1995. Enonciations et formes syntaxiques. In *Relations discursives et traduction*, M. Ballard (ed.), 39–54. Lille: Presses Universitaires.

Gosselin, L. 1996. *Sémantique de la temporalité*. Bruxelles: DeBoexk-Duculot.

Gosselin, L. 2005. *Temporalité et modalité*. Louvain-la-Neuve: Duculot.

Gosselin, L. 2009. *Les modalités en français*. Amsterdam: Rodopi.

Gotti, M., Dossena, M., Dury, R., Facchinetti, R. & Lima, M. 2002. *Variation in Central Modals. A Repertoire of Forms and Usage in Late Middle English and Early Modern English*. Bern: Peter Lang.

Greenwood, P.M. 2007. Functional plasticity in cognitive aging: review and hypothesis. *Neuropsychology* 21: 657–673.

Grevisse, M. 1993. *Le bon usage*. Paris: Duculot.

Grevisse, M. & Goosse, A. 1980. *Nouvelle grammaire française*, 2nd edn. Paris: Duculot.

Grondin, N. & White, L. 1993. Functional categories in child L2 acquisition of French. *McGill Working Papers in Linguistics* 9: 121–145.

de Groot, A.M.B & Kroll, J.F. 1997. *Tutorials in Bilingualism: Psycholinguistic Perspectives*. Mahwah, NJ: Lawrence Erlbaum Associates.

Hakuta, K., Bialystok, E. & Wiley, A. 2003. A test for the critical-period hypothesis for second language acquisition. *Psychological Science* 14: 31–38.

Halle, M. 1962. Phonology in generative grammar. *Word* 18: 54–72.

Halle, M. & Marantz, A. 1993. Distributed morphology and the pieces of inflection. In *The View from Building 20. Essays in Linguistics in Honor of Sylvain Bromberger*, K. Hale & S.J. Keyser (eds), 111–176. Cambridge, MA: The MIT Press.

Hammond, R.M. 1988. Accuracy versus communicative competency: The acquisition of grammar in the second language classroom. *Hispania* 71: 408–417.

Han, Y. & Ellis, R. 1998. Implicit knowledge, explicit knowledge and general language proficiency. *Language Teaching Research* 2: 1–23.

Hardison, D.M. 2004. Generalization of computer-assisted prosody training: Quantitative and qualitative findings. *Language Learning & Technology* 8: 34–52.

Hardison, D.M. 2005. Contextualized computer-based L2 prosody training: Evaluating the effects of discourse context and video input. *CALICO Journal* 22: 175–190.

Harley, B. 1985. Second language proficiency and classroom treatment in early French immersion. Paper presented at the FIPLV/Eurocentres Symposium on Error in Foreign Language Learning: Analysis and Treatment. University of London.

Harley, B. 1986. *Age in Second Language Acquisition*. Clevedon: Multilingual Matters.

Harley, B. 1989. Functional grammar in French immersion: A classroom experiment. *Applied Linguistics* 10: 331–359.

Harley, B. 1992. Patterns of second language development in French immersion. *Journal of French Language Studies* 2: 159–183.

Harley, B., Cummins, J., Swain, M. & Allen, P. 1990. The nature of language proficiency. In *The Development of Second Language Proficiency*, B. Harley, P. Allen, J. Cummins & M. Swain (eds), 7–25. Cambridge: CUP.

Harley, B. & Swain, M. 1978. An analysis of verb form and function in the speech of French immersion pupils. *Working Papers on Bilingualism* 14: 31–46.

Harley, B. & Swain, M. 1984. The interlanguage of immersion students and its implications for second language teaching. In *Interlanguage*, A. Davies, C. Criper & A. Howatt (eds), 291–311. Edinburgh: EUP.

Harley, B. & Wang, W. 1997. The critical period hypothesis: Where are we now? In de Groot & Kroll (eds), 19–51.

Harrington, M. 2004. Commentary: Input Processing as a theory of processing input. In VanPatten (ed.), 79–92.

Hasegawa, M., Carpenter, P. & Just, M.A. 2002. An fMRI study of bilingual sentence comprehension and workload. *Neuroimage* 15: 647–660.

Hatch, E. 1978. Apply with caution. *Studies in Second Language Acquisition* 2: 123–143.

Hauser, M.D., Chomsky, N. & Fitch, W.T. 2002. The faculty of language: What it is, who has it, how did it evolve? *Science* 298: 1569–1579.

Hawkins, R. 2001. *Second Language Syntax: A Generative Introduction*. Malden, MA: Blackwell.

Hawkins, R. 2003. 'Representational deficit' theories of adult SLA: Evidence, counterevidence and implications. Plenary paper presented at EuroSLA, Edinburgh, UK.

Hawkins, R. 2005. Revisiting *wh*-movement: the availability of an uninterpretable [wh] feature in interlanguage grammars. In *Proceedings of the 7th Generative Approaches to Second Language Acquisition Conference (GASLA 2004)*, L. Dekydtspotter, D. Sprouse & A. Liljestrand (eds), 124–137. Somerville, MA: Cascadilla Proceedings Project.

Hawkins, R. & Casillas, G. 2008. Explaining frequency of verb morphology in early L2 speech. *Lingua* 118: 595–612.

Hawkins, R. & Chan, C.Y.-H. 1997. The partial availability of Universal Grammar in second language acquisition: The 'Failed Functional Features Hypothesis'. *Second Language Research* 13: 187–226.

Hawkins, R. & Hattori, H. 2006. Interpretation of multiple *wh*-questions by Japanese speakers: A missing uninterpretable feature account. *Second Language Research* 22: 269–301.

Hawkins, R. & Liszka, S. 2003. Locating the source of defective past tense marking in advanced L2 English speakers. In *The Interface Between Syntax and Lexicon in Second Language Acquisition* [Language Acquisition and Language Disorders 30], R. van Hout, H. Aafke, F. Kuiken & R. Towell (eds), 21–44. Amsterdam: John Benjamins.

Hawkins, R., Casillas, G., Hattori, H., Hawthorne, J., Husted, R., Lozano, C., Okamoto, A., Thomas, E. & Yamada, K. 2008. The semantic effects of verb raising and its consequences for second language grammars. In *The Role of Formal Features in Second Language Acquisition*, J. Liceras, H. Zobl & H. Goodluck (eds), 328–351. Mahwah, NJ: Lawrence Erlbaum Associates.

Haznedar, B. 2001. The acquisition of the IP system in child L2 English. *Studies in Second Language Acquisition* 23: 1–39.

Haznedar, B. 2003. The status of functional categories in child second language acquisition: Evidence from the acquisition of CP. *Second Language Research* 19: 1–41.

Haznedar, B. & Schwartz, B. 1997. Are there optional infinitives in child L2 acquisition? In *Proceedings of the 21st Annual Boston University Conference on Language Development*, E. Hughes, M. Hughes & A. Greenhill (eds), 257–68. Somerville, MA: Cascadilla Press.

Hegarty, M. 2005. *A Feature-Based Syntax of Functional Categories*. Berlin: Mouton de Gruyter.

Hedgcock, J. 1993, Well-formed *vs.* ill-formed strings in L2 metalingual tasks: Specifying features of grammaticality judgments. *Second Language Research* 91: 1–21.

Heift, T. & Schulze, M. 2007. *Errors and Intelligence in Computer-Assisted Language Learning: Parsers and Pedagogues*. New York, NY: Routledge.

Henshaw, F. 2012. How effective are affective activities? Relative benefits of two types of structured input-activities as part of a computer-delivered lesson on the Spanish subjunctive. *Language Teaching Research* 16: 393–414.

Herdina, P. & Jessner, U. 2000. The dynamics of third language acquisition. In *English in Europe: The Acquisition of a Third Language*, J. Cenoz & U. Jessner (eds), 84–98. Clevedon: Multilingual Matters.

Herschensohn, J. 2000. *The Second Time Around: Minimalism and L2 Acquisition* [Language Acquisition and Language Disorders 21]. Amsterdam: John Benjamins.

Herschensohn, J. 2001. Missing inflection in L2 French: Accidental infinitives and other verbal deficits. *Second Language Research* 17: 273–305.

Herschensohn, J. 2003. Verbs and rules: Two profiles of French morphology acquisition. *Journal of French Language Studies* 13: 23–45.

Herschensohn, J. 2004. Functional categories and the acquisition of object clitics in L2 French. In *The Acquisition of French in Different Contexts* [Language Acquisition and Language Disorders 32], P. Prévost & J. Paradis (eds), 207–242. Amsterdam: John Benjamins.

Herschensohn, J. 2009. Fundamental and gradient differences in language development. *Studies in Second Language Acquisition* 31: 259–289.

Herschensohn, J. & Arteaga, D. 2007. Parameters and processing: Gender agreement in L2 French. Paper presented at EuroSLA, Newcastle, UK.

Herschensohn, J. & Arteaga, D. 2009. Tense and verb raising in advanced L2 French. *French Language Studies* 19: 291–318.

Herzog, C. 1981. *Le passé simple dans les journaux du XXᵉ siècle*. Berne: Francke.

Hinkel, E. (ed.). 2011. *Handbook of Research in Second Language Teaching and Learning*, Vol. 2. London: Routledge.

Hokanson, S. 2000. Foreign language immersion homestays. Maximizing the accommodation of cognitive styles. *Applied Language Learning* 11: 239–264.

Hopp, H. 2010. Ultimate attainment in L2 inflection: Performance similarities between non-native and native speakers. *Lingua* 120: 901–931.

Horst, M., Cobb, T. & Nicolae, I. 2005. Expanding academic vocabulary with an interactive on-line database. *Language Learning & Technology* 9: 90–110.

Horvath, J. & Siloni, T. 2002. Against the little-*v* hypothesis. *Rivista di Grammatica Generativa* 27: 107–122.

Housen, A. 1994. Tense and aspect in second language acquisition: The Dutch interlanguage of a native speaker of English. In *Tense and Aspect in Discourse*, C. Vet & C. Vetters (eds), 257–291. Berlin: Mouton de Gruyter.

Housen, A. 2006. Developmental stages and educational context: The acquisition of verbal morphology by advanced learners of French as a second language. *Cahier de l'Institut de linguistique de Louvain* 32: 273–293.

Howard, M. 2002. Prototypical and non-prototypical marking in the advanced learner's aspectuo-temporal system. *EUROSLA Yearbook* 2: 87–113.

Howard, M. 2005. The emergence and use of the *plus-que-parfait* in advanced French interlanguage. In *Focus on French as a Foreign Language*, M. Dewaele (ed.), 63–85. Clevedon: Multilingual Matters.

Howard, M. 2008. Morpho-syntactic development in the expression of modality: the subjunctive in French L2 acquisition. *Revue Canadienne de Linguistique Appliquée* 11: 171–191.

Howard, M. 2012. From tense and aspect to modality: the acquisition of future, conditional and subjunctive morphology in L2 French. A preliminary study. *Cahiers Chronos* 24: 201–223.

Hoye, L.F. 2005. You may think that; I couldn't possibly comment! Modality studies: Contemporary research and future directions, Part I. *Journal of Pragmatics* 37: 1295–1321.

Hsien-jen Chin, D. 2008. A cross-linguistic investigation on the acquisition of Spanish aspect. In *Selected Proceedings of the* 10th *Hispanic Linguistics Symposium*, J. Bruhn de Garavito & E. Valenzuela (eds), 36–50. Somerville, MA: Cascadilla Press.

Hubbard, P. (ed.). 2009. *Computer Assisted Language Learning*, Vols I-IV. New York, NY: Routledge.

Huddleston, R. 1976. *An Introduction to English Transformational Syntax*. London: Longman.

Hulstijn, H. 1997. Second language acquisition research in the laboratory. Possibilities and limitations. *Studies in Second Language Acquisition* 19: 131–143.

Hurford, J. 1991. The evolution of the critical period for language acquisition. *Cognition* 40: 159–201.

Hurford, J. & Kirby, S. 1999. Co-evolution of language size and the Critical Period. In Birdsong (ed.), 39–63.

Hyams, N. 1986. *Language Acquisition and the Theory of Parameters*. Dordrecht: Reidel.

Hyltenstam, K. & Abrahamsson, N. 2003. Maturational constraints in SLA. In *The Handbook of Second Language Acquisition*, C. Doughty & M.H. Long (eds), 539–588. Oxford: Blackwell.

Hymes, D. 1972. On communicative competence. In *Sociolinguistics*, J.B. Pride & J. Holmes (eds), 269–293. Harmondsworth: Penguin.

Iverson, M., Kempchinsky, P. & Rothman, J. 2008. Interface vulnerability and knowledge of the subjunctive/indicative distinction with negated epistemic predicates in L2 Spanish. *EUROSLA Yearbook* 8: 135–163.

Iverson, M. & Rothman, J. 2008. Adverbial quantification and perfective/imperfective interpretive nuances in L2 Portuguese. In *Proceedings of the 9th Generative Approaches to Second Language Acquisition Conference (GASLA 2007)*, R. Slabakova, J. Rothman, P. Kempchinsky & E. Gavruseva (eds), 70–80. Somerville, MA: Cascadilla Proceedings Project.

Izquierdo, M.J. 2008. Multimedia Environments in the Foreign Language Classroom: Effects on the Acquisition of the French Perfective and Imperfective Distinction. Ph.D., McGill University.

Izumi, S. 2003. Comprehension and production processes in second language learning: in search of the linguistic rationale of the output hypothesis. *Applied Linguistics* 24: 168–196.

Jackendoff, R. 1977. *X-bar Syntax: A Study of Phrase Structure* [Linguistic Inquiry Monograph 2]. Cambridge, MA: The MIT Press.

Jackendoff, R. & Pinker, S. 2005. The nature of the language faculty and its implications for evolution of language (Reply to Fitch, Hauser & Chomsky). *Cognition* 97: 211–225.

Jakobson, R., Fant, G. & Halle, M. 1963. *Preliminaries to Speech Analysis*. Cambridge, MA: The MIT Press.

James, F. 1986. *Semantics of the English Subjunctive*. Vancouver: University of British Columbia Press.

Jean, G. & Simard, D. 2011. Grammar learning in English and French L2: Students' and teachers' beliefs and perceptions. *Foreign Language Annals* 44: 465–492.

Jernigan, T., Trauner, D., Hesselink, R. & Tallal, P. 1991. Maturation of human cerebrum observed *in vivo* during adolescence. *Brain* 114: 2037–2049.

Jin, J. 2011. An evaluation of the role of consciousness in second language learning. *International Journal of English Linguistics* 1: 126–136.

Johnson, J.S. & Newport, E.L. 1989. Critical period effects in second language learning: The influence of maturational state on the acquisition of English as a second language. *Cognitive Psychology* 21: 60–99.

Johnson, J., Prior, S. & Artuso, M. 2000. Field dependence as a factor in second language communicative production. *Language Learning* 50: 529–567.

Jones, L. 2006. Listening comprehension in multimedia environments. In Ducate & Arnold (eds), 99–125.

Jones, L. & Plass, J. 2002. Supporting listening comprehension and vocabulary acquisition in French with multimedia annotations. *The Modern Language Journal* 86: 546–561.

Judge, A. 2002. Ecarts entre manuels et réalité: Un problème pour l'enseignement des temps du passé à des étudiants d'un niveau avancé. *Cahiers Chronos* 9: 135–156.

Kaplan, M. 1987. Developmental patterns of past tense acquisition among foreign language learners of French. In *Foreign Language Learning: A Research Perspective*, B. VanPatten (ed.), 52–60. Rowley, MA: Newbury House.

Kaplan, R. & Bresnan, J. 1982. Lexical-Functional Grammar: A formal system for grammatical representation. In *The Mental Representation of Grammatical Relations*, J. Bresnan (ed.), 173–281. Cambridge, MA: The MIT Press.

Kempler, D. 2005. *Neurocognitive Disorders in Aging*. Thousand Oaks, CA: Sage.

Kern, R.G. 1995. Restructuring classroom interaction with networked computers: Effects on quantity and characteristics of language production. *The Modern Language Journal* 79: 457–476.

Kern, R.G. 2000. *Literacy and Language Teaching*. Oxford: OUP.

Kihlstedt, M. 1994. Le mode d'action du verbe. Son rôle dans l'acquisition du français et quelques problèmes liés à sa classification. Ms, University of Stockholm.

Kihlstedt, M. 2002. Reference to past events in dialogue: The acquisition of tense and aspect by advanced learners of French. In *The L2 Acquisition of Tense/Aspect Morphology* [Language Acquisition and Language Disorders 27], R. Salaberry & Y. Shirai (eds), 323–361. Amsterdam: John Benjamins.

Kiparsky, P. 1997. Remarks on denominal verbs. In *Complex Predicates*, A. Alsina, J. Bresnan & P. Sells (eds), 473–499. Stanford, CA: CSLI.

Kornuc, S.P. 2004. L2 Use and Development of Mood Selection in Spanish Complement Clauses. Ph.D. dissertation, University of Southern California.

Kowal, M. & Swain, M. 1994. Using collaborative language production tasks to promote students' language awareness. *Language Awareness* 3: 73–93.

Kozhevnikov, M. 2007. Cognitive styles in the context of modern psychology: Toward an integrated framework of cognitive style. *Psychological Bulletin* 133: 464–481.

Krashen, S. 1973. Lateralization, language learning and the critical period. *Language Learning* 23: 63–74.

Krashen, S. 1982. *Input and Practice in Second Language Acquisition*. Oxford: Pergamon.

Krashen, S. 1993. *The Power of Reading*. Inglewood, CO: Libraries Unlimited.

Krashen, S. & Terrell, T. 1983. *The Natural Approach: Language Acquisition in the Classroom*. Oxford: Pergamon.

Kronning, H. 1996. *Modalité, cognition et polysémie: Sémantique du verbe modal 'devoir'* [Studia romanica Upsaliensia 54]. Uppsala: Acta universitatis Upsaliensis.

Kronning, H. 2001. Pour une tripartition des emplois de 'devoir'. In *Les verbes modaux*, P. Dendale & J. van der Auwera (eds), 67–84. Amsterdam: Rodopi.

Krug, M. 2000. *Emerging Modals: A Corpus-based Study of Grammaticalization*. Berlin: Mouton de Gruyter.

Labeau, E. 2004. Le(s) temps du compte rendu sportif. *Journal of French Language Studies* 14: 129–148.

Labeau, E. 2007. Pas si simple! La place du PS dans l'interlangue d'apprenants. *Cahiers Chronos* 19: 177–197.

Labeau, E. 2009. Le PS: Cher disparu de la rubrique nécrologique? *Journal of French Language Studies* 19: 61–86.

Lakshmanan, U. & Selinker, L. 1994. The Status of CP and the tensed complementizer *that* in the developing L2 grammars of English. *Second Language Research* 10: 25–48.

Lamb, S. 1999. *Pathways of the Brain. The Neurocognitive Basis of Language*. Amsterdam: John Benjamins.

Lambert, W. & Tucker, R. 1972. *Bilingual Education of Children: The St. Lambert Experiment*. Rowley, MA: Newbury House.

Langacker, R. 1982. Remarks on English aspect. In *Tense-Aspect: Between Syntax and Pragmatics* [Typological Studies in Language 1], P. Hopper (ed.), 265–305. Amsterdam: John Benjamins.

Lardiere, D. 1998a. Case and tense in the 'fossilized' steady state. *Second Language Research* 14: 1–26.

Lardiere, D. 1998b. Dissociating syntax from morphology in a divergent end state grammar. *Second Language Research* 14: 359–375.

Lardiere, D. 2000. Mapping features to forms in second language acquisition. In *Language Acquisition and Syntactic Theory*, J. Archibald (ed.), 102–129. Oxford: Blackwell.

Lardiere, D. 2003. Second language knowledge of [±Past] vs. [±Finite]. In *Proceedings of the 6th Generative Approaches to Second Language Acquisition: L2 Links*, J. Liceras, H. Zobl & H. Goodluck (eds), 176–189. Somerville, MA: Cascadilla Proceedings Project.

Lardiere, D. 2006a. Attainment and acquirability in second language acquisition. *Second Language Research* 22: 239–242.

Lardiere, D. 2006b. *Ultimate Attainment in Second Language Acquisition: A Case Study*. Mahwah, NJ: Lawrence Erlbaum Associates.

Lardiere, D. 2007. Acquiring (or assembling) functional categories in second language acquisition. In *Proceedings of the 2nd Conference on Generative Approaches to Language Acquisition North America*, A. Belikova, L. Meroni & M. Umeda (eds), 233–244. Somerville, MA: Cascadilla Proceedings Project.

Lardiere, D. 2008. Feature assembly in second language acquisition. In *The Role of Formal Features in Second Language Acquisition*, J.M. Liceras, H. Zobl & H. Goodluck (eds), 106–140. New York, NY: Lawrence Erlbaum Associates.

Larjavaara, M. 1999. Primarily transitive verbs without objects in Modern French. *French Language Studies* 9: 105–111.

Larreya, P. 1996. Le temps grammatical: une question de mode? In *Dynamique du Temps*, A. Suberchicot (ed.), 139–153. Clermont-Ferrand: CRLMC (Université Blaise Pascal).

Larreya, P. 2000. Modal verbs and the expression of futurity in English, French and Italian. *Belgian Journal of Linguistics* 14: 115–129.

Larreya, P. 2003. Irrealis, past time reference and modality. In *Modality in Contemporary English*, R. Facchinetti, K., Manfred & F. Palmer (eds), 21–45. Berlin: Mouton de Gruyter.

Larsen-Freeman, D. 1998. On the scope of second language acquisition research: 'The learner variety perspective' and beyond – A response to Klein. *Language Learning* 48: 551–556.

Larson-Hall, J. 2004. Predicting perceptual success with segments: A test of Japanese speakers of Russian. *Second Language Research* 20: 32–76.

Lasagabaster, D. & Sierra, J.M. 2005. Error correction: students' versus teachers' perceptions. *Language Awareness* 14: 112–127.

Lasnik, H. 1981. On two recent treatments of disjoint reference. *Journal of Linguistic Research* 1: 48–58.

Lasnik, H. 1999. On feature strength: Three minimalist approaches to overt movement. *Linguistic Inquiry* 30: 197–217.

Lazard, G. 2001. On the grammaticalization of evidentiality. *Journal of Pragmatics* 33: 359–368.

Lealess, A. 2005. En français il faut qu'on parle bien: Assessing Native-like Proficiency in L2 French. MA thesis, University of Ottawa.

Lee, J. & Tonhauser, J. 2010. Temporal interpretation without tense: Korean and Japanese coordination constructions. *Journal of Semantics* 27: 304–341.

Leeman, J. 2003. Recasts and second language development: Beyond negative evidence. *Studies in Second Language Acquisition* 25: 37–63.

Le Goffic, P. & Lab, F. 2001. The present *pro futuro*. *Cahiers Chronos* 7: 77–98.

Lenneberg, E. 1967. *Biological Foundations of Language*. New York, NY: Wiley.

Leopold, W.F. 1939–1949. *Speech Development of a Bilingual Child*. Evanston, IL: Northwestern University Press.

Leow, R. 1993. To simplify or not to simplify. A look at intake. *Studies in Second Language Acquisition* 15: 333–355.

Lepetit, D. 2001. Subjonctif: descriptions et manuels. *The French Review* 74: 1176–1192.

Leung, Y.-k. I. 2002. Functional Categories in Second and Third Language Acquisition: A Cross-linguistic Study of the Acquisition of English and French by Chinese and Vietnamese Speakers. Ph.D. dissertation, McGill University, Montreal.

Leung, Y.-k. I. 2005. L2 vs. L3 initial state: A comparative study in the acquisition of French DPs by Vietnamese monolinguals and Cantonese-English bilinguals. *Bilingualism: Language & Cognition* 8: 39–61.

Levis, J. 2008. Computer technology in teaching and researching pronunciation. *Annual Review of Applied Linguistics* 27: 184–202.

Lewis, M. 1986. *The English Verb*. Hove: Language Teaching Publications.

L'Huillier, M. 1999. *Advanced French Grammar*. Cambridge: CUP.

Li, A. Y.-H. 1990. *Order and Constituency in Mandarin Chinese*. Dordrecht: Kluwer.

Liceras, J.M., Zobl, H. & Goodluck, H. (eds). 2008. *The Role of Formal Features in Second Language Acquisition*. Mahwah, NJ: Lawrence Erlbaum Associates.

Lightbown, P. 1985. Can language acquisition be altered by instruction? In *Modelling and Assessing Second Language Acquisition*, K. Hyltenstam & M. Pienemann (eds), 101–112. Clevedon: Multilingual Matters.

Lightbown, P. 2000. Anniversary article: Classroom SLA research and second language teaching. *Applied Linguistics* 21: 431–462.

Lin, J.-W. 2003. Temporal reference in Mandarin Chinese. *Journal of East Asian Linguistics* 12: 259–311.

Lin, J.-W. 2006. Time in a language without tense: The case of Chinese. *Journal of Semantics* 23: 1–53.

Lin, J.-W. 2010. A tenseless analysis of Mandarin Chinese revisited: A response to Sybesma 2007. *Linguistic Inquiry* 41: 305–329.

Liszka, S.A. 2006. Advanced grammars and pragmatic processes. Exploring the interface. *EUROSLA Yearbook* 6: 79–99.

Liszka, S.A. 2009. Associating meaning to form in advanced L2 speakers: An investigation into the acquisition of the English present simple and present progressive. In *Representational Deficits in SLA: Studies in Honor of Roger Hawkins* [Language Acquisition and Language Disorders 47], N. Snape, Y.-K.I. Leung & M. Sharwood Smith (eds), 229–246. Amsterdam: John Benjamins.

Littlemore, J. 2001. An empirical study of the relationship between cognitive style and the use of communication strategy. *Applied Linguistics* 22: 241–265.

Locke, J. 1993. *The Child's Path to Spoken Language.* Cambridge, MA: Harvard Press University.

Loengarov, A. 2005. *Le fait que...*et la question du subjonctif: La directionalité de la grammaticalisation. *Cahiers Chronos* 12: 67–81.

Lomicka, L. 2006. Understanding the other: intercultural exchange and CMC. In Ducate & Arnold (eds), 211–236.

Long, M. 1988. Instructed interlanguage development. In *Issues in Second Language Acquisition: Multiple perspectives*, L. Beebe (ed.), 115–141. Rowley, MA: Newbury House.

Long, M. 1990. Maturational constraints on language development. *Studies in Second Language Acquisition* 12: 251–285.

Long, M. 1991. The design and psycholinguistic motivation of research in foreign language learning. In *Foreign Language Acquisition Research and the Classroom*, B. Freed (ed.), 309–320. Lexington, MA: Heath.

Long, M. 2005. Problems with supposed counter-evidence to the Critical Period Hypothesis. *International Review of Applied Linguistics* 43: 287–317.

Long, M. & Crookes, G. 1992. Three approaches to task-based syllabus design. *TESOL Quarterly* 26: 27–56.

Long, M. & Robinson, P. 1998. FonF: Theory, research and practice. In *Focus on Form in Classroom Second Language Acquisition*, C. Doughty & J. Williams (eds), 15–41. Cambridge: CUP.

Loschky, L. & Bley-Vroman, R. 1993. Grammar and task-based methodology. In *Tasks and Language Learning: Integrating Theory and Practice*, G. Crookes & S. Gass (eds), 123–167. Clevedon: Multilingual Matters.

Lunn, P.V. 1995. The evaluative function of the Spanish subjunctive. In *Modality and Grammar in Discourse* [Typological Studies in Language 32], J. Bybee & S. Fleischman (eds), 419–449. Amsterdam: John Benjamins.

Lyons, J. 1977. *Semantics.* Cambridge: CUP.

Lyster, R. 1994. The effect of functional-analytic teaching on aspects of French immersion students' sociolinguistic competence. *Applied Linguistics* 15: 263–287.

Lyster, R. 2004a. Research on form-focused instruction in immersion classrooms: Implications for theory and practice. *Journal of French Language Studies* 14: 321–341.

Lyster, L. 2004b. Differential effects for prompts and recasts in form-focused instruction classroom. *Studies in Second Language Acquisition* 26: 399–432.

Lyster, R. 2007. *Learning and Teaching Languages Through Content: A Counterbalanced Approach* [Language Learning & Language Teaching 18]. Amsterdam: John Benjamins.

Lyster, R. 2008. Learning French as a second language through immersion. In *Studies in French Applied Linguistics* [Language Learning & Language Teaching 16], D. Ayoun (ed.), 3–36. Amsterdam: John Benjamins.

Lyster, R. & Mori, H. 2006. Interactional feedback and instructional counterbalance. *Studies in Second Language Acquisition* 28: 269–300.

Lyster, R. & Mori, H. 2008. Instructional counterbalance in immersion pedagogy. In *Pathways to Bilingualism and Multilingualism: Evolving Perspectives on Immersion Education*, R. Fortune & D. Tedick (eds), 133–151. Clevedon: Multilingual Matters.

Lyster, R., Saito, K. & Sato, M. 2013. Oral corrective feedback in second language classrooms. *Language Teaching* 46: 1–40.

MacWhinney, B. 1997. Second language acquisition and the Competition Model. In de Groot & Kroll (eds), 113–142.

Mandell, P.B. 1999. On the reliability of grammaticality judgment tests in second language acquisition research. *Second Language Acquisition* 15: 73–99.

Marchman, V.A., Martínez-Sussman, C. & Dale, P.S. 2004. The language-specific nature of grammatical development: Evidence from bilingual language learners. *Developmental Science* 7: 212–224.

Marsden, E. 2004. Teaching and Learning French Verb Inflections: A Classroom Experiment Using Processing Instruction. Ph.D. dissertation, University of Southampton.

Marsden, E. 2006. Exploring input processing in the classroom: an experimental comparison of Processing Instruction and enriched input. *Language Learning* 56: 507–566.

Masgoret, A.-M. & Gardner, R. 2003. Attitudes, motivation, and second language learning: A meta-analysis of studies conducted by Gardner and associates. *Language Learning* 53: 123–163.

Matte, E. 1989. *French and English Verbal Systems*. Bern: Peter Lang.

Mayberry, R. 1993. First language acquisition after childhood differs from second language acquisition: The case of American Sign Language. *Journal of Speech and Hearing Research* 36: 1258–1270.

McCormick, D. 2008. Teaching the English Present Perfect in the Second Language Classroom. Ph.D. dissertation, University of Toronto.

McLaughlin, B. 1987. *Theories of Second Language Learning*. London: Arnold.

Mégharbi, N. 2007. The Acquisition of the Perfective/imperfective Aspectual Distinction in French: Output-based Instruction *vs.* Processing Instruction. MA thesis, University of Texas at Austin.

Meisel, J. 1999. Parametric change in language development: Psycholinguistic and historical perspectives on second language acquisition. *LynX* 6: 18–36.

Meisel, J. 2000. Revisiting Universal Grammar. *Revista de Documentacao de Estudos em Linguistica Teorica e Aplicada* 16: 129–140.

Mellet, S. 2000. Le présent. *Travaux de Linguistique* 40: 97–111.

Merzenich, M., Nelson, M., Stryker, R., Cynader, M., Schoppmann, A. & Zook, J. 1984. Somatosensory cortical map changes following digit amputation in adult monkeys. *Journal of Comparative Neurology* 224: 591–605.

Mitchell, R. & Myles, F. 2004. *Second Language Learning Theories*. London: Arnold.

Montrul, S. 2002. Incomplete acquisition and attrition of Spanish tense/aspect distinctions in adult bilinguals. *Bilingualism: Language and Cognition* 5: 39–68.

Montrul, S. 2007. Interpreting mood distinctions in Spanish as a heritage language. In *Spanish in Contact. Policy, Social and Linguistic Inquiries*, K. Potowski & R. Cameron (eds), 113–149. Dordrecht: Kluwer.

Montrul, S. 2012. Is the heritage language like the second language? *Eurosla Yearbook* 12: 1–29.

Montrul, S. & Perpiñán, S. 2011. Assessing differences and similarities between instructed heritage language learners and L2 learners in their knowledge of Spanish tense-aspect and mood (TAM) morphology. *Heritage Language Journal* 8: 90–133.

Montrul, S. & Slabakova, R. 2002. Acquiring morphosyntactic and semantic properties of preterit and imperfect tenses in L2 Spanish. In *The Acquisition of Spanish Morpho-syntax: The L1-L2 Connection*, A.T. Perez-Leroux & J. Liceras (eds), 113–149. Dordrecht: Kluwer.

Montrul, S. & Slabakova, R. 2003. Competence similarities between native and near-native speakers: An investigation of the preterit/imperfect contrast in Spanish. *Studies in Second Language Acquisition* 25: 351–398.

Moses, J. 2002. The Development of Future Expression in English-speaking Learners of French. Ph.D. dissertation, Indiana University, Bloomington.

Mourelatos, A. 1978. Events, processes and states. *Language and Philosophy* 2: 415–434.

Mourelatos, A. 1981. Events, processes, and states. In *Syntax and Semantics, Vol. 14: Tense and Aspect*, P.J. Tedeschi & A. Zaenen (eds), 191–212. New York, NY: Academic Press.

Muñoz, C. & Singleton, D. 2011. A critical review of age-related research on L2 ultimate attainment. *Language Teaching* 44: 1–35.

Murray, L. & Hourigan, T. 2006. Using micropublishing to facilitate writing in the foreign language. In Ducate & Arnold (eds), 149–179.

Nadasdi, T., Mougeon, R. & Rehner, K. 2003. The use of the future tense in the spoken French of French immersion students. *Journal of French Language Studies* 13: 195–219.

Nagata, N. 1999. The effectiveness of computer-assisted interactive glosses. *Foreign Language Annals* 32: 469–479.

Nassaji, H. 2012. The relationship between SLA research and language pedagogy: Teachers' perspectives. *Language Teaching Research* 16: 337–365.

Nassaji, H. & Fotos, S. 2004. Current developments in research on the teaching of grammar. *Annual Review of Applied Linguistics* 24: 126–145.

Nassaji, H. & Fotos, S. 2010. *Teaching Grammar in Second Language Classrooms: Integrating Form-focused Instruction in Communicative Context*. London: Routledge.

Neville, H. 1995. Developmental specificity in neuro-cognitive developments in humans. In *The Cognitive Neuro-Sciences*, M. Gazzaniga (ed.), 219–231. Cambridge, MA: The MIT Press.

Neville, H. & Weber-Fox, C. 1994. Cerebral subsystems within language. In *Structural and Functional Organization of the Neocortex*, B. Albowirz, K. Albus, U. Kuhnt, H.-C. Norhdurft & P. Wahle (eds.), 424–438. Berlin: Springer.

Nicoladis, E., Palmer, A. & Marentette, P. 2007. The role of type and token frequency in using past tense morphemes correctly. *Developmental Science* 10: 237–254.

Nicoladis, E., Song, J. & Marentette, P. 2012. Do young bilinguals acquire past tense morphology like monolinguals, only later? Evidence from French-English and Chinese-English bilinguals. *Applied Psycholinguistics* 33: 457–479.

Nobuyoshi, J. & Ellis, R. 1993. Focused communication tasks and second language acquisition. *ELT Journal* 47: 203–210.

Norris, J. & Ortega, L. (eds). 2006. *Synthesizing Research on Language Learning and Teaching* [Language Learning & Language Teaching 13]. Amsterdam: John Benjamins.

Norris, J. & Ortega, L. 2000. Effectiveness of L2 instruction: A research synthesis and quantitative meta-analysis. *Language Learning* 50: 417–528.

Nyberg, L. 2005. Cognitive training in healthy aging: A cognitive neuroscience perspective. In *Cognitive Neuroscience of Aging: Linking Cognitive & Cerebral Aging*, R. Cabeza, L. Nyberg & D. Park (eds), 309–323. New York, NY: OUP.

O'Brien, M.G. 2006. Teaching pronunciation and intonation with computer technology. In Ducate & Arnold (eds), 127–148.

O'Dowd, R. & Ritter, M. 2006. Understanding and working with failed communication in tele-collaborative exchanges. *CALICO Journal* 23: 623–642.

O'Grady, W. 2003. The radical middle: Nativism without Universal Grammar. In *The Handbook of Second Language Acquisition*, C. Doughty & M. Long (eds), 43–62. Oxford: Blackwell.

Ouhalla, J. 1991. *Functional Categories and Parametric Variation*. London: Routledge.

Oyama, J. 1976. A sensitive period for the acquisition of a nonnative phonological system. *Journal of Psycholinguistic Research* 5: 261–283.

Pallier, C., Dehaene, S., Poline, J.-B., LeBihan, D., Argentini, A.-M., Dupoux, E. & Mehler, J. 2003. Brain imaging of language plasticity in adopted adults: Can a second language replace the first? *Cerebral Cortex* 13: 155–161.

Palmer, F.R. 1979. *Modality and the English Modals*. London: Longman.

Palmer, F.R. 1986. *Mood and Modality*. Cambridge: CUP.

Palmer, F.R. 1990. *Modality and the English Modals*. Cambridge: CUP.

Palmer, F.R. 2001. *Mood and Modality*. Cambridge: CUP.

Palmer, F.R. 2003. Modality in English: theoretical, descriptive and typological issues. In *Modality in Modern English*, R. Facchinetti, M. Krug & F. Palmer (eds), 1–17. Berlin: Mouton de Gruyter.

Papafragou, A. 1998. Inference and word meaning: The case of modal auxiliaries. *Lingua* 105: 1–47.

Paradis, M. 2006. Implicit competence and explicit knowledge in second language acquisition and learning. Talk given at Georgetown University.

Paradis, J., Le Corre, M. & Genesee, F. 1998. The emergence of tense and agreement in child L2 French. *Second Language Research* 14: 227–257.

Paradis, J. & Crago, M. 2001. The morphosyntax of Specific Language Impairment in French: Evidence for an Extended Optional Default Account. *Language Acquisition* 9: 269–300.

Paradis, J., Nicoladis, E., & Crago, M. 2007. French-English bilingual children's acquisition of the past tense. In *BUCLD 31 Proceedings*, H. Caunt-Nulton, S. Kulatilake & I.-H. Woo (eds), 497–507. Somerville, MA: Cascadilla Press.

Paradis, J., Nicoladis, E., Crago, M. & Genesee, F. 2011. Bilingual children's acquisition of the past tense: A usage-based approach. *Journal of Child Language* 37: 1–25.

Patard, A. 2011. The epistemic uses of the English simple past and the French *imparfait*. When temporality conveys modality. In *Cognitive approaches to Tense, Aspect and Epistemicity* [Human Cognitive Processing 29], A. Patard & F. Brisard (eds), 279–310. Amsterdam: John Benjamins.

Patard, A. & Richard, A. 2011. Attenuation in French simple tense. *Cahiers Chronos* 22: 157–178.

Patowski, M. 1980. The sensitive period for the acquisition of syntax in a second language. *Language Learning* 30: 449–472.

Patowski, M. 1990. Age and accent in a second language. A reply to James Emil Flege. *Applied Linguistics* 1: 73–89.

Payne, J.S. & Ross, B.M. 2005. Synchronous CMC, working memory, and L2 oral proficiency development. *Language Learning & Technology* 9: 35–54.

Penfield, W. & Roberts, L. 1959. *Speech and Brain Mechanism*. Princeton, NJ: Princeton University Press.

Pereltsvaig, A. 2002. Aspect Lost, Aspect Regained: Restructuring of Aspectual Marking in American Russian. Ms, University of Tromsø.

Perkins, M.R. 1983. *Modal Expressions in English*. London: Frances Pinter.

Pesetsky, D. & Torrego, E. 2001. I to C movement: Causes and consequences. In *Ken Hale. A Life in Language*, M. Kenstowicz (ed.), 355–426. Cambridge, MA: The MIT Press.

Pesetsky, D. & Torrego, E. 2004. Tense, case, and the nature of syntactic categories. In *The Syntax of Time*, J. Gueron & J. Lecarme (eds), 495–538. Cambridge, MA: MIT Press.

Philip, J. & Mackey, A. 2010. Interaction research: What can socially informed approaches offer to cognitivists (and vice versa)? In *Sociocognitive Perspectives on Language Use and Language Learning*, R. Batstone (ed.), 210–224. Oxford: OUP.

Pica, T. 2005. Second language acquisition research and applied linguistics. In *Handbook of Research in Second Language Teaching and Learning*, E. Hinkel (ed.), 263–280. Mahwah, NJ: Lawrence Erlbaum Associates.

Pienemann, M. 1984. Psychological constraints on the teachability of languages. *Studies in Second Language Acquisition* 6: 186–214.

Pienemann, M. 1987. Psychological constraints on the teachability of languages. In *First and Second Language Acquisition Processes*, C.W. Pfaff (ed.), 143–168. Rowley, MA: Newbury House.

Pienemann, M. 1989. Is language teachable? Psycholinguistic experiments and hypotheses. *Applied Linguistics* 10: 52–79.

Pienemann, M. 1998. *Language Processing and Second Language Development: Processability theory* [Studies in Bilingualism 15]. Amsterdam: John Benjamins.

Pienemann, M. 2005. An introduction to processability theory. In *Cross-linguistic Aspects of Processability Theory* [Studies in Bilingualism 30], M. Pienemann (ed.), 1–60. Amsterdam: John Benjamins.

Pinker, S. 1994. *The Language Instinct*. New York, NY: W. Morrow.

Pinker, S. [1999] 2000. *Words and Rules: The Ingredients of Language*. London: Phoenix. (Original edition, New York, NY: Morrow).

Pinker. S. & Jackendoff, R. 2005. The faculty of language: What's so special about it? *Cognition* 95: 201–236.

Polinsky, M. 1995. American Russian: language loss meets language acquisition. In *Formal Approaches to Slavic Linguistics. Cornell Meeting*, W. Browne (ed.), 370–406. Ann Arbor: Michigan Slavic Publications.

Polinsky, M. 1997. American Russian. Language loss meets language acquisition. In *Proceedings of the Annual Workshop on Formal Approaches to Slavic Linguistics*, 370–406. Ann Arbor, MI: Michigan Slavic Publications.

Polinsky, M. 2006. Incomplete acquisition: American Russian. *Journal of Slavic Linguistics* 14: 191–262.

Polinsky, M. 2011. *Annotated Bibliography of Research in Heritage Languages*. Oxford: OUP.

Pollard, C. & Sag, I. 1994. *Head-Driven Phrase Structure Grammar*. Chicago, IL: University of Chicago Press.

Pollock, J.-Y. 1989. Verb movement, Universal Grammar, and the structure of IP. *Linguistic Inquiry* 20: 365–424.

Poole, A. 2005. FonF instruction: Foundations, application and criticism. *The Reading Matrix* 5: 47–56.

Poplack, S. 1992. The inherent variability of the French subjunctive. *Theoretical Analyses in Romance Linguistics* [Current Issues in Linguistic Theory 74], C. Laeufer & T. Morgan, 235–263. Amsterdam: John Benjamins.

Poplack, S. 2001. Variability, frequency and productivity in the irrealis domain of French. In *Frequency and the Emergence of Linguistic Structure* [Typological Studies in Language 45], J. Bybee & P. Hopper, 405–428. Amsterdam: John Benjamins.

Posner, M. & Snyder, C.R. 1975. Attention and cognitive control. In *Information Processing and Cognition: The Loloya Symposium*, R.L. Solso (ed.), 55–85. Mahwah, NJ: Lawrence Erlbaum Associates.

Postal, P. 1966. On so-called 'pronouns' in English. In *Monograph Series on Language and Linguistics*, Vol. 19, F. Dinneen (ed.), 177–206. Washington, DC: Georgetown University Press.

Prasada, S. & Pinker, S. 1993. Generalization of regular and irregular morphological patterns. *Language and Cognitive Processes* 8: 1–56.

Prévost, P. 2009. *The Acquisition of French. The Development of Inflectional Morphology and Syntax in L1 Acquisition, Bilingualism, and L2 Acquisition* [Language Acquisition and Language Disorder 51]. Amsterdam: John Benjamins.

Prévost, P. & White, L. 2000a. Missing surface Inflection or impairment in second language acquisition? Evidence from tense and agreement. *Second Language Research* 16: 103–134.

Prévost, P. & White, L. 2000b. Accounting for morphological variability in second language acquisition: Truncation or missing inflection? In *The Acquisition of Syntax*, M.-A. Friedemann & L. Rizzi (eds), 202–235. London: Longman.

Price, L. 2004. Individual differences in learning: cognitive control, cognitive style, and learning style. *Journal of Educational Psychology* 24: 681–698.

Pulvermüller, F. & Schumann, J. 1994. Neurobiological mechanisms of language acquisition. *Language Learning* 44: 681–734.

Quirk, R., Greenbaum, S., Leech, G. & Svartvik, J. 1985. *A Comprehensive Grammar of the English Language*. London: Longman.

Ramat Giacalone, A. & Banfi, E. 1990. The acquisition of temporality. A second language perspective. *Folia Linguistica* 24: 405–428.

Ramsay, V. 1990. Developmental Stages in the Acquisition of the Perfective and the Imperfective Aspects by Classroom L2 Learners of Spanish. Ph.D. dissertation, University of Oregon.

Ranta, L. & Lyster, R. 2007. A cognitive approach to improve immersion students' oral language abilities: The awareness-practice-feedback sequence. In *Practice in a Second Language*, R. DeKeyser (ed.), 141–160. Cambridge: CUP.

Reichenbach, H. 1947. *Elements of Symbolic Logic*. Berkeley, CA: University of California Press.

Reichle, R.V. 2010. Judgments of information structure in L2 French: Nativelike performance and the critical period hypothesis. *IRAL* 48: 53–85.

Rideout, D. 2002. The perfective/imperfective opposition in the French past tense. *Cahiers Chronos* 9: 15–29.

Ritter, B. & Wiltschko, M. 2004. The lack of tense as a syntactic category: Evidence from Blackfoot and Halkomelem. *UBC Working Papers in Linguistics* 14: 341–370.

Rizzi, L. 2004. *The structure of IP and CP. The Cartography of Syntactic Structures*, Vol. 2. Oxford: OUP.

Roberts, I. 1985. Agreement parameters and the development of English modal auxiliaries. *Natural Language and Linguistic Theory* 3: 21–58.

Roberts, I. 1998. *Have/Be* raising, Move F, and Procrastinate. *Linguistic Inquiry* 29: 113–125.

Robinson, P. 1995. Attention, memory and the noticing hypothesis. *Language Learning* 45: 283–331.

Robinson, P. 2003. Attention and memory during SLA. In *The Handbook of Second Language Acquisition*, C. Doughty & M. Long (eds), 631–678. Oxford: Blackwell.

Robison, R. 1990. The primacy of aspect: Aspectual marking in English interlanguage. *Studies in Second Language Acquisition* 12: 315–330.

Robison, R. 1995. The aspect hypothesis revisited: A cross-sectional study of tense and aspect marking in interlanguage. *Applied Linguistics* 16: 344–371.

Romaine, S. 2001. Multilingualism. In *The Handbook of Linguistics*, M. Aronoff & J. Rees-Miller (eds), 512–532. Oxford: Blackwell.

Romanova, N. 2008. Mechanisms of verbal morphology processing in heritage speakers of Russian. *Heritage Language Journal* 6: 105–126.

Rothman, J. 2008. Aspect selection in adult L2 Spanish and the competing systems hypothesis. When pedagogical rules and linguistic rules conflict. *Languages in Contrast* 8: 74–106.

Rothman, J. & Iverson, M. 2007. Beyond morphological use: What semantic knowledge tells us about aspect in L2 Portuguese. Paper presented at the XXXVII Linguistic Symposium on Romance Languages, University of Pittsburgh, PA.

Rothman, J. & Iverson, M. 2008. Poverty of the stimulus and SLA epistemology: Considering L2 knowledge of aspectual phrasal semantics. *Language Acquisition* 15: 270–314.

Rowlett, P. 2007. Cinque's functional verbs in French. *Language Sciences* 29: 755–786.

Sabeau-Jouannet, E. 1975. Les premières acquisitions syntaxiques chez des enfants unilingues français. *La Linguistique* 11: 105–122.

Salaberry, R. 1997. The acquisition of aspect in past tense French among L2 classroom learners. In *The 1996 Twenty-Third LACUS Forum*, A. Melby (ed.), 521–532. Chapel Hill, NC: Linguistic Association of Canada and the United States.

Salaberry, R. 1998. The development of aspectual distinctions in classroom L2 French. *Canadian Modern Language Review* 54: 504–542.

Salaberry, R. 1999. The development of past tense verbal morphology in classroom L2 Spanish. *Applied Linguistics* 20: 151–178.

Salaberry, R. 2000a. The acquisition of English past tense in an instructional setting. *System* 28: 135–152.

Salaberry, R. 2000b. L2 morphosyntactic development in text-based computer communication. *Computer Assisted Language Learning* 13: 5–27.

Salaberry, R. 2005. Evidence for transfer of knowledge about aspect from L2 Spanish to L3 Portuguese. In Ayoun & Salaberry (eds), 179–210.

Salaberry, R. 2008. *Marking Past Tense in Second Language Acquisition: A Theoretical Model.* London: Continuum.

Salaberry, R. & Ayoun, D. 2005. The development of L2 tense-aspect in the Romance languages. In *Tense and Aspect in Romance Languages: Theoretical and Applied Perspectives*, D. Ayoun & R. Salaberry (eds), 1–33. Amsterdam: John Benjamins.

Salkie, R. 2000. Does French have a relative past tense? *Journal of French Language Studies* 10: 245–271.

Sanz, M. 1999. Aktionsart and transitive phrases. In *Semantic Issues in Romance Syntax* [Current Issues in Linguistic Theory 157], E. Treviño & J. Lema (eds), 247–261. Amsterdam: John Benjamins.

Sanz, M. 2000. *Events and Predication. A New Approach to Syntactic Processing in English and Spanish* [Current Issues in Linguistic Theory 207]. Amsterdam: John Benjamins.

Sanz, M. & Morgan-Short, K. 2004. Positive evidence vs. explicit rule presentation and explicit negative feedback: A computer-assisted study. *Language Learning* 54: 35–78.

Saussure de, L., Moeschler, J. & Puskás, G. (eds). 2009. *Recent Advances in the Syntax and Semantics of Tense, Aspect and Modality.* Berlin: Mouton de Gruyter.

Schell, K. 2000. Functional Categories and the Acquisition of Aspect in L2 Spanish: A Longitudinal Study. Ph.D. dissertation, University of Washington.

Schlyter, S. 1990. The acquisition of French temporal morphemes in adults and in bilingual children. In *La Temporalità nell'Acquisizione di Lingue Seconde*, G. Bernini & A. Giacalone-Ramat (eds), 293–310. Milano: Franco Angeli.

Schlyter, S. 1994. Morphologie verbale dans différents types de texte chez les apprenants naturels de français L2 (suédophones). Talk given at EUROSLA, Aix-en-Provence.

Schlyter, S. 1996. Bilingual children stories: French *passé composé/imparfait* and their correspondences in Swedish. *Linguistics* 34: 1059–1085.

Schmidt, R. 1990. The role of consciousness in language learning. *Applied Linguistics* 11: 129–158.

Schmidt, R. 1993. Awareness and second language acquisition. *Annual Review of Applied Linguistics* 13: 206–226.

Schmidt, R. 1994. Deconstructing consciousness in search of useful definitions for applied linguistics. *AILA Review* 11: 11–26.

Schmidt, R. 1995. Consciousness and foreign language learning: A tutorial on the role of attention and awareness in learning. In *Attention and Awareness in Foreign Language Learning*, D. Schmidt (ed.), 1–65. Honolulu, HI: University of Hawai'i Press.

Schmidt, R. 2001. Attention. In *Cognition and Second Language Instruction*, P. Robinson (ed.), 3–32. Cambridge: CUP.

Schmidt, R. & Frota, S. 1986. Developing basic conversational ability in a second language: A case study of an adult learner of Portuguese. In *Talking to Learn: Conversation in Second Language Acquisition*, R. Day (ed.), 237–326. Rowley, MA: Newbury.

Schneider, N. & Shiffrin, R.M. 1977. Controlled and automatic processing: Detection, search and attention. *Psychological Review* 84: 1–64.

Schumann, J. 1975. Affective factors and the problem of age in second language acquisition. *Language Learning* 25: 209–235.

Schumann, J. 2001. Appraisal psychology, neurobiology and language. *Annual Review of Applied Linguistics* 21: 23–42.

Schütze, C. 1996. *The Empirical Base of Linguistics*. Chicago, IL: University of Chicago Press.

Schwartz, B. 1993. On explicit and negative data effecting and affecting competence and linguistic behavior. *Studies in Second Language Acquisition* 15: 147–163.

Schwartz, B. & Sprouse, R. 1994. Word order and nominative Case in non-native language acquisition: A longitudinal study of L1 Turkish German interlanguage. In *Language Acquisition Studies in Generative Grammar* [Language Acquisition and Language Disorders 8], T. Hoekstra & B. Schwartz (eds), 317–368. Amsterdam: John Benjamins.

Schwartz, B. & Sprouse, R. 1996. L2 cognitive states and the Full Transfer/Full Access model. *Second Language Research* 12: 40–72.

Scovel, T. 1988. *A Time to Speak: A Psycholinguistic Inquiry into the Critical Period for Human Speech*. Rowley, MA: Newbury House.

Shaer, B. 2003. Toward the tenseless analysis of a tenseless language. *Proceedings of SULA* 2, 139–146. Amherst, MA: GLSA.

Sharwood Smith, M. 1986. Comprehension versus acquisition: Two ways of processing input. *Applied Linguistics* 7: 239–274.

Shiffrin, R.M. & Schneider, N. 1977. Controlled and automatic human information processing II: Attending and a general theory. *Psychological Review* 84: 127–190.

Shirai, Y. & Kurono, A. 1998. The acquisition of tense-aspect marking in Japanese as a second language. *Language Learning* 48: 245–279.

Shlonsky, U. 2010. The Cartographic enterprise in syntax. *Language and Linguistics Compass* 4: 417–429.

Singleton, D. 2005. The critical period hypothesis: A coat of many colors. *IRAL* 43: 269–285.

Skehan, P. 1998. *A Cognitive Approach to Language Learning*. Oxford: Oxford University Press.

Slabakova, R. 2000. L1 transfer revisited: The L2 acquisition of telicity marking in English by Spanish and Bulgarian native speakers. *Linguistics* 38: 739–770.

Slabakova, R. 2001. *Telicity in the Second Language* [Language Acquisition and Language Disorders 26]. Amsterdam: John Benjamins.

Slabakova, R. 2003. Semantic evidence for functional categories in interlanguage grammars. *Second Language Research* 19: 42–75.

Slabakova, R. & Montrul, S. 2000. Acquiring semantic properties of preterit and imperfect tenses in L2 Spanish. In *Proceedings of the 24th Boston University Conference on Language Development*, S.C. Howell, S.A. Fish & T. Keith-Lucas (eds), 534–545. Somerville, MA: Cascadilla Press.

Slabakova, R. & Montrul, S. 2002. On viewpoint aspect interpretation and its L2 acquisition: A UG perspective. In *The L2 Acquisition of Tense-Aspect Morphology* [Language Acquisition and Language Disorders 27], R. Salaberry & Y. Shirai (eds), 363–395. Amsterdam: John Benjamins.

Slabakova, R. & Montrul, S. 2003. Genericity and aspect in L2 acquisition. *Language Acquisition* 11: 165–196.

Slobin, D. 1985. Crosslinguistic evidence for the language-making capacity. In *The Cross-linguistic Study of Language Acquisition: Theoretical Issues*, Vol. 2, D. Slobin (ed.), 1157–1256. Hillsdale, NJ: Lawrence Erlbaum Associates.

Smith, B.2013. Eye-tracking & classroom interaction. In *New Perspectives on Classroom Interaction in Second Language Acquisition* [Language Learning & Language Teaching 34]. K. McDonough & A. Mackey (eds). Amsterdam: John Benjamins.

Smith, C.S. 1991/1997. *The Parameter of Aspect*. Dordrecht: Kluwer.

Smith, N. & Tsimpli, I–M. 1995. *The Mind of a Savant. Language learning and modularity.* Oxford: Blackwell.

Snow, C. 1995. Issues in the study of input: Fine-tuning, universality, individual and developmental differences, and necessary causes. In *The Handbook of Child Language Acquisition*, P. Fletcher & B. MacWhinney (eds), 180–193. Oxford: Blackwell.

Sorace, A. 1996. The use of acceptability judgments in second language acquisition research. In *Handbook of Second Language Acquisition*, W. Ritchie & T. Bhatia (eds), 375–409. San Diego, CA: Academic Press.

Sorace, A. 2011. Pinning down the concept of interface in bilingualism. *Linguistic Approaches to Bilingualism* 1: 1–33.

Sorace, A. & Filiaci, F. 2006. Anaphora resolution in near-native speakers of Italian. *Second Language Research* 22: 339–368.

Spada, N. 1997. Form-focused instruction and second language acquisition: A review of classroom and laboratory research. *Language Teaching* 30: 73–87.

Spada, N. & Lightbown, P. 2008. Form-focused instruction: isolated or integrated? *TESOL Quarterly* 42: 181–207.

Sperber, D. & Wilson, D. 1986[1995]. *Relevance: Communication and Cognition,* 2nd edn. Oxford: Blackwell.

Steinmeyer, G. 1987. Le futur antérieur comme temps du passé. Remarques sur un emploi particulier fréquent du futur antérieur en français. *IRAL* 25: 119–29.

Sterr, A., Muller, M., Elbert, T., Rockstroh, B., Pantev, C. & Taub, E. 1998. Changed perceptions in Braille readers. *Nature* 391: 134–135.

Stowe, L. & Sabourin, L. 2005. Imaging the processing of a second language: Effects of maturation and proficiency on the neural processes involved. *IRAL* 43: 329–353.

Svenonius, P. 2002. Icelandic case and the structure of events. *Journal of Comparative Germanic Linguistics* 5: 197–225.

Squartini, M. 2001. The internal structure of evidentiality in Romance. *Studies in Language* 25: 297–334.

Squartini, M. 2004. Disentangling evidentiality and epistemic modality in Romance. *Lingua* 114: 873–895.

Swain, M. 1985. Communicative competence. Some roles of comprehensible input and comprehensible output in its development. In *Input and Second Language Acquisition*, S. Gass & C. Madden (eds), 235–256. Rowley, MA: Newbury House.

Swain, M. 1993. The output hypothesis. Just speaking and writing aren't enough. *The Canadian Modern Language Review* 50: 158–164.

Swain, M. 1995. Three functions of output in second language learning. In *Principles and Practice in Applied Linguistics: Studies in Honor of H.G. Widdowson*, G. Cook & B. Seidlhofer (eds), 125–144. Oxford: OUP.

Swain, M. 1998. Focus on form through conscious reflexion. In *Focus on Form in Classroom Second Language Acquisition*, C. Doughty & J. Williams (eds), 64–81. Cambridge: CUP.

Swain, M. & Lapkin, S. 1982. *Evaluating Bilingual Education: A Canadian Case Study*. Clevedon: Multilingual Matters.

Swain, M. & Lapkin, S. 1986. Immersion French in secondary schools: The goods and the bads. *Contact* 5: 2–9.

Swain, M. & Lapkin, S. 1990. Aspects of the sociolinguistic performance of early and late immersion students. In *Developing Communicative Competence in a Second Language*, R. Scarcella, E. Andersen & S. Krashen (eds), 41–54. Rowley, MA: Newbury House.

Swain, M. & Lapkin, S. 1995. Problems in output and the cognitive processes they generate: A step towards second language learning. *Applied Linguistics* 16: 371–391.

Swain, M., Lapkin, S., Knouzi, I., Suzuki, W. & Brooks, L. 2009. Languaging: University students learn the grammatical concept of voice in French. *The Modern Language Journal* 93: 5–29.

Sweetser, E. 1990. *From Etymology to Pragmatics*. Cambridge: CUP.

Sykes, J. 2005. Synchronous CMC and pragmatic development: Effects of oral and written chat. *CALICO Journal* 22: 399–431.

Sybesma, R. 2007. Whether we tense-agree overtly or not. *Linguistic Inquiry* 38: 580–587.

Tarone, E. 1983. On the variability of interlanguage systems. *Applied Linguistics* 4: 142–163.

Tarone, E., Gass, S. & Cohen, A. (eds). 1994. *Research Methodology in Second Language Acquisition*. Hillsdale, NJ: Lawrence Erlbaum Associates.

Tarone, E., Swain, M. & Fathman, A. 1976. Some limitations to the classroom applications of current second language acquisition research. *TESOL Quarterly* 10: 9–32.

Taub, E., Uswatte, G. & Elbert, T. 2002. New treatments in neuro-rehabilitation founded on basic research. *Nature Reviews Neuroscience* 3: 228–236.

Taylor, A. 2006. The effects of CALL versus traditional L1 glosses on L2 reading comprehension. *CALICO Journal* 23: 309–318.

Terrell, T. 1986. Acquisition in the natural approach: The binding/access framework. *The Modern Language Journal* 75: 52–63.

Thuillier, F. 2004. Synonymie et différences: Le cas de 'paraître' et 'sembler'. In *Le verbe dans tous ses états. Grammaire, sémantique, didactique*, C. Vaguer & B. La Vien (eds), 161–178. Namur: Presse universitaire de Namur.

Tracy-Ventura, N. 2008. Developmental Readiness and Tense/aspect: An Instructional Study of L2 Preterit and Imperfect Acquisition in Spanish. Ph.D. dissertation, Northern Arizona University.

Travis, L. 1991. Inner aspect and the structure of VP. *Cahiers de Linguistique,* 132–146.

Travis, L. 1994. Event phrase and a theory of functional categories. In *Proceedings of the 1994 Canadian Linguistic Association Meeting at the University of Calgary*, P. Koskinen (ed.), 559–570. Toronto: University of Toronto.

Travis, L. 2008. The role of features in syntactic theory and language variation. In *The Role of Formal Features in Second Language Acquisition*, J. Liceras, H. Zobl & H. Goodluck (eds), 22–47. New York, NY: Lawrence Erlbaum Associates.

Truscott, J. 1998. Noticing in second language acquisition: A critical review. *Second Language Research* 14: 103–135.

Tsimpli, I.-M. 2003. Clitics and determiners in L2 Greek. In *Proceedings of the 6th Generative Approaches to Second Language Acquisition Conference (GASLA 2002)*, J. Liceras, H. Zobl & H. Goodluck (eds), 331–339. Somerville, MA: Cascadilla Proceedings Project.

Tsimpli, I.-M. & Dimitrakopoulou, M. 2007. The interpretability hypothesis: Evidence from *wh*-interrogatives in second language acquisition. *Second Language Research* 23: 215–242.

Tsimpli, I. & Roussou, A. 1991. Parameter setting in L2? *University College of London Working Papers in Linguistics* 3: 149–169.

Tsimpli, I.-M. & Smith, N. 1991. Second language learning: Evidence from a polyglot savant. *UCLA Working Papers in Linguistics* 3: 171–84.

Turnbull, M., Lapkin, S. & Hart, D. 2001. Grade 3 immersion students' performance in literacy and mathematics: Province-wide results from Ontario (1989–99). *The Canadian Modern Language Review* 58: 9–26.

Vainikka, A. & Young-Scholten, M. 1994. Direct access to X-bar theory: Evidence from Korean and Turkish adults learning German. In *Language Acquisition Studies in Generative Grammar* [Language Acquisition and Language Disorders 8], T. Hoekstra & B. Schwartz (eds), 265–316. Amsterdam: John Benjamins.

Vainikka, A. & Young-Scholten, M. 1996a. Gradual development of L2 phrase structure. *Second Language Research* 12: 7–39.

Vainikka, A. & Young-Scholten, M. 1996b. The early stages in adult L2 syntax: Additional evidence from Romance speakers. *Second Language Research* 12: 140–176.

Vainikka, A. & Young-Scholten, M. 1998. Morphosyntactic triggers in adult SLA. In *Morphology and its Interface in Second Language Knowledge* [Language Acquisition and Language Disorders 19], M.-L. Beck (ed.), 89–113. Amsterdam: John Benjamins.

VanPatten, B. 1985. Communicative value and information processing in second language acquisition. In *On TESOL '84: A Brave New World*, P. Larson, E. Judd & D. Messerschmitt (eds), 89–100. Washington, DC: TESOL.

VanPatten, B. 1990. Attending to form and content in the input. An experiment in consciousness. *Studies in Second Language Acquisition* 12: 287–301.

VanPatten, B. 1996. *Input Processing and Grammar Instruction: Theory and Research*. Westport, CT: Ablex.

VanPatten, B. 2002. Processing instruction: An update. *Language Learning* 52: 755–803.

VanPatten, B. 2004. Input processing in SLA. In VanPatten (ed.), 5–31.

VanPatten, B. (ed.). 2004. *Processing Instruction: Theory, Research and Commentary*. Mahwah, NJ: Lawrence Erlbaum Associates.

VanPatten, B. 2005. Processing instruction. In *Mind and Context in Adult Second Language Acquisition*, C. Sanz (ed.), 267–281. Washington, DC: Georgetown University Press.

VanPatten, B. & Cadierno, T. 1993. Explicit instruction and input processing. *Studies in Second Language Acquisition* 15: 225–43.

VanPatten, B. & Oikkenon, S. 1996. Explanation vs. structured input in processing instruction. *Studies in Second Language Acquisition* 18: 495–510.

VanPatten, B. & Wong, W. 2004. Processing Instruction and the French causative: Another replication. In *Processing Instruction: Theory, Research and Commentary*, B. VanPatten (ed.), 97–118. Mahwah, NJ: Lawrence Erlbaum Associates.

Van Wuijtswinkel, K. 1994. Critical Period Effects on the Acquisition of Grammatical Competence in a Second Language. BA thesis, Katholieke Universiteit. Nijmegen, Netherlands.

Vendler, Z. 1967. Verbs and times. In *Linguistics and Philosophy*, Z. Vendler (ed.), 97–121. Ithaca, NY: Cornell University Press. (Reprinted from *Philosophical Review* 1957, 66: 143–160).

Verkuyl, H. 1993. *A Theory of Aspectuality: The Interaction between Temporal and Atemporal Structure*. Cambridge: CUP.

Vet, C. 1992. Le passé composé: Contextes d'emploi et interprétation. *Cahiers de Praxématique* 19: 37–59.

Vet, C. 1993. Conditions d'emploi et interprétations des temps futurs du français. *Verbum* 16: 71–84.

Visser, T. 1963–73. *An Historical Syntax of the English Language*, Vols. I-IIIb. Leiden: E.J. Brill.

von Wright, G.H. 1951. *An Essay in Modal Logic*. Amsterdam: North Holland.

Vuillaume, M. 2001. L'expression du futur et du passé en français et en allemand. *Recherches Linguistiques* 25: 105–124.

Wagner, R.L. & Pinchon, J. 1991. *Grammaire du français classique et moderne*. Paris: Hachette.

Wärnsby, A. 2006. *(De)coding Modality. The Case of Must, May, Måste, and Kan*. Lund: Lund University.

Warschauer, M. 2001. Millennialism and media: Language, literacy, and technology in the 21st century. *AILA Review* 14: 49–59.

Warschauer, M. 2004. Technological change and the future of CALL. In *New Perspectives on CALL for Second and Foreign Language Classrooms*, S. Fotos & C. Browne (eds), 15–25. Mahwah, NJ: Lawrence Erlbaum Associates.

Waugh, L.R. 1987. Marking time with the *passé composé*: Toward a theory of the perfect. *Lingvisticae Investigationes* XI: 1–47.

Weber-Fox, C. & Neville, H. 1999. Functional neural subsystems are differentially affected by delays in second language immersion: ERP and behavioral evidence in bilinguals. In Birdsong (ed.), 23–38.

Weinart, R. 1994. Some effects of a foreign language classroom on the development of German negation. *Applied Linguistics* 15: 76–101.

White, L. 2003. On the nature of interlanguage representation: Universal Grammar in the second language. In *The Handbook of Second Language Acquisition*, C. Doughty & M. Long (eds), 19–42. Oxford: Blackwell.

White, L. & Genesee, F. 1996. How native is near-native? The issue of ultimate attainment in adult second language acquisition. *Second Language Research* 11: 233–265.

White, J. & Goulet, C. 1995. Getting your primary ESL students hooked on books. *Speaq-Out* 24: 7–13.

Wiberg, E. 2002. Information structure in dialogic future plans: a study of Italian native speakers and Swedish preadvanced and advanced learners of Italian. In *Tense-Aspect Morphology in L2 Acquisition* [Language Acquisition and Language Disorders 27], R. Salaberry & Y. Shirai (eds), 285–321. Amsterdam: John Benjamins.

Widdowson, H.G. 1989. Knowledge of language and ability for use. *Applied Linguistics* 10: 128–137.

Williams, E. 1976. The natural philosophy of language acquisition. Ms, University of Massachusetts.

Williams, E. 1977a. Discourse and logical form. *Linguistic Inquiry* 8: 101–39.

Williams, E. 1977b. Presentation, international Conference on Child Language, Tokyo.

Williams, E. 1978. Language acquisition, markedness and phrase structure. In *Language Acquisition and Linguistic Theory*, S. Tavakolian (ed.), 8–34. Cambridge, MA: The MIT Press.

Williams, E. 1987. Introduction. In *Parameter setting*, T. Roeper & E. Williams (eds), vii–xix. Dordrecht: D. Reidel.

Wilmet, M. 1976. *Etude de morpho-syntaxe verbale*. Paris: Klincksieck.

Wilmet, M. 1997. *Grammaire critique du français*. Paris: Hachette.

Wilmet, M. 2001. *L'architectonique du conditionnel*. *Recherches linguistiques* 25: 21–44.

Wingfield, A. & Grossman, M. 2006. Language and the aging brain: Patterns of neural compensation revealed by functional brain imaging. *Journal of Neurophysiology* 96: 2830–2839.

Wingfield, A. & Stine-Morrow, E.A.L. 2000. Language and speech. In *Handbook of Aging and Cognition*, 2nd edn., F. Craik & T. A. Salthouse (eds), 359–416. Mahwah, NJ: Lawrence Erlbaum Associates.

Wong, W. 2004. Processing instruction in French: The roles of explicit information and structured input. In *Processing Instruction: Theory, Research and Commentary*, B. VanPatten (ed.), 187–206. Mahwah, NJ: Lawrence Erlbaum Associates.

Yang, Y. & Lyster, R. 2010. Effects of form-focused practice and feedback on Chinese EFF learners' acquisition of regular and irregular past tense forms. *Studies in Second Language Acquisition* 32: 235–263.

Yang, S. & Yuan Huang, Y. 2004. The impact of the absence of grammatical tense in L1 on the acquisition of the tense-aspect system in L2. *International Review of Applied Linguistics* 42: 49–70.

Yanguas, I. 2009. Multimedia glosses and their effect on L2 text comprehension and vocabulary learning. *Language Learning & Technology* 13: 48–67.

Yvon, H. 1953. Indicatif futur antérieur, ou suppositif probable d'aspect composé? *Le français moderne* 21: 169–177.

Zafar, S. & Meenakshi, K. 2012. A study on the relationship between extroversion-introversion and risk-taking in the context of second language acquisition. *International Journal of Research Studies in Language Learning* 1: 33–40.

Zagona, K. 1994. Perfectivity and temporal arguments. In *Issues and Theory in Romance Linguistics: Selected Papers from the Linguistic Symposium on Romance Languages XXIII April 1–4, 1993*, M. Mazzola (ed.), 523–546. Washington, DC: Georgetown University Press.

Name index

Subject index